Linked Histories:

POSTCOLONIAL STUDIES IN A GOBALIZED WORLD

Edited by Pamela McCallum & Wendy Faith

UNIVERSITY OF
CALGARY
PRESS

Published by the
University of Calgary Press
2500 University Drive NW
Calgary, Alberta, Canada T2N 1N4
www.uofcpress.com

We acknowledge the financial
support of the Government of Canada
through the Book Publishing Industry
Development Program (BPIDP) and the
Alberta Foundation for the Arts. We
acknowledge the support of the Canada
Council for the Arts for our publishing
program.

Canada Council   Conseil des Arts
for the Arts   du Canada

Canadä

LIBRARY AND ARCHIVES OF CANADA
CATALOGUING IN PUBLICATION:

Linked histories : postcolonial studies in
a globalized world / edited by
Pamela McCallum & Wendy Faith.

Includes bibliographical references
and index.

ISBN   1-55238-088-2

1   Postcolonialism.
2   Globalization – Social aspects.
3   Marginality, Social.
I   McCallum, Pamela, 1949–
II   Faith, Wendy, 1963–

HM1136.L55 2005   305.5'6
C2005-906920-1

Cover design, Mieka West.
Internal design & typesetting,
    Jason Dewinetz.

This book is printed on 60 lb.
Rolland Enviro Natural.
Printed and bound in Canada by
AGMV MARQUIS.

Contents

Acknowledgements *vii*

1 Introduction: *1*
The Linked Histories in a Globalized World
Pamela McCallum & Wendy Faith

2 The Fascist Longings in our Midst *21*
Rey Chow

3 Queer with Class: *45*
Absence of Third World Sweatshop in Lesbian/Gay
Discourse and a Rearticulation of Materialist Queer Theory
Rob Cover

4 Cross-Mirrorings of Alterity: *63*
The Colonial Scenario
and Its Psychological Legacy
Monika Fludernik

5 Mythologies of Migrancy: *91*
Postcolonialism, Postmodernism,
and the Politics of (Dis)location
Revathi Krishnaswamy

6 Postcolonial Differend: *111*
Diasporic Narratives of Salman Rushdie
Vijay Mishra

7 At the Margins of Postcolonial Studies *145*
Kalpana Sheshadri-Crooks

8 Keeping History at Wind River and Acoma *167*
Mary Lawlor

9 Modernity's First Born: *189*
Latin America and Postcolonial Transformation
Bill Ashcroft

10 Toward Articulation: *209*
Postcolonial Theory and Demotic Resistance
Victor Li

11 Postcolonial Theory and the "Decolonization"
of Chinese Culture *231*
Wang Ning

Notes on Contributors *245*
Index *249*

Acknowledgements

Many colleagues have assisted us in preparing this book. We are grateful to Victor Ramraj, the former editor of *ARIEL*, under whose direction many of these articles appeared, and to his associate editors Lorne Macdonald and Patricia Srebrnik.

We appreciate the encouragement of the editorial staff at University of Calgary Press throughout this project. Joyce Hildebrandt's vigilant copyediting helped us clarify many issues. At different stages of the project, Ann Becze and Erin Wunker were excellent research assistants. The Graduate Program in the Department of English at the University of Calgary brought us together, and we are grateful for the funding that the Faculty of Humanities and the Faculty of Graduate Studies provided for our work. Part of the introduction was drafted when Pamela McCallum was a Visiting Fellow at Clare Hall, Cambridge University, whose gracious fellowship provided a stimulating space for reflection. Finally we would like to thank our families – Keith McCallum, Hendrikus van Ginneken and Damon van Ginneken – for their unfailing patience and support in matters large and small.

The Fascist Longings
in our Midst   Queer with Class: Absence
of Third World Sweatshop in Lesbian/
Gay Discourse and a Rearticulation
of Materialist Queer Theory   Cross-
Mirrorings of Alterity: The Colonial
Scenario and Its Psychological
Legacy   Mythologies of Migrancy: Post-
colonialism, Postmodernism, and the
Politics of (Dis)location   Postcolonial
DefferendDifferend: Diasporic Narratives
of Salman Rushdie   At the Margins of
Postcolonial Studies   Keeping History
at Wind River and Acoma   Modernity's
First Born: Latin America and Postcolonial
Transformation   Towards Articulation:
Postcolonial Theory and Demotic
Resistance   Postcolonial Theory and
the "Decolonization" of Chinese Culture

Introduction:

Linked Histories
in a Globalized World

PAMELA MCCALLUM & WENDY FAITH

In the spring of 2000, marking the twenty-fifth anniversary of the end of the Vietnam war, a Toronto newspaper published a story about the new economy of that formerly ravaged country. Journalist Miro Cernetig began the account by describing a familiar and conventionalized image of the Third World: on the outskirts of Hanoi, visitors are met by peasant farmers who hold out plastic bags, calling "Buy! Buy!" But the bags do not contain the expected produce from local fields; rather, they are filled with golf balls, carefully recovered from the grasses around a newly constructed course that was built as a joint venture with the South Korean company Daewoo. The club's membership – mostly Japanese, American, and French, with some newly wealthy Vietnamese – invokes the successive imperialisms that have marked Vietnam, while the name of the Scottish golf pro Ian Fleming ironically recalls the author whose James Bond thrillers popularized a nostalgically orientialized view

1

of the British presence in East Asia. Peasant farmers braving unexploded American bombs buried more than twenty-five years ago in the surrounding fields to collect golf balls for the recreational pleasures of a small number of affluent club members provides an astonishing image of the intertwining of past histories and present possibilities in globalized economies.

Alongside this unsettling depiction of peasant "labour" in the new globalized world, other images, which also invoke cultural memories of the Vietnam war and the protests against it, have become familiar in recent years: the photographs and television coverage of mass demonstrations in various capitals of Western countries – Seattle, Quebec City, Prague, Goteburg, Genoa, and others – against the meetings of the powerful organizations (the World Bank, the World Trade Organization, the International Monetary Fund, the G8) that have presided over the reshaping of national economies in recent decades. The unstructured and diverse coalition of groups that have come together in the anti-capitalist movement has focussed attention on the linkages between the glittering, enticing commodities in the shops of Western cities and the impoverished populations of the countries where they are produced. The Nike running shoes or Gap T-shirts or stuffed Disney characters carefully stacked in polished and mirrored shops tell stories of sweatshop exploitation in conditions that cannot fail to bring to mind the nineteenth-century factories of the industrial revolution, conditions many had believed long since superseded. The new economics of globalization has come to be represented in the designer T-shirt that sells for eighty dollars and is made by a young woman in a faraway factory who is paid two dollars a day, perhaps the daughter of the peasant who risks bombs buried a quarter of a century ago to collect lost golf balls.

What are the implications of globalization for postcolonial studies? In a recent essay, Simon During relates the category of postcolonialism with that of globalization, despite their different focuses: whereas the first exposes the fictiveness of the colonial imaginary (dehistoricization) and, in its more critical expression, replaces Western meta-narratives with local accounts, the second peruses the effects of the deregulated global economy (deterritorialization). While During clarifies these perspectives, he argues that postcolonialism and globalization are "names for forces which work, and long have worked, in transaction with one another" in ways both progressive and reactionary (392). Although widespread deregulation has "delegitimized the whole history of settlement" (391), leading to unprecedented moral support for indigenous claims to cultural autonomy and geographic territory, the "contemporary world unification is simultaneously reconfiguring the past in its own image and renewing colonial struggles" (393). Thus, within During's overlapping interplay of forces, the larger question persists: to what extent will postcolonial contests for self-representation and equality be diminished by the transnational displacement of national hegemonies?

Layered onto the world-shaping projects of various colonialisms and imperialisms since the Renaissance, the concept of globalization has renewed attention to the ways in which advanced capitalist systems of the early twenty-first century strive to extend and integrate modes of domination. Indeed, the use of the term *globalization* has itself been questioned by scholars on the left. Samir Amin calls it a "euphemism for that forbidden word, imperialism" (45). Taking up a similar position, anthropologist David Harvey asks, "[W]hat significance attaches to the fact that even among many 'progressives' and 'leftists' in the advanced capitalist world, much more politically loaded words like 'imperialism,' 'colonialism,' and 'neo-colonialism' have increasingly taken a back seat to 'globalization' as a way to organize thoughts and to chart political possibilities?" (53). And yet, when Harvey comes to consider whether new configurations in the world economy – a series of financial deregulations, a proliferation of technology transfer, the effects of the "information revolution," the rapid movement of commodities across the world – constitute a qualitative difference from earlier colonizing projects, his answer is "a qualified 'yes'" (68).

The difficulties in conceptualizing globalization can perhaps be located in Fredric Jameson's trenchant analysis of two opposed but equally affective and resonant responses to conceptualizing the implications of the contemporary world systems. The first, more positive image of globalization has its roots in the expansion of communications technology and celebrates "the emergence of a whole immense range of groups, races, genders, ethnicities, into the speech of the public sphere, a falling away of those structures that condemned whole segments of the population to silence and to subalternity" (57). At the same time, a more negative image arises from the economics of a globalized world: "the rapid assimilation of hitherto autonomous national markets and productive zones into a single sphere, the disappearance of national subsistence (in food, for example), the forced integration of countries all over the globe into precisely that new global division of labor" (57). Heterogeneous difference or relentless identity? In Jameson's view, globalization represents both at one and the same time; in his words, they seem "somehow to be dialectically related, at least on the mode of the unresolvable antinomy" (57). If globalization has imposed such a contradictory template, such divergent expectations, on the contemporary world, it is not surprising that a critical understanding of its processes and implications appears to be an urgent task.

Within such a context, a renewed focus on global patterns and structural markings of continents and peoples may prove especially illuminating for postcolonial studies. Critics working in this field, Arif Dirlik argues, must

3

be particularly vigilant against the comforting illusion that postcolonial studies have always-already-been global. Rather, he suggests, the contrary is true. Postcolonial studies have all too often rejected global categories as fatally tied to the overriding master narratives so devastatingly critiqued by poststructuralism. In his view, "postcolonialism in its most popular forms (in the United States, at least) eschews questions of the structurations of the world in terms of 'foundational categories,' and stresses local encounters in the formation of identities; it is in many ways driven by a radical individualism, and [is] situationist in its historical explanations" (4). This differential movement, as Bill Ashcroft, Gareth Griffiths, and Helen Tiffin observe in *The Empire Writes Back*, stems ironically from the very policies and practices of imperialism. "In pushing the colonial world to the margins of experience," they write, "the 'centre' pushed consciousness beyond the point at which monocentrism in all spheres of thought could be accepted without question. In other words the alienating process which initially served to relegate the post-colonial world to the 'margin' turned upon itself and acted to push that world through a kind of mental barrier into a position from which all experience could be viewed as uncentred, pluralistic, and multifarious" (12). While strategies of difference have generated insightful and empowering readings, especially in demonstrating how postcolonial texts have appropriated, resisted, and rewritten colonial Euro-American cultures, Dirlik nevertheless argues that this orientation runs the risk of "elevating culture to primacy in social and cultural theory" (24). A refocusing on the global structures of capitalism is imperative, he suggests, for "without an account between Eurocentrism, and the enormous power that enabled Euroamerican expansion, the criticism of Eurocentrism may not only perpetuate Eurocentrism in new guises, but also disguise the ways in which globalism itself is imbued with a Eurocentric worldview" (15). In other words, Dirlik advocates a reconnection of cultural and discursive analyses with the material conditions in and through which they were articulated. Such a position does not seek to privilege political economy, as in old materialisms, but attempts to open up new ways of envisioning the connections between the cultural and the material.

Frederick Buell has underlined the complexity of globalization in which local identities and the global whole are worked and reworked in complicated and continuing inter-relationships: "global interactiveness," he writes, "has become more significantly decentered and much more overt than before, no longer managed so restrictively and ideologically obscured by bordered nation-states and national economies" (46). Such fluid and interactive ongoing connections raise urgent questions for postcolonial studies. How might it be possible to articulate and facilitate potential sites of cross-cultural exchange without situating genders, races, classes as the "others" of Europe? How does a renewed interest in the intersections of culture and materialism challenge postcolonial criticism to rethink categories of marginality and subalternity? How might identity be reconceived by a postcolonial criticism sensitive to the nuances of complicity and compromise within global economic structures? What new configurations of social transformation are emerging? These are the kinds of questions that the articles in *Linked Histories* seek to open up and to illuminate.

Rey Chow's "The Fascist Longings in our Midst" examines the present state of North American academic politics through the historical lens of European and Japanese fascism. Unlike commonplace critiques that interpret fascistic atrociousness, in the Freudian sense of "projection," as the violent externalization of repressed fear, Chow construes this phenomenon, in "the more obvious sense of projection," as the technological display of cultural imagery. She thus shifts attention away from fascism's speculative essence toward its historical-material existence or "surface." Taking Hitler's statement that "the masses need illusion" at face value, she compares the lure of fascistic ideals to the appeal of polished filmic images; fascism takes hold when members of the population – eager to be seen as pure and righteous – seek identification with figures who appear godlike or "larger than life." Such monstrous exhibitions of idolatry are indicative not of baleful unconscious drives but rather of "good intentions shining forth in dazzling light." By associating themselves with exemplars of the flawless, the beautiful, the brave, or the ecstatic, fascists aim to displace the harsh reality of lived history with the "glossy" dream of utopian living.

Chow draws a parallel between fascism's "massive submission" to the ideal of the absolutely heroic leader and academia's uniform acquiescence to the perception of the purely oppressed racial other. This "new liberal fascism," through its wholesale valorization of cultural pluralism and corresponding neglect of historical and class differences, treats all persons of colour as intrinsically "correct and deserving of support." Such willful "disbelief in fraudulence," she observes, serves the fascistic manufacture of self-aggrandizing phantasmagoria. By identifying with an idealized appearance of racial otherness, "these supporters receive an image of *themselves* that is at once enlightenedly humble ('I submit to you, since you are a victim of our imperialism') and beautiful ('Look how decent I am by submitting to you')." While Chow applauds academic challenges to white hegemony, she warns that prejudicial discrimination and preconceived indiscrimination of persons of colour are two sides of the same fascistic coin. Both views rely on the imagistic division between us and them: the former, typical of "territorial colonialism," avoids the contaminating touch of the impure, vilified other; the latter, characteristic of scholastic postcolonialism, desires redemptive contact with the pure, exotic other.

In "Queer with Class," Rob Cover examines the ethical implications of queer theory's focus on desire to the exclusion of needs. He notes that while this emphasis is used complexly in academic discourse to transgress the normalization of sexual identity, it is applied reductively in gay/lesbian media publications to establish a homosexual identity "in opposition to" the heterosexual construct, thereby fostering the illusion of an essential queer subjectivity that transcends all cultural and regional boundaries. This homogenization of queerness forms the basis for a definable market niche, which is exploited by corporate advertisers who profess to champion gay/lesbian rights in the interest of social progress but still reproduce the (classist, sexist, racist) status quo by targeting the bourgeois, white, Euro-American male as representative of the queer subject. Cover is boldly critical of this marketing strategy. By assigning the expression of desire exclusively to the most affluent members of gay communities, mainstream advertisers and queer magazines collude to establish a new sexual norm that both marginalizes relatively poor queer persons in the West (non-whites, indigenous persons, women, youth, migrants, and the disabled) and subsumes culturally specific sexualities into a Western paradigm. Moreover, the gay/lesbian media's reliance on advertisers who promote middle-class patterns of spending blindly supports, and thereby helps to obscure, capitalism's exploitation of labour throughout the world.

Cover argues that the insidious relation between (non-hetero) sexual identity and corporate economic vision necessitates the rearticulation of queer theory through a broad materialist analysis. This approach will always be difficult for, as Cover takes pains to note, gay and lesbian magazines represent queer persons as sufficiently aware of "other worldly injustices," by virtue of "having suffered the ills of homophobia," and as necessarily "apart from other middle-class consumers." Materialist theory provides a corrective for such assumptions by foregrounding how the stakes of global capitalism have contributed to the construction of sexualities, dividing Third and First World bodies into labourers and consumers respectively and Western (queer) consumers into desirable and undesirable subjects. A materialist approach does not abandon theories of desire as a means of disrupting heteronormative patriarchy but focuses, additionally, on the ways in which the queer celebration of pleasure and longing is indebted to the deprivation and alienation of others.

Monika Fludernik's "Cross-Mirrorings of Alterity: The Colonial Scenario and Its Psychological Legacy" explores the class-based assumptions embedded in the circulation of long-standing colonial clichés. Within Western cosmopolitan environments, she notes, gendered stereotypes of "the bad native" are transferred in various complex ways to the poor and underprivileged. The recirculation of old colonial categories in the new context of global capitalism is facilitated by non-white middle- and upper-class émigrés, who internalize Euro-American racist perceptions (the "native other" is conniving, dirty, lazy, etc.) and, in a strategy of psychoanalytic compensation, project them onto lower-class exiles and minorities. Fludernik suggests that postcolonial scholars, in their sweeping celebration of migrancy and hybridity, have become insensible to the ways in which such urban professional expatriates "participate in the processes of cultural dominance." Her argument here parallels Chow's analysis that academics, in their indiscriminate valorization of persons of colour, can prove to be blind to the strategies through which class privilege reproduces itself across the political economies of higher education.

In a nostalgic attempt to establish a native identity abroad, Fludernik argues, it is not uncommon for expatriates to adopt Western stereotypes and "exoticist fantasies" about their home countries. At times, the replication of such cultural imagery is employed reflexively "to prove [indigenous, ethnic, or national] worth against Western allegations of unworth." At other times, it is used more strategically to "deflect the feelings of inferiority generated by racial remarks" onto other minorities, such as less desirable foreigners or welfare recipients. In the latter case, it is a means by which elite migrants ascend to the ranks of (white, Euro-American) respectability and aspire, increasingly, "to the idealized status of the moneyed." Indeed, in the touristic and migrant global economy, wherein the fetishistic appeal and marketability of cultural symbols supersede their colonial and "counter-colonial specificity," it is only the higher-class cosmopolitan émigré who occupies the relatively enviable position of manipulating and "exploiting" Western "clichés for his or her own purposes."

Revathi Krishnaswamy raises similar cautions about an undifferentiated marginality in "Mythologies of Migrancy: Postcolonialism, Postmodernism and the Politics of (Dis)location." She charges that present cultural discourses, by conflating all experiences of subalternity and lack with those of the prosperous voluntary migrant (epitomized here by the intellectual and literary luminary Salman Rushdie) obscure both transcultural and Third World hierarchies of class and gender. In opposition to this leveling of historically and culturally specific narratives of subalternity, Krishnaswamy stresses that working-class exiles and economic refugees, unlike professional emigrants, are often victims of either the global trade in cheap labour or the worldwide "traffic in female flesh." Elite Third World intellectuals generally ignore such "grim [material] realities of migrant labour" and focus instead

7

on the personal and psychological trials of migrancy. Moreover, as a means of legitimizing their relative power and privilege, they appropriate the "vocabulary of protest," with its fears of persecution and hopes of emancipation, from superexploited groups and assign it to the upper-middle class "public (literary) persona."

This persona, notes Krishnaswamy, involves the concept of the exiled writer as a "champion of the oppressed" and evokes modernism's image of the alienated artist as a critic of bourgeois modernity. But whereas the modernist author-hero both denounced and conceded the dislocation, destabilization, and fragmentation of the humanistic subject, postmodern and postcolonial "celebrities" such as Rushdie flatly valorize these conditions in the names of fluidity, detachment, contingency, hybridity, and diversity. Indeed, far from being distressed by feelings of alienation, as were his modernist predecessors, Rushdie constructs a romantic image of himself as a man-of-the-world who belongs "everywhere by belonging nowhere." He is thus able to identify with either the sophisticated cosmopolite, the struggling subaltern, or both. It is ironic, however, that by laying claim to a "deterritorialized consciousness freed from such collectivities as race, class, gender, or nation" he recreates "a postmodernist avatar" of the bourgeois autonomous subject (more specifically, the avant-garde transcendent artist).

But, as Krishnaswamy warns, geographical displacement and cultural alienation are not the exclusive domain of elite migrants. Much Third World literature is not written by exiles; nor is it "postcolonial in ways recognized by the postmodern West." In addition, the ongoing struggle against hegemony demands an awareness of the ways that hierarchical relations are performed not only across nations but also "within societies." With these caveats in mind, Krishnaswamy reproves Third World intellectuals for self-indulgently failing to acknowledge that the prevailing "mythologies of migrancy" perpetuate long-standing economic and social inequalities.

Approaching Rushdie from a different perspective in "Postcolonial Differend: Diasporic Narratives of Salman Rushdie," Vijay Mishra assesses the intense controversy that surrounded the publication of *The Satanic Verses*. In so doing, he recasts the notorious oppositional stance between Islamic fundamentalists and Western literati – which, according to Homi Bhabha, overshadowed the debate's "irresolvable" heterogeneities – in terms of Lyotard's differend: the discursive incommensurability between sacrosanct tradition and secular aestheticism. The ideology of the sacred, claims Mishra, demands allegiance to totalizing, transhistorical narratives that secure its inviolability. Such homogeneity, he continues, is nostalgically promoted by members of diasporic settlements, who reduce shared religious doctrines to a single millenarian politic in an effort to establish ethnic solidarity abroad: "The fatwa against Rushdie originated in the diaspora – in Bradford – and not in Iran." In contrast, the ideology of liberal humanism perpetuates narratives of individualism and difference (but perhaps only those that "can be footnoted adequately in the grand history of Empire").

Mishra's main emphasis is that the diasporic religious denunciation of *The Satanic Verses*, which denies special status (or political immunity) to the creative writer, is irreconcilable with the Western humanistic valorization of the aesthetic object, which grants "non-negotiable privilege" to the author-as-genius. According to Rushdie, whose sensibility is aligned with this latter discourse of modernity, Islamic fundamentalists cruelly aimed to censor his right to freedom of expression. But from the perspective of Islamic devotees, Rushdie, in his promiscuous aestheticization of the sacred, aggressively sought to undermine their freedom from secular corruption. For the Westernized diasporic author, "the choice for civilization" is between the "Enlightenment and barbarism"; for the insular diasporic settler, who does not presume a separation between the spheres of religion and the state, the choice is between holy enlightenment and philistinism.

In focusing this differend, Mishra's point "is not that every dispute must be resolved but how to argue for a nonresolvable heterogeneity (the basis for all true discussion) that is not a simple pluralism." However, his plea for indeterminacy and radical plurality is not as impartial as it first appears. Indeed, it entails the idea that the opposition between sacred scripture, which he presents as necessarily monolithic and closed, and the postmodernist text, which he poses as characteristically multifaceted and open, can ever only be illuminated through the (secular) ideology of heterogeneity itself: it is the humanistic aesthetic domain that "signals the possibility of alternative worlds that do not seek legitimation purely through facts." In the final analysis, Mishra defends *The Satanic Verses* on the basis that it "bears witness to differends by finding idioms for them."

How can postcolonial studies avoid lapsing into a hegemonic mode characteristic of the dominant discourses that it attempts to critique? In an innovative observation, Kalpana Seshadri-Crooks's "At the Margins of Postcolonial Studies" identifies the crux of this well-rehearsed theoretical problem as the "inadequately enunciated notion of the margin." Her main point of contention lies in the treatment of the margin as a "spatial category" or discursive "turf" whose boundaries are drawn in monolithic opposition to an ostensible centre. This concept of marginality, she argues, is better associated with the consonance of affirmative action and ethnic/minority studies, which are rooted in the Western liberalistic "positive discourse of rights," rather than with the "amorphousness" of postcolonial studies, which is situated in a postmodern "discourse of limits" that negates the "identifiable object" and the unified subject. She observes that the conflation of the clearly delineated margin of minorities with the "irreducible other" of the postcolonial dynamic persists, however, revealing a utopian neo-assimilative impulse, which she aligns with the American "melting pot" brand of multiculturalism. (Parenthetically, it is important to note here that Seshadri-Crooks writes from a perspective within cultural debates in the United States; there is a significant difference between the way that multiculturalism takes shape within the internationally dominant United States and the way that it plays out in the relatively powerless settler colonies of, for instance, Canada or New Zealand.) She asserts that if postcolonial studies is to preserve its critical edge – that is, its distance from bourgeois liberal humanism – then it must remain suspicious of categories of identity and attend to the ways that hierarchy is performed in current contexts as "the lived condition of unequal power-sharing globally" instead of the way it is theorized in static terms as "a particular historical phenomenon such as colonialism, which may be plotted as a stage of capitalist imperialism."

Seshadri-Crooks focuses on two recent conceptions of the margin, which advocate homogeneousness (under the guise of multiculturalism). The first attributes the inferior status of the marginalized to their lack of self-fulfillment and social recognition and seeks to alleviate this malady by inviting the generic (and fetishized) other "to partake in the privileges of the center." The second defines the margin in terms of an increasingly hybrid subject position, which generates a disruptive postmodern aesthetic wrought not so much by late capitalism as by global migration. The first treats the margin as a weak appendage of U.S. mainstream culture that can only be rejuvenated by receiving validation from "its" larger body. The second, by viewing all postcolonial subjects as essentially migrant, posits an "undifferentiated" margin. In opposition to these reductions of otherness, Seshadri-Crooks insists that postcolonial studies must explore marginality both as an (unlocatable) site of political exclusion and as an impossible category of identity. Indeed, she claims that only by its "failure to recoup the margin" can this field remain critically effective.

Mary Lawlor's "Keeping History at Wind River and Acoma" explores issues of representation through a discussion of two Native-hosted museums, whose displays of culture seem to comply with Euro-American historiography. Such apparent capitulation of Native identity to the market of tourism is often countered in postcolonial discourse by appeals to "authenticity," which oppose the promotion of assimilationist narratives of indigenousness to the preservation of "genuinely aboriginal" accounts. But, as Lawlor argues, self-representations that appear at first glance to reproduce stereotypical perceptions of Native culture as static and exotic, in keeping with the themes of the "doomed" and "noble savage," may in fact work to monitor the touristic expression of colonial fantasy and to preserve the "exclusivity" of Native communities.

How, then, are we to conceive of Native history and identity? In response to this question, Lawlor moves beyond the old lure of "authentic" aboriginal subjectivity to examine more recent models of hybridity and "cultural doubling." The first, usually viewed as a point of strength in postcolonial studies because it circumvents the monolithic narratives of the past, recognizes the colonized's simultaneous identification with and opposition to the dominant culture. The second locates an unspeakable cultural space "in between" the presumably distinct lineages of Euro- and Native America, implying the need for a double vision of history. Lawlor rejects the former on the grounds that it signals, through its assumption that hybridity is a "rich way of being," a glib acceptance of the alienating effects of cultural displacement. She dismisses the latter on the basis that it suggests an inconceivably "compartmentalized" or puristic notion of historical development.

Whereas the ideas of hybridity and "doubling" presuppose a binary model of cultural identity (centre/margin; subject/other) and merely extend the "either/or" proposition to one of "both/neither," Lawlor imagines a "kaleidoscopic" vision of history in which oppositional terms are "shuffled into different and still-changing relations." Her main point is that Fourth World narratives – those produced by aboriginal peoples of former settler colonies – are in a position, within the colonial legacy of popular culture, to capitalize on shifting patterns and inherent contradictions. By appropriating mainstream historiography, and by selling it back to Euro-American tourists, Native-hosted museums gain some measure of control over the fetishistic, public consumption of their traditions. Indeed, insofar as they select which aspects of their lives to expose to the popular gaze, they restore a degree of self-determination to their communities. Thus, Lawlor concludes that the displays at Wind River and Acoma have "consumed" dominant cultural representations so as, in effect, not to be consumed by them.

In "Modernity's First Born: Latin America and Postcolonial Transformation," Bill Ashcroft also considers questions that can be located in the intersection of postcolonialist discourse and the Americas. He notes that most postcolonial theorists analyze exclusively the global consequences of British imperialism from 1757 (the year Robert Clive captured the Indian province of Bengal), and thus turn away from the comparable regional effects of Spanish imperialism from 1492. In turn, many Latin American thinkers are reluctant to engage in postcolonial discourse, which they view as a new way of consolidating "the English speaking centres of global power." In response to these stances stressing separation, Ashcroft calls for the postcolonial inclusion of the Latin American paradigm. Although he concedes that the fifteenth- and sixteenth-century colonization of Latin America bears little historical resemblance to the more recent occupation of formerly British territories, he argues that the region's characteristic ambivalence and hybridity are manifest, to some degree, in all settler societies. Moreover, because the European imperial expansion into Latin America heralds the very emergence of modernity, it "obliges us to address the question of postcolonialism at its [conquistadorial and capitalistic] roots." By refusing to treat postcolonial discourse either Anglocentrically in terms of the decline of the British empire or hyper-vigilantly in terms of the establishment of a neo-hegemonic field, Ashcroft aims to widen its theoretical scope.

Like other settler colonies, Latin American culture is marked by ambivalence – that is, by "the conscious desire for separation" from the imperialist regime and, in keeping with the Althusserian notion of interpellation, by "the unconscious desire for the persistence of colonial relations." But unlike other settler colonies, stresses Ashcroft, Latin America "still lies at the edges of the world system" and thus lays bare the workings of imperialism and capitalism in the continuing exploitation of Third World labour. More specifically, this colonial paradigm reveals that the so-called underdeveloped region is not simply in "an earlier state of a transition to industrialization" as compared to the First World, in accordance with the bourgeois myth of progress, but is engaged in a hard and painful struggle against the leading industrialized nations, which use it as a "peripheral, raw-material producing" area – that is, as a colony. In the process, this model illuminates not only the problem of interpellation but also the power of what Ashcroft calls interpolation, which involves "the extraordinary capacity of indigenous and indigenized forms to appropriate and reform the powerful discursive practices of the colonizer."

No anti-colonial strategy, claims Ashcroft, exemplifies the act of interpolation better than the Latin American *testimonio*. Through its use of a communal speaking position, which disrupts both the Enlightenment affirmation of individuality and the poststructuralist/postmodern critique of presence, it bears witness to the material effects of imperialism. In so doing, it blurs the distinctions between orality and writing, mythos and history, and the personal and the political, thus offering "a fascinating confrontation with modernity." In total, it brazenly discloses the "socially transformative dimension of postmodernity," which is suppressed by postmodern aestheticism. Ashcroft stresses that this politically resistant approach should not be viewed as a naïve appeal to the transparency of language, the truthfulness of the text, or the value of identity politics, but should be seen rather as "the urgent representation of the experience of a reality." Thus, the Latin American colonial paradigm and its *testimonio* allows Ashcroft to redefine postcolonial discourse as a means by which the colonized disruptively insert or interpolate "their own realities and cultural activities into the global arena." In this way Ashcroft's assertion that *testimonio* "produces, if not the real, then certainly a sensation of experiencing the real" has affinities with magic realism, which is, of course, well rooted in Latin America. As Stephen Slemon has shown, magic realism reconstructs colonial discourse in much the same way that *testimonio* interpolates it. "Magic realism," he perceptively comments, "can be seen to provide a positive and liberating response to [both] the codes of imperial history and its legacy of fragmentation and discontinuity. [...] This process [...] can transmute the 'shreds and fragments' of colonial violence and otherness into new 'codes of recognition' in which the dispossessed, the silenced, and the marginalized of our own dominating systems can again find voice, and enter into the dialectic of on-going community" (21).

Victor Li's "Toward Articulation: Postcolonial Theory and Demotic Resistance" re-evaluates the binary opposition, axiomatic in certain strains of postcolonialism, between theoretical and popular modes of resistance. This binarism, notes Li, is used to level suspicion at both "collective identity and action," as exemplified by Said's admonishment of "nativism," and academic interpretation and remove, as epitomized by Simon During's critique of postcolonial discourse. It is chiefly to the latter, however, that Li speaks. While he acknowledges that appeals to demotic renitency are prompted by the desire to protect indigenous cultures from assimilation, he warns that such strategies of "separatism" lead to the political trap of essentialism, in which the concept of "authentic" difference is exploited to justify oppressive practices of segregation. In addition, the demand for the preservation of seemingly genuine features of the "indigenous" entails that subaltern cultures resist not only the perils of cultural domination but also the vitalities of cultural change.

The benumbing worry that postcolonial theory itself is hegemonic, says Li, results from the field's characteristic "wariness of all monocultural discourses," which in turn stems from its humanistic valorization of autonomy and difference. But because a potentially exploitive "performative contradiction" occurs whenever privileged First World theorists – either "nativist" or elitist – speak for the subaltern, Li advocates that the theoretical/demotic or centre/margin poles be articulated (linked) through a transcultural dialectic, in contrast to Sheshadri-Crooks's call to dissolve this binarism through amorphousness. This interactive approach, while attentive to uneven relations of power, would recognize that the subaltern has often managed to "resist, influence, or even redirect and shape the dominant culture." By allowing for the hazards and contingencies that Li associates with agency, this approach empowers "us"

– in the Marxist sense –"to make our history even under conditions not of our own choosing."

From a different cultural positioning, Chinese scholar Wang Ning explores the implications of linguistic and discursive globalization, the new technologies and mass-marketed Western cultures that have made English the global language and "Americanness" the global style. Like Wang Fengzhen, he shares the sense that in the past decade "the privileges or special policies given to foreign companies for their investments seem to me to be an unconscious or covert subjection of the nation state to world capital" (Wang 148). In "Postcolonial Theory and the 'Decolonization' of Chinese Culture," Wang Ning goes on to ask: should academics and aesthetes in China contest the "colonization," or Westernization, of Chinese language and literature? His answer stresses that this concern cannot be adequately addressed until we first clarify the sense in which China may be deemed a postcolonial entity. Because of its low technological and economic status, the country can rightly be seen to share concerns with other former colonies of the Third World; but because its culture has always "been deeply rooted in the soil of the Chinese nation," it cannot properly be viewed as a colonized region.

Is there a productive niche, then, for the discipline of postcolonial studies in Chinese intellectual circles? Can it be used to halt the invasion of anglicisms and Western advertising into China, for instance? In response to these questions, Wang endorses a cautious acceptance of postcolonialism. On one hand, from a Chinese perspective, the theoretical approaches of eminent "hybrid Western–non-Western" critics such as Said, Spivak, and Bhabha betray an ignorance of "the practical situations" faced by Third World cultures. Strategies that appear anti-hegemonic in the West may thus seem neo-imperialistic in the East. On the other hand, Asian intellectuals can appropriate postcolonialism's centre/margin (active invader/passive invaded) binarism and reconceptualize the "colonization" of China, in dialectical terms, as a cultural exchange between East and West. Here Wang seems to share Victor Li's assertion that the subaltern can "redirect" the centre. This approach would foreground the potential benefits of cross-cultural contact for both the Third World and the Occident. Such advantages would include the "modernization of Chinese culture," which would improve communication between the formerly isolationist country and the international public, and the introduction of "fresh methodologies" and new ideas to Western thought. Although Wang admits that this method would inevitably result in the loss of some aspects of traditional Chinese culture and identity, he argues that "no society" in our global village, "be it Oriental or Occidental, can avoid the influence of, or even 'colonization' by, other societies." He concludes that Chinese intellectuals should adopt postcolonial theory with the awareness that it is "unnecessary"– indeed, futile – to use it to combat the so-called colonization of Chinese language and literature (or what could be called Chinese/Western transculturation).

Wang Ning's reflections on postcolonial theory and globalization in China raise other questions for Western scholars. Can the language of the colonizer, as Chinua Achebe has pointedly asked in another context, "carry the weight" of the colonized's experiences (103)? In *Postcolonialism: Theory, Practice or Protest?* Ato Quayson cautions against a postcolonial historiography that would erase local oral traditions of storytelling about the past. Knowledges based solely on documents, he argues, "serve ultimately to overdetermine the very ways by which indigenous peoples later imagine their histories" (74). What implications does the dominance of Western forms of knowledge production have for cross-cultural exchange? How, as John Mowitt asks, might the categories of cross-cultural exchange be reconfigured so that classes, genders, races, and nations outside the West are no longer required to construct their experience as the "other" of Western thought (3–4)? The essays collected here do not claim to hold the answers to such pressing and urgent questions. Rather, they contribute to an ongoing process of "thinking through" these and other issues in postcolonial studies.

One of the most visionary recent attempts to map the configurations of globalization is Michael Hardt and Antonio Negri's *Empire*. In an innovative and conceptually wide-ranging analysis of contemporary global modes of domination and potential forms of resistance, Hardt and Negri suggest that postcolonial studies must rethink its (sometimes implicit) reliance on a binary model that posits an external colonizing power and a resistant colonized locality. In the writings of many postcolonial critics, they argue, the influential work of Homi Bhabha being their primary example, the act of colonizing is assumed to impose a hierarchy of binary oppositions through which a dominant term overshadows an excluded one (Europe and colony; First and Third Worlds; North and South). The resistance of the colonized can be read in the subversion of power structures through hybridity, mimicry, multiple or unstable identities, and other strategies that refuse and complicate the binary divisions of colonial rule (Hardt and Negri 143–45). And yet, Hardt and Negri contend, however useful such constructions might be for reading history, they ultimately fall short of recognizing the unique "logics of power" (145) in a world reconfigured by contemporary Empire. They go on to point out the irony of how thoroughly the concepts valorized by postmodernism, and freely adopted by postcolonial studies, have been integrated into the economics of globalization: "[T]he ideology of the world market has always been the anti-foundational and anti-essentialist discourse par excellence. Circulation, mobility, diversity, and mixture are its very conditions of possibility" (150). If the historical divisions of colonizer and colonized have been eroded by the sweep and eddies of the global flows of capital, how is resistance to be understood in these new configurations of power and subordination?

The sections of *Empire* that attempt to imagine resistance in a globalized world inspire Hardt and Negri's most speculative vocabulary. In conceiving of a "multitude" – a word they use to avoid the passivity implied in "masses" or the Enlightenment revolutions echoed in "the people" – they seek to imagine a group within whom resistance is immanent. The multitude embodies a great refusal, an existential stance of "being-against" (211), in the forms of "desertion, exodus and nomadism" (212). Paradoxically, although flight from the spaces of pain that characterize much of the globe may only bring the nomadic subject to "a new rootless condition of poverty and misery" (213), Hardt and Negri also exalt the subversive energies of the multitude that cannot be controlled by national boundaries and that exert an insurgent will against any forces of containment. Alluding to Marx's opening words in the *Communist Manifesto*, they comment succinctly, "[A] specter haunts the world and it is the specter of migration" (213). Here, as in postcolonial studies, the terms *migrant* and *migrancy* – which encompass everyone from a middle-class professional seeking advancement, to an impoverished peasant leaving a remote village for the metropolis, to a destitute refugee fleeing the devastation of war – prove to be central figures in understanding potential tropes of emancipation in the new globalized world. In the "diffuse, anonymous network of all-englobing power" that is Empire (Balakrishnan 143), the flow of bodies in migrancy comes to represent an unwillingness to tolerate "miserable cultural and material conditions" and, more significantly, an "irrepressible desire for free movement" (Hardt and Negri 213).

There can be no doubt that *Empire* offers an imaginative and insightful analysis of globalization in a resonant language that attempts to articulate the utopian longings of Leftist traditions. And yet, Hardt and Negri's construction of the "multitude" remains decidedly unsettling. What are the implications of assigning equivalence to a well-educated professional who decides to accept a position on one continent rather than another and an impoverished worker who illegally enters Europe or the U.S. seeking labour? Both choose to become part of the global "flow of bodies," but under very different circumstances. How are the continuing displacements of aboriginal peoples within settler colonies to be conceptualized? How should we understand the "desire for free movement" across such divergent situations as characterize global migrancy? These questions, and others, underline the necessity we have stressed of re-examining the enormously divergent group of those marginalized by race, class, ethnicity, sexual orientation, gender, or geographical location. One strategy might be to develop Arjun Appadurai's discrimination among "diasporas of hope, diasporas of terror, and diasporas of despair," all of which carry "the force of imagination" (6). It might be equally productive to retrieve and rethink the functioning of "class" in and through the globalized world of the twenty-first century. To the pressing challenges of mapping new configurations of domination and resistance, postcolonial studies brings a wealth of histories, methodologies, and creativities.

Our title, *Linked Histories*, is taken from an installation by the Canadian aboriginal artist Joanne Cardinal-Schubert entitled "Kitchen Works: sstorsiinao'si," exhibited at the Alberta Biennial in the fall of 1998. The installation is unquestionably striking: the size of a small room, it confronts viewers with diverse representations of aboriginal peoples' histories under colonization. One wall consists of a mural of contorted, distressed figures, presided over by two soldiers; in the distance the viewer can make out a church and a flag recognizable as the Union Jack. Above the mural is a large blackboard covered with writing, extending the length of the wall, some seven or eight meters long. The conjuncture of church, settlement, and blackboard evokes memories of the infamous residential schools run by Roman Catholic and Protestant denominations where, in the name of cultural integration, young aboriginal children were separated from their families and communities, forced to abandon their languages and cultures, and sometimes subjected to physical and sexual abuse. While these representations work to preserve the memories of sufferings under colonization and at the same time call the dominant society to account, Cardinal-Schubert also strives to move beyond the markings of the past: "As an artist," she writes on the blackboard, "I can dare to look into the future." She goes on to challenge her viewers to move toward an "understanding of our linked histories [...] and the imposition of those histories on each other." From Cardinal-Schubert's perspective, it is not enough to address only the colonization of aboriginal peoples; rather, it is crucial to grasp the intertwining of shared histories, to understand how the cultural memories of the past might both block and, in different ways, facilitate movement toward the future. Such a perspective implies an attentive openness to how aboriginal cultures might offer emancipatory strategies to settler cultures and a willingness to question vigorously the assumption that cultural critique of colonization simply addresses the victimization of the colonized. In her view it is crucial to understand the linked histories in which pasts, presents, and futures are intersecting projects that cannot be easily disentangled or separated.

Links are also forged, and it is worth reflecting on this significant verb. In its evocation of fashioning and shaping, *forge* implies the historical and material conditions at work in the making of the contemporary world. Such a recognition is crucial, for if linkages can be understood as humanly and socially constructed, then they are also susceptible to alteration and change. This process is reminiscent of Victor Li's evocation of Marx when he writes that "the practice of articulation reopens the dimension of agency, change, risk, and uncertainty. In short, it enables us to make our own history even under conditions not of our choosing." And yet, from another point of view, *forge* signifies the act of counterfeiting, of falsifying, which underscores how linked histories have been nuanced and mobilized to carry diverse ideological inflections. Histories told by the victors are obvious examples of counterfeited, "forged" histories, but they are not the only examples. In forms as diverse as "writing back to the empire," *testimonio*, and magic realism, histories and cultural practices have reappropriated, refabricated and rewritten – one might say "reforged" – in order to represent new and unfolding projects.

In the spirit of linkages, it is appropriate to address our affiliations to an earlier publication. In 1990 Ian Adam and Helen Tiffin published *Past the Last Post: Theorizing Post-Colonialism and Post-Modernism*, a collection of essays drawn from a special issue of *ARIEL* (*A Review of International English Literature*), the postcolonial journal published by the University of Calgary Department of English. At a time when postcolonialism was beginning to reflect on its status as a disciplinary field, *Past the Last Post* provided spirited reflections on a range of theoretical and textual questions. A little more than a decade later when, to borrow the black British writer Biyi Bandele's timely comment in his *Brixton Stories*, "every post seemed to have been postponed," *Linked Histories* brings together subsequent articles from *ARIEL* that have moved the discussion forward into considerations of cultural materialism, a politics of resistance, and globalization. It would be mistaken to represent such shifts in focus as the inevitable advancement of knowledge within the traditional practices of academic disciplines. Rather, it is a process of defamiliarization and reconstitution, of a return to cultural memories and a rethinking of their implications for the future. As Diana Brydon has written,

> The "post" in "postcolonial" refers to the survival of certain ways of seeing and not-seeing from the past into the present, sometimes in rigidified forms [...] but other times in more subtle and dissimulating modes: in the rhetoric through which the media manage difference; in the way key public choices are posed; in the way knowledge is conceived, produced and exchanged and research conducted; in the way citizenship is understood and practised. (56)

In Brydon's formulations, the "post" in postcolonial does not signal a movement beyond a certain point, but rather signals the persistence of the past ("the survival of certain ways of seeing and not-seeing from the past into the present"). The implications of these persistences are changing and diverse; there is no definitive plotline into the future, but only a sense of mapping that is negotiated across shared and linked histories.

Works Cited

Achebe, Chinua. *Morning Yet on Creation Day*. New York: Doubleday, 1975.

Adam, Ian, and Helen Tiffin, eds. *Past the Last Post: Theorizing Post-Colonialism and Post-Modernism*. Calgary: University of Calgary Press, 1990.

Amin, Samir. *Specters of Capitalism: A Critique of Current Intellectual Fashions*. New York: Monthly Review, 1998.

Appadurai, Arjun. *Modernity at Large: Cultural Dimensions of Globalization*. Minneapolis: University of Minnesota Press, 1996.

Ashcroft, Bill, Gareth Griffiths, and Helen Tiffin. *The Empire Writes Back: Theory and Practice in Post-Colonial Literatures*. London: Routledge, 1989.

Balakrishnan, Gopal. "Virgilian Visions." *New Left Review* 5 (Sept.-Oct. 2000): 142–48.

Brixton Stories. By Biyi Bandele. The Pit Theatre, Barbican, London. 18 Apr. 2001.

Brydon, Diana. "Canada and Postcolonialism: Questions, Inventories and Futures." *Is Canada Postcolonial? Unsettling Canadian Literature*. Ed. Laura Moss. Waterloo: Wilfrid Laurier University Press, 2003. 49–77.

Buell, Frederick. "Globalization without Environmental Crisis: The Divorce of Two Discourses in U.S. Culture." *Symplokē* 9. 1–2 (2001): 45–73.

Cardinal-Schubert, Joane. *Kitchen Works: sstorsiinao'si*. Installation. Glenbow Museum and The Edmonton Art Gallery, Calgary and Edmonton. Alberta Biennial, 1998.

Cernetig, Miro. "Apocalypse Revisited: A visit to the Mekong Delta 25 years after the U.S. was defeated." *Globe and Mail* 29 Apr. 2000: A16–A17.

Dirlik, Arif. "Is There History after Eurocentrism? Globalism, Postcolonialism and the Disavowal of History." *Cultural Critique* 42 (1999): 1–34.

During, Simon. "Postcolonialism and Globalization: Towards a Historicization of Their Inter-relation." *Cultural Studies* 14.3–4 (2000): 385–404.

Hardt, Michael, and Antonio Negri. *Empire*. Cambridge: Harvard University Press, 2000.

Harvey, David. *Spaces of Hope*. Berkeley: University of California Press, 2000.

Jameson, Fredric. "Notes on Globalization as a Philosophical Issue." *The Cultures of Globalization*. Ed. Fredric Jameson and Masao Miyoshi. Durham: Duke University Press, 1998. 54–77.

Mowitt, John. "In the Wake of Eurocentrism." *Cultural Critique* 47 (2001): 3–15.

Quayson, Ato. *Postcolonialism: Theory, Practice or Protest?* Cambridge: Polity Press, 2000.

Slemon, Stephen. "Magic Realism and Post-Colonial Discourse." *Canadian Literature* 116 (1988): 9–24.

Wang, Fengzhen. "Mapping the Globalization in Chinese Culture." *ARIEL* 32.2 (Apr. 2001): 145–62.

Introduction: The Linked Histories of the Globalized World

Queer with Class: Absence of Third World Sweatshop in Lesbian/ Gay Discourse and a Rearticulation of Materialist Queer Theory   Cross-Mirrorings of Alterity: The Colonial Scenario and Its Psychological Legacy   Mythologies of Migrancy: Postcolonialism, Postmodernism, and the Politics of (Dis)location   Postcolonial DefferendDifferend: Diasporic Narratives of Salman Rushdie   At the Margins of Postcolonial Studies   Keeping History at Wind River and Acoma   Modernity's First Born: Latin America and Postcolonial Transformation   Towards Articulation: Postcolonial Theory and Demotic Resistance   Postcolonial Theory and the "Decolonization" of Chinese Culture

*Evil is never done so thoroughly
and so well as when it is done
with a good conscience.*

— Blaise Pascal
THOUGHTS (279)

*Fascism is not the prohibition of saying
things, it is the obligation to say them.*

— Roland Barthes
LEÇON (14)

The Fascist Longings
in Our Midst

REY CHOW

Fascism is a banal term.[1] It is used most often not simply to refer to the historical events that took place in Hitler's Germany and Mussolini's Italy but also to condemn attitudes or behaviour that we consider to be excessively autocratic or domineering.[2] Speaking in the mid-1970s, Michel Foucault referred to the popularized use of the term *fascism* as "a general complicity in the refusal to decipher what fascism really was." The non-analysis of fascism, Foucault goes on, is "one of the important political facts of the past thirty years. It enables fascism to be used as a floating signifier, whose function is essentially that of denunciation" ("Power and Strategies" 139).

In this essay, I attempt to study this – what amounts to a collective – denunciation of fascism by examining not only what is being denounced but also the major conceptual paths through which denunciation is produced. My argument is hence not exactly one that avoids the "floatingness" of the word *fascism* by grounding it in a particular time or space. Instead, I take fascism as a commonplace in the many ways it is used to indicate what is deemed questionable and unacceptable. In the process, I highlight what I think is fascism's most significant but often neglected aspect – what I will refer to as its technologized idealism. In my argument, fascism is not simply the disguised or naturalized "ideology" that we find in Louis Althusser and Roland Barthes;[3] rather it is a term that indicates the production and consumption of a glossy surface image, a crude style, for purposes of social identification even among intellectuals. In lieu of a conclusion, I also comment on the affinities between fascism as a "large" historical force and the mundane events of academic life in North America in the 1990s by foregrounding the idealizing tendencies in what is called multiculturalism.

Monstrous Visions

For those of us who do not have personal experience of the period of the Second World War in Europe and Asia, the picture that comes to mind when we think of fascism is always a photograph, a scene from a film, a documentary, or some graphic account narrated by survivors. The visual association we have with fascism is usually one of horror and destruction. Recently, for instance, I had the chance to view a video called *Magee's Testament* (produced and distributed by the Alliance in Memory of the Victims of the Nanking Massacre, 1991) about Japan's invasion of the city of Nanjing during December 1937 to February 1938. These newsreel pictures of rape and massacre constitute the only known filmed documentation of the atrocities committed by Japanese soldiers during what the Chinese call "Nanjing da tusha," the Nanjing Massacre or the Rape of Nanjing. Shot by an American missionary, John Magee, and recently rediscovered after fifty-five years, the cans of amateur film from the 1930s have been incorporated into a thirty-minute video by the Chinese American filmmaker Peter Wang. According to Magee's account, about 300,000 Chinese were killed in a week. This number would be among the fifteen to twenty million generally estimated to have been killed during Japan's aggression against China from 1931 to 1945.[4]

What comes across most powerfully in *Magee's Testament* is the aesthetic of Japanese brutality. I use the term *aesthetic* not in its narrow sense of principles of beauty or good taste, but in the broader, Kantian sense of principles of perception and cognition, principles that are in turn manifested in outward behaviour, as behavioural style. Among the Chinese survivors interviewed some forty-five years after the war, the memories of that aesthetic unfold in narratives that are juxtaposed with pictures taken in 1937 and 1938 of heartrending wounds, amputations, disabilities, and deaths. I was struck most of all by the pictures of a still-living woman the back of whose neck had been sawed at with a bayonet. A large portion of the head, which must have at one time been dangling in mid-air without being completely chopped off, was surgically stitched back onto this woman's body. At the time the newsreel was made, it was as if the camera, simply because it captured so vividly the painful physicality of this event, was an accomplice to the original act of brutality. So was the doctor who manipulated the woman's head for the camera, and so were those watching the film.

No words would do justice to the monstrosity of such an aesthetic. But what exactly is monstrous? No doubt it is the calamitous destruction that descended upon the victims. And yet a monstrous aesthetic is also an aesthetic of *making* something monstrous, of demonstrative magnification and amplification. As one writer points out, the Japanese soldiers who committed such acts of atrocity were able to do so because, like the Nazis, their loyalty to their ideology was so absolute that it freed them from all other restraints (Lestz 105). Unlike the Nazis, who were Christians mindful of the close relations between "body" and "spirit" and who regarded physical involvement with their victims' bodies as a form of spiritual contamination, the Japanese showed no such compunction. The point about their fascism was not enthusiasm in discipline but enthusiasm in unharnessed cruelty. It was thus not enough simply to extinguish the enemy's life *tout court*; they must torture and mutilate in ways that prolong and aggravate their victims' suffering and thus maximize their own pleasure. There was no sense of being contaminated by the enemy because the enemy was just raw material into which they poked their swords or discharged their urine and semen.

Like all graphic records of fascist destructiveness, the images of *Magee's Testament* clarify two things about fascism. The first, which is the easier to grasp, is that fascism is a form of technology. This does not simply refer to the fact that fascism deploys technological means for its purposes, but also that fascism is a kind of demonstrative culture/writing whose magnitude – whose portent – can only be that of the technological. The Japanese soldier did not simply use technological weapons; he was a murder machine that happened to take the form of a man. The second thing about fascism, which is closely related to the first but not as readily acceptable, is that the most important sentiment involved in fascism is not a negative but a positive one: rather than hatefulness and destructiveness, fascism is about love and idealism. Most of all it is a search for an idealized self-image through a heart-felt surrender to something higher and more beautiful. Like the Nazi officer who killed to purify his race, the Japanese soldier raped and slaughtered in total devotion to emperor and in the name of achieving the "Great East

Asia Co-Prosperity Sphere." Like the Nazi concentration camp official who was genuinely capable of being moved to tears by a Beethoven sonata being played by Jewish prisoners, the Japanese officer, we may surmise, was probably also genuinely capable of being moved by the delicate feelings inscribed in cultured practices such as haiku poetry, calligraphy, or the tea ceremony. In each case, what sustains the aesthetics of monstrosity is something eminently positive and decent.

Projection I: The Violence "In Us All"

The question of the relationship between the destructive and idealizing sentiments in fascism is thus much more difficult than it first appears. Let us think, once again, of Foucault's criticism that we have only used the term *fascism* to denounce others. On another occasion, in the preface to Gilles Deleuze and Félix Guattari's *Anti-Oedipus*, Foucault writes that the strategic adversary combated by *Anti-Oedipus* is fascism, adding that by this he means "not only historical fascism, the fascism of Hitler and Mussolini [...] but also the fascism in us all, in our heads and in our everyday behaviour, the fascism that causes us to love power, to desire the very thing that dominates and exploits us" (xiii).

By moving from events in the world outside back to the fascism "in us all," Foucault suggests an ancient piece of philosophical advice: "Know thyself." At the same time, by calling attention to the fascism within us as opposed to that outside us, Foucault articulates a specific conceptual mechanism used in many accounts of fascism, the mechanism of projection as defined by Freud. The function of projection is described by Freud as a defence: when we sense something dangerous and threatening in ourselves, we expel and objectify it outward, so as to preserve our own stability. The best social example of Freud's understanding of projection is anti-Semitism. The "Jew" is the name and the picture of all those things we cannot admit about ourselves; it is thus a symptom of our fears and anxieties.[5] Even though it is not always consciously stated as such, Freudian projection is crucial to some of the most sophisticated accounts of fascism.[6] However, what emerges interestingly from Foucault's brief comments on fascism is that if the fascist discrimination against the "Jew" is a projection in Freud's sense, then our denunciatory use of the term "fascism," insofar as it remains a "floating signifier," is also such a projection. *Fascism* has become for us the empty term, the lack, onto which we project all the unpleasant realities from which we want to distance ourselves. This is why fascism is associated alternately with colonialism, authoritarianism, mysticism, populism, socialism, banality, and so forth.[7] Ortega y Gasset summarizes fascism's emptiness perceptively when he writes that it is "simultaneously one thing and the contrary, A and not-A" (qtd. in Laclau 81–82). The extreme logical conclusion to this is that those who most violently denounce fascism – who characterize others as fascists – may themselves be exhibiting symptoms of fascism.

But what is it that we cannot admit about ourselves? Like many of his other concepts, Freud's definition of projection hinges on an act of negation: projection is the outward manifestation of a basic denial or refusal (of knowledge) in the individual organism. Once we focus on the indispensable negativity involved in projection, we notice that the premise for this projection is something like "human nature," which is treated as the source of the problems at hand. A critique of fascism by way of Freudian projection would hence always emphasize fascism as an expression of *our own* repression – our oppression of ourselves – and most critics of fascism, it follows, see fascism first of all as an inner or internalized violence from which we need to be "liberated." The belief in repression and liberation as such has the effect of turning even the perpetrators of fascism – those who rape, mutilate, and slaughter – into victims who are ultimately pardonable. For instance, in his classic study, *The Mass Psychology of Fascism*, Wilhelm Reich argues that fascism, like many forms of organized religion and mysticism, is the mass expression of orgiastic impotence or repressed sexual energies. Citing Hitler as his type case, Reich locates the social origin of fascism in the authoritarian patriarchal family, in which feelings of fear and rebellion toward the father are combined with those of reverence and submission (37–40). While Reich's interpretation made up in a significant way for the neglect of sexuality that characterized most Marxist and economic approaches to fascism of his day, it nevertheless reads like a vulgarized use of Freud's notion of repression: fascism becomes the compensatory "sublimation" (in distorted form) of the energy that had nowhere else to go. Not surprisingly, therefore, the solution offered by Reich is finally that of "love" and "work" – the proper sublimation of sexual energies that should, he writes, govern our lives.

Similarly, in *Anti-Oedipus*, Deleuze and Guattari explain the repressive violence characteristic of Western society by way of Nietzsche's notion of *ressentiment*. For them, *ressentiment*, which is active life force turned inward, has a name – Oedipus. Freudian psychoanalysis, insofar as it helps perpetuate the ideological baggage of a metaphysics of interiority, is for Deleuze and Guattari the place to begin criticism of the everyday fascism of Western society.[8]

The "internalized violence" model is so persuasive that it captures even a Marxist political philosopher like Ernesto Laclau. In *Politics and Ideology in Marxist Theory*, Laclau's project is that of finding ways to articulate the popular forces that motivated fascism in Europe. While Laclau does not fail to see the problems in Reich's interpretation (84–86), his own criticism of

Nicos Poulantzas's well-known study of fascism is precisely that Poulantzas reduced every contradiction to a class contradiction and failed to take into account the processes of subjectivization involved. Using Althusser's notion of "interpellation," Laclau thus reformulates fascism as a kind of populism that interpellated masses as "a people" in ways that went beyond their class distinctions. It does not seem problematic to Laclau that Althusser's notion of interpellation is still, arguably, dependent upon an outside (ideology) versus an inside (the individual), and that the moment the individual responds to the hailing "Hey, you!" is also the moment when the force of ideology is "internalized."

Despite the differences among these critics of fascism – Deleuze and Guattari mock and deterritorialize Freudian psychoanalysis while Reich, Althusser, and Laclau continue to adapt it to their own purposes – they all implicitly agree that fascism's effectiveness has to do with its being a violence – a negative force – that has been internalized, a violence that is somehow "in us all" by nature or by culture. This leaves us with the question of how exactly fascism is internalized. What does it mean for fascism to be in us? Do we violate ourselves the way the Nazis and the Japanese violated Jews, Gypsies, and Asians? How does the lack in us (in Freud's terms, fear and denial) turn into a concrete thing outside us? How does the nameless in us acquire the external name "Jew"? Conversely, how does that monstrous picture out there signify/become what is in us? How are we to understand that proclamation by Göring which epitomizes this basic problem of fascist projection – "I have no conscience. My conscience is Adolf Hitler" (qtd. in Mitscherlich 288)?

In other words, when we move from acts of brutality to internalized violence, or when we move from the lack that is supposedly in us to external atrocities, some change, presupposed and yet unexplained, has taken place. This change, which is the unarticulated part of all of these theories of internalized violence, is metaphorical, imaginary, and, as I will argue, technological. It indicates that which happens but which we cannot actually see or hear – and which we must therefore explain in terms other than itself. The filmic image, because it is obvious and palpable, offers a convenient way of staging these other terms.

But there is a more fundamental reason why fascism can be explained by way of film. Not that film expresses the images of fascism effectively. Rather, like film, fascism as an ideology has "its foundation in projection." I take this phrase from Alice Yaeger Kaplan's illuminating study of French fascism, *Reproductions of Banality*. Basing her notion of fascism not on the profound but on the banal and obvious (46), Kaplan calls for a different kind of attention to be paid to fascism – not a convoluted search in the depths of our selves for the *ressentiment* imposed by religion or family, but attention to fascism as projection, surface phenomena, everyday practice, which does away with the distinction between the inside and the outside: "The fascist ideal is being swallowed by the subject at the same time as it is being projected onto the leader. Projection and introjection are not always even that distinguishable" (6).[9] The indistinguishability of introjection from projection means that there is a mutual implication between fascism and technology, including the technology that is psychoanalysis. When authors like Freud used terms such as *projection* and *screen memory*, Kaplan writes, they were already speaking to the mediatized makeup of our experience (5).

What is internalized – if the language of internalization still makes sense – is thus not so much the atrocious ideology of cruelty as its monstrous, propagandist form:

> The crowd comes to know itself as film. Subjects knowing themselves as film – that is, internalizing the aesthetic criteria offered in film – have a radically different experience, than if they knew themselves through film. In the film experience the spectators do not merely control a model that remains exterior to their untouched subjectivity; rather, their subjectivity is altered and enlarged by the film. (155)

What is internalized in the age of film is the very projectional mechanism of projection. If individuals are, to use Althusser's term, interpellated, they are interpellated not simply as watchers of film but also as film itself. They "know" themselves not only as the subject, the audience, but as the object, the spectacle, the movie. In his study of the cinema of Fassbinder, Thomas Elsaesser makes a similar argument about German fascism – namely, that German fascism was based in the state of being-looked-at, which cinema's proclivity toward visual relations conveniently exemplifies. Elsaesser holds that the Fassbinder trademark of exhibitionism – the persistent foregrounding of being-looked-at and its significance for the formation of social identity – should be understood in this light:

> What, Fassbinder seems to ask, was fascism for the German middle and working-class which supported Hitler? We know what it was for Jews, for those actively persecuted by the regime, for the exiles. But for the apolitical Germans who stayed behind? Might not the pleasure of fascism, its fascination have been less the sadism and brutality of SS officers than the pleasure of being seen, of placing oneself in view of the all-seeing eye of the State? Fascism in its Imaginary encouraged a moral exhibitionism, as it encouraged denunciation and mutual surveillance. Hitler appealed to the *Volk* but always by picturing the German nation,

> standing there, observed by "the eye of the world." The massive
> specularization of public and private life [...] might it not have helped
> to institutionalize the structure of "to be is to be perceived" that
> Fassbinder's cinema problematizes? (545)[10]

In Elsaesser's phrase "to be is to be perceived," we see that projection, instead of being preceded by "being," is itself the basis from which "being" arises. Such psychologizing implies a reversal of Freud's model of projection. While Freud begins with the "being" that is the individual organism – the inner something that, sensing something unpleasant, projects it outward – Elsaesser's reading of Fassbinder enables us to begin instead with the projection that is obviously "out there" – the projection that is "being perceived," the projection that is film. While the Freudian model describes projection as being based upon an original lack, as an externalized concretization or objectification of that lack, we can now ask instead: how does the projection that is film become us? How does visual technology inhabit the human shape?

In order to answer these questions, we need to recall the more conventional meaning of projection as an act of thrusting or throwing forward, an act that causes an image to appear on a surface. Despite the suggestive association of fascism with film, what remains unarticulated in Kaplan's (and to some extent Elsaesser's) account is the difference between this obvious sense of projection and Freud's definition. While the common conceptual path taken by most critics of fascism is projection in Freud's sense – that is, projection as a subject's refusal to recognize something in order to defend itself – film, as external image, operates with the more obvious sense of projection – as objects already out there, objects that may not necessarily be a compensation or substitution for an original (subjective) lack or inability. Once the premise of projection is changed from "inside" to "surface" in this manner, it becomes possible to think of projection as a positing rather than a negating function. It would also, I propose, be possible to rethink fascism away from the projection-as-compensated-lack model provided by Freud.

Projection II: Angels of Light

By turning to film and to the formal mutuality between film and fascism, I am not saying that film offers a means of illustrating the principles of fascism. What I am saying is that fascism cannot be understood without a certain understanding of the primacy of the image, which is best exemplified by the relations of receptivity involved in film. My point can be stated in a different way: film, because it is obviously imagistic, stands as a good way of analyzing the abstract problem of projection, which is also the problem of that imaginary and metaphoric change between external and internal violence that remains unexplained in the writers I mentioned earlier.[11]

It is hence not an accident that critics of fascism frequently turn to film for their discussions. Consider, for instance, Susan Sontag's classic "Fascinating Fascism," from which the title of the present essay is taken.[12] In her essay, Sontag repudiates the judgement that the work of filmmaker and photographer Leni Riefenstahl, who received generous support from the German government for her productions during the Nazi period, is nevertheless in some significant manner "apolitical." By refusing to separate artistic technique from ideology, Sontag persuasively shows how the creation of beauty in Riefenstahl's films is intimately linked to fascist ideals. Toward the end of the essay, Sontag writes:

> [I]t is generally thought that National Socialism stands only for brutishness and terror. But this is not true. National Socialism – or, more broadly, fascism – also stands for an ideal, and one that is also persistent today, under other banners: the ideal of life as art, the cult of beauty, the fetishism of courage, the dissolution of alienation in ecstatic feelings of community; the repudiation of the intellect; the family of man (under the parenthood of leaders). (43)

Insofar as she identifies the positive messages of fascism as an inalienable part of its functioning, I am in total agreement with Sontag. Her charge that the most widely appreciated qualities of Riefenstahl's work – its beauty, its technical refinement – are precisely what speak most effectively to "the fascist longings in our midst" is so perceptive that it is unsettling.[13] Yet peculiarly, in an essay that so clearly insists on the inseparability of art and ideology, Sontag nonetheless makes a distinction between art and ideology as soon as she tries to contrast fascist art with communist art:

> The tastes for the monumental and for mass obeisance to the hero are common to both fascist and communist art. [...] But fascist art has characteristics which show it to be, in part, a special variant of totalitarian art. The official art of countries like the Soviet Union and China is based on a utopian morality. Fascist art displays a utopian aesthetics – that of physical perfection. [...] In contrast to the asexual chasteness of official communist art, Nazi art is both prurient and idealizing. [...] The fascist ideal is to transform sexual energy into a "spiritual" force, for the benefit of the community. (40–41)

If Sontag's judgement about fascist art does away with the distinction between propaganda and aesthetics, her reading of the difference between communist and fascist art reintroduces it. We can only speculate that, as a Jewish intellectual writing in the United States of the 1970s, Sontag was absolutely clear-eyed about the fascism of the earlier decades, but like all left-leaning Eurocentric intellectuals of that period, she retained a sense of illusion about communism. Hence even though she writes that fascist art shares with totalitarian art the same tastes for the monumental and for mass obeisance to the hero, she seems to imply, ultimately, that because fascism beautifies and thus hides its totalitarian motives in aesthetically impeccable images, it is the more pernicious and dangerous of the two. Once ideology and art are distinguished as content and façade in this way, however, aesthetics returns to the more narrow and conventional sense of the beautiful alone.

By describing fascism as fascinating aesthetics in the narrow sense, Sontag, in spite of her own insights, rejoins the tendency of most discussions of fascism, in which attention is almost always focussed, negatively, on the deceptiveness of fascist authorities: these fascists, it is thought, paint beautiful (that is, delusive) pictures about their ugly (that is, real) behaviour. Such pictures, in other words, have the status of deliberate lies. Fascist atrocities thus become the "real" that sets the records straight, that exposes the deceit and error of fascist rhetoric.

But it is precisely in this kind of interpretive crossover from rhetoric to deed, from "lies" to "truth," from "beautiful pictures" to "ugly reality" that critics have downplayed the most vital point about fascism – its significance as image and surface; its projectional idealism. The false-true dichotomization leads us to believe that good intentions cannot result in cruel behaviour, and conversely, that the fact of cruelty can only be the result of hidden evil motives dressed up as beautiful pictures. We see how the substitutive or compensatory logic of Freud's notion of projection is fully at work here: the fascists, according to this logic, project to the outside what they (secretly) deny about themselves; we the critics thus have to negate their negation and rewind their projection from that false outside back into their hidden inside. According to this logic, not only are intentions and behaviour transparently linked; they are also linked through opposition and negation: hence, the "good" image is an index to "bad" motives. But what if the declared ideals were not lies (projection in Freud's sense) but projections (projection in the common sense of throwing forward)? How then do we understand the relation between noble intentions and atrocious deeds?

Without the illusion about communism – that its propaganda, unlike the beautiful façade of fascism, has after all some real connection to a utopian morality – Sontag would in fact have come close to saying that the aesthetics of fascism (aesthetics in the broad sense of cognition and perception) resides precisely in images – not so much images-as-the-beautiful but images-as-the-positivistic-and-self-evident. The beautiful images are not images that hide (the content of horror); rather they are the cognitive form of the technological age, the surface or superficial phenomena that present themselves as evidence of themselves instead of some other, inner meaning. What is fascist about fascism's idealized images is not only that they are positive, but also that they pose and posit, and are positivistic. This positivity is the projection that the followers of fascism internalize.

What Sontag correctly identifies as the idealizing tendencies of fascism can thus be explained by the projectional nature of film. To present something in idealized terms is literally to enlarge and embolden it – in short, to blow it up as a picture. While it takes its materials from everyday life, this picture, by its very positivity, also becomes mythic. It holds a promise and turns the everyday into the primitive and archetypal. In the process of consuming it, we become infantilized. As Kaplan writes, "the machinery of the media gave birth to a new kind of ideological vulnerability. It was mother bound" (23). In what amounts to the same argument, Kaplan writes: "When fascism took power, it took charge of the imaginary" (34).[14]

André Bazin provides an astute analysis of these relations between film and idealism, relations that are based on projection, in an essay called "The Stalin Myth in Soviet Cinema." Unlike Sontag, who still attributes to communist art a utopianism that would set it off from fascist art, Bazin calls attention precisely to the idealizing – that is, fascistic – logic in the Soviet films about Stalin. Writing around 1950, Bazin was amazed by the fact that these mythically positive images of Stalin – as a hyper-Napoleonic military genius, as an omniscient and infallible leader, but also as a friendly, avuncular helper to the common people – were made while the man was still alive. Bazin's point is that only the dead are larger than life: "If Stalin, even while living, could be the main character of a film, it is because he is no longer 'human,' engaging in the transcendence which characterizes living gods and dead heroes" (36). The glorifying films have the effect of mummifying and monumentalizing Stalin, so that it is the Stalin-image that becomes the ultimate authority, which even Stalin himself had to follow in order to "be" (40).

Thus, according to Bazin, the idealizing power of cinema is not only positivistic but also retroactive, calling for a submission to that which has always, in the process of being idealized, already become past or dead. The Stalin myth in Soviet cinema commands an absolute surrender – an identification that is possible only with the cessation of history. Bazin illustrates the retroactive logic of fascist idealization with another, non-filmic example: the Stalinist trials. For Bazin, the major accomplishment of the trials is their success in remaking – that is, falsifying – history with the pre-emptiveness of retroaction:

> According to the Soviet "Stalinist" communist perspective, no one can
> "become" a traitor. That would imply that he wasn't always a traitor, that
> there was a biographical beginning to this treason, and that, conversely,
> a person who became a menace to the Party would have been considered
> useful to the Party before becoming evil. The Party could not simply bust
> Radek to the lowest rank, or condemn him to death. It was necessary to
> proceed with a retroactive purge of History, proving that the accused was,
> since birth, a willful traitor whose every act was satanically camouflaged
> sabotage. Of course, this operation is highly improbable and far too
> serious to be used in every case. That is why the public *mea culpa* can be
> substituted concerning minor figures whose historical action is indirect –
> such as artists, philosophers, or scientists. These solemn hyperbolic *mea
> culpas* can seem psychologically improbable or intellectually superfluous
> to us if we fail to recognize their value as exorcism. As confession is
> indispensable to divine absolution, so solemn retraction is indispensable
> to the reconquering of historical virginity. (37)

By inserting this discussion of the logic of totalitarian interrogation in an
essay about cinematic representation, Bazin enables us to see retroaction
as the crucial common ground for both the Stalinist trials and the filmic
construction of Stalin. Moreover, he enables us to see that retroaction works
hand in hand with positivism: like the interrogative erasure of the history
of communist "traitors" – an erasure (of counter-evidence) that, in effect,
becomes the self-validating "evidence" of their guilt – the very (retroactive)
idealization of Stalin's goodness in the form of (positivistic) images is part
of a manipulation of history that uses images as their own alibi by making
them appear self-evident. The effect is mass sacrifice – the sacrifice of the
masses' own knowledge of history in submission to the mythic image.

Bazin's analysis offers us a way out of Freud's definition of projection.
Instead of operating negatively as refusal, compensated lack, and defence
mechanism, projection here is the positive instrument of transparency, of
good intentions shining forth in dazzling light. Stalin as the angel of light – not
only in the sense that he was bringing enlightenment to the people but also in
the sense that he was himself transparent, thus allowing for an identification
that dissolves the boundary between the inside and the outside: this was the
magic of his image. It is therefore not by focussing on the atrocious deeds,
the evil of fascists, but on their moments of idealism production, their good
conscience, that we can understand the effectiveness of fascist aesthetics.
The voice of Emperor Hirohito, heard for the first time by his people over the
radio after the bombing of Hiroshima and Nagasaki, speaking solemnly of the
sadness of national defeat, was one example of this aesthetic. The voice and

image of Mao Zedong telling the Red Guards that "revolution is not criminal, revolt is reasonable" in the form of massive street slogans and pamphlets was another. The sincere altruistic rhetoric we hear in U.S. presidential campaigns, complete with the candidates' demonstrations of their ordinariness (their love of family, for instance), is a third. In all of these cases, it is the force of light, transparency, and idealized image that works in the service of interpellating the masses, who receive the leaders as a mesmerizing film. To say that the leaders are lying to the masses would be to miss the point of our thoroughly mediatized feelings and perceptions, which accept this aesthetic without coercion, and which accept it as positive and good.[15]

That fascism is primarily a production of light and luminosity is an argument Paul Virilio makes in *War and Cinema: The Logistics of Perception*, among other works. Virilio's point over and over again is the fatal interdependence of the technologies of warfare and vision, "the conjunction between the power of the modern *war* machine [...] and the new technical performance of the *observation* machine" (71). Hitler and Mussolini clearly understood the coterminous nature of perception and destruction, of cinematic vision and war. While the former commented in 1938, "The masses need illusion – but not only in theatres or cinemas," the latter declared, "Propaganda is my best weapon" (qtd. in Virilio 53).

These remarks show us the technical nature of fascism, not only in the sense that fascism deploys technological weapons, but also in the sense that the scale of illusion/transparency promised by fascism is possible only in the age of film, the gramophone, and the loudspeaker. The mediatized image and voice – machines in human form rather than humans using machines – are, in Heidegger's terms, fascism's *teche*. Virilio writes:

> If photography, according to its inventor Nicéphore Niepce, was simply
> a method of engraving with light, where bodies inscribed their traces by
> virtue of their own luminosity, nuclear weapons inherited both the dark
> room of Niepce and Daguerre and the military searchlight. (81)

To paraphrase Virilio, we might add that fascism is an engraving with light on people's minds: fascist leaders inscribed their traces by virtue of their own luminosity; fascist propaganda inherited both the dark room of Niepce and Daguerre and the military searchlight.

The Story of O, or, the New Fascism

In the foregoing pages, I have tried to argue that fascism needs to be understood not only in its negative but, more importantly, in its positive aspects, and that fascism's production of idealism is a projectional production of luminosity-as-self-evidence. In an essay entitled "The Evidence of Experience," which does not at first seem to have anything to do with the topic of fascism, Joan Scott has made comparable observations about the use of experience in the North American academy today. In the general atmosphere of a felt need to deconstruct universalist claims about human history, Scott writes, scholars of various disciplines have increasingly turned to personal experience as a means of such deconstruction. However, she argues, by privileging experience as the critical weapon against universalisms, we are leaving open the question as to what authorizes experience itself. Scott charges that the appeal to experience "as uncontestable evidence and as an originary point of explanation" for historical difference has increasingly replaced the necessary task of exploring "how difference is established, how it operates, how and in what ways it constitutes subjects who see and act in the world (777)."[16]

For me, what is especially interesting is the manner in which Scott emphasizes the role of vision and visibility throughout her essay. Beginning her discussion with Samuel R. Delany's autobiographical meditation, *The Motion of Light in Water*, Scott notes that "a metaphor of visibility as literal transparency is crucial to his project." She concludes that for Delany, "[k]nowledge is gained through vision; vision is a direct apprehension of a world of transparent objects" (775). What Scott articulates here is the other side of Virilio's argument about the coterminous nature of visual perception and destruction – that is, the coterminous nature of visual perception and knowledge: "Seeing is the origin of knowing" (776). While the technology of seeing, or seeing-as-technology, has become an inalienable part of the operation of militarism and fascist propaganda, Scott shows how it has also come to dominate our thinking about identity, so much so that visibility and luminosity are the conditions toward which accounts of difference and alternative histories derived from "personal experience" now aspire. Such aspiration, Scott implies, is an aspiration toward the self-evidence of the self's (personal) experience. The self as evidence: this means that the self, like the Stalin myth in Soviet cinema, is so transparent, so shone through with light, that it simply *is*, without need for further argument about its history or what Scott calls its "discursive character" (787).

By alerting us to the technology (what she calls metaphor) of visibility, which is now engraved in the attitudes toward knowledge, history, and identity, Scott's argument provides a way of linking the "large" historical issues of fascism and totalitarianism we have been examining with the "small" sphere of North American academic life in the 1990s. In the remainder of this essay, I will elaborate this linkage further with the help of a fictional scenario. As many readers will recognize, the features of this scenario are a composite drawn from the recent general trends of multiculturalism in the academy. By portraying these features in a deliberately exaggerated form, my point is not to slight the significance of the work that is being done by non-Western intellectuals on the non-Western world, but rather to deconstruct our increasingly fascistic intellectual environment, in which facile attitudes, pretentious credentials, and irresponsible work habits can be fostered in the name of "cultural pluralism." The heroine in my fictional scenario is ultimately a mock heroine, the victim of a dangerous collective culture that all of us working in the West perpetrate in different ways.

We will call this imaginary heroine O. A "person of colour" from a Third World country, O is enrolled in a graduate program in a North American university. Despite her upper-class background, O tells people that she is from poor peasant stock in order to enhance her credibility as a Third World intellectual. After muddling and bluffing through her coursework, O launches a "multidisciplinary" dissertation that deals with various types of social protest by underdogs in her culture of origin. For two or three years O does virtually nothing by way of serious reading and research, though she makes her presence known regularly by speaking extemporaneously at different conferences. Much as she holds Western capitalism in contempt and tirelessly brandishes slogans of solidarity with downtrodden classes in the Third World, O seems even more determined to get her share of fame, privilege, and material well-being in the First World by hook or by crook. But even while O has no qualms about faking her way through graduate school, and even while no one can, when asked, say what her project really is apart from repeating the vague generalities that O habitually recites, the support O receives from well-established academics across the U.S. is tremendous. Many of these supporters are white. Some of them assert that O is the most talented young intellectual from a Third World country they have ever encountered. With their glowing recommendations, O eventually finds herself a job teaching at a U.S. university.

What is behind such sincere support of a great impostor from what are undoubtedly intelligent and accomplished people? A mass process similar to that described in the classic story of the Emperor's new clothes is mobilized here, as someone willing to occupy the position of the Emperor accidentally appears. Obviously, we cannot say to O's supporters – "But can't you see…?!" – because another kind of seeing is taking place. By seeing a student of colour, no matter how pretentious and fraudulent, as self-evidently correct and deserving of support, these supporters receive an image of themselves that is at once enlightenedly humble ("I submit to you, since you are a victim of our imperialism") and beautiful ("Look how decent I am by submitting to you"), and thus eminently gratifying.

Even though O may be cheating her way through the system, she alone is not to blame for this ridiculous situation. As I already emphasized, it is our

flagrantly irresponsible environment of "cultural pluralism" that nurtures
her behaviour and allows her to thrive.[17] In the white liberal enthusiasm
for "people of colour" that is currently sweeping through North American
academic circles, something of the fascism we witnessed in earlier decades
has returned in a new guise. The basis for this fascism is, once again, the
identification with an idealized other placed in the position of unquestion-
able authority. Like the fascism of the 1920s and 1930s, a feeling of rebellion
is definitely present; like the old fascism also, there is a massive submission
to a kind of figure of experience that is assumed to be, to use the terms of
Scott's analysis, luminously self-evident. This time, what is rebelled against is,
fashionably, the canon of the West or "Western imperialism," and the figure
onto whom such feelings are projected is the "person of colour," regardless
of that person's actual personal or professional politics.[18]

Once fascism starts taking effect, it is useless to point out that the person
being put in the position of the Emperor wearing new clothes is a fraud.
Debunking O as an impostor by pointing out her fraudulence – that she
is actually ignorant, lazy, and deceitful, for instance – would be to miss
the point that fascism happens when people willingly suspend disbelief in
fraudulence and that, in fact, it is precisely with such fraudulence that they
identify. The trait-of-identification between O and her supporters is the
glossy surface image of a righteous "person of colour" who, simply by being
(herself), simply by making loud proclamations against the West at all times,
brings justice to everyone who has suffered under Western imperialism.
Since the identification is precisely with this truth/illusion about O – that she
simply *is*, without work or effort – debunking it would reinforce rather than
destroy O's appeal.[19] Fascism here is the force of an "in spite of" turning into
a "precisely because": in spite of the fact that the Emperor has no clothes on,
people see him as the opposite; precisely because he has no clothes on, people
themselves provide the vision that makes up for this lack. In this vision, an
impostor like O looms with irresistible charm, as an angel of light. For those
who love her with benevolence, O is a cipher, an automaton performing the
predictable notions of the Third World intellectual they desire.

This story of O is but one among many that characterize the politically
correct atmosphere of the North American academy of the 1990s. In using
the term *politically correct*, what I intend is not the kind of conservative,
right-wing bashing of the academy gone to hell with feminism, cultural
pluralism, multidisciplinarity, and the like, but rather the phrase's original
sense of a criticism of our own moral self-righteousness having gone haywire.
In this original sense, political correctness is a machinery of surveillance that
encourages certain kinds of exhibitionism. To borrow from Elsaesser's study
of Fassbinder, we may say that "[i]n the face of a bureaucratic surveillance

system ever more ubiquitous," the O's of the academy, like the German middle-class citizens in Fassbinder's films, take on "an act of terrorist exhibitionism which turns the machinery of surveillance [...] into an occasion for self-display" (545).

As a person of colour from the Third World, as a student doing a project about lower classes in the Third World, O occupies a number of positions that are currently considered, in an *a priori* manner, as "other" and "marginalized." But are such positions alone, especially when they are self-consciously adopted and promoted simply in order to draw attention and in place of hard work, a genuine contribution to change? Does otherness itself automatically suffice as critical intervention? By subscribing to the "evidence of experience" as embodied by the likes of O, those who support people of colour insult the latter a second time: this time people of colour are not being colonized territorially and ideologically; rather they are uniformly branded as the "virtuous other" regardless of their own class, gender, race, and other differences, and are thus, to cite Edward Said, orientalized all over again. To put all this in blunter terms, we can draw an analogy between what is happening to O and the much-criticized white fantasy about the sexuality of, say, black people. According to this fantasy, the black man or woman simply *is* sex, primitive rhythm, unrepressed nature, and so forth. To this wish list we may now add the oppressed, revolution, and political correctness as well.[20]

The machines of surveillance here are not war airplanes but the media – the networks of communication, which, in the academic world, include the classroom, conferences, publications, funding agencies, and even letters of recommendation. With the large number of students (rightly) eager for alternative histories, of academic conferences (rightly) devoted to the constructions of differences, and of publishers (rightly) seeking to publish new, unexplored materials, fascism has reasserted itself in our era. And, as even my brief discussion shows, fascism's new mode is very much complicated by postcoloniality. The question facing intellectuals in the contemporary West is how to deal with peoples who were once colonized and who are now living and working in the First World as "others."[21] In the early days of colonialism, when actual territorial conquests were made and relocation from the mother country to the colonies was a fact of life for those from what eventually came to be called the First World, the questions for white people finding themselves removed from home were questions of what Nancy Armstrong and Leonard Tennenhouse call "the imaginary puritan": How to preserve whiteness while in the brown and black colonies? How to stay English in America? How to fabricate a respectable national origin against the onslaught of barbaric natives – that is, how to posture as the invaded and colonized while invading and colonizing others? All in all, these questions amount to how *not* to "go native."[22] As Armstrong and Tennenhouse argue, the English novel, which was conceptually based not so much on previous cultural developments in Europe but rather on the captivity narratives that found their way back to Europe from the New World, bears symptoms of this white anxiety about cultural purity. In this sense, the English novel is perhaps the earliest example – to use Fredric Jameson's classic pronouncement on Third World literature – of a "national allegory."

Toward the end of the twentieth century, as the aftermath of the grand imperialist era brings about major physical migrations of populations around the globe, it is no longer a question of white people going to the colonies, but rather of formerly colonized peoples settling permanently in their former colonizers' territories. The visible presence of these formerly colonized peoples in the First World leads to violent upheavals in Western thought. The overriding preoccupation among First World intellectuals has now become how to become "other." How to claim to be a minority – to claim to be black, Native American, Hispanic, or Asian, even if one has only 1/64th share of these "other" origins. In other words, how to "go native." Instead of imagining themselves to be a Pamela or Clarissa being held captive, resisting rape, and writing volumes in order to preserve the purity of their souls (and thus their "origins," to quote again from Armstrong and Tennenhouse), First World intellectuals are now overtaken by a new kind of desire: "Make me other!" And so, with expediency, we witness the publication of essays that are studded with names of nations and territories in order to convey a profile of "cosmopolitanism"; journals that amass the most superficial materials about lesser known cultures and ethnicities in the name of being "public," "global," or "transnational"; and book series which (en)list "indigenous" histories and narratives in the manner of a world fair – all this, while so-called postcolonial criticisms of former European imperialist strategies of representing, objectifying, and exhibiting the other are going on.

If there is one thing that unites the early territorial colonialism and the contemporary white liberalist intellectual trends that I am describing, it is the notion of a clear demarcation between self and other, between us and them – a demarcation that is mediated through the relations between consciousness and captivity. The myth, in the days of territorial colonialism, was that (white) consciousness had to be established in resistance to captivity – even while whites were holding other peoples and lands captive – so that (white) cultural origins could be kept pure. In the postcolonial era, by contrast, the myth is that (white) consciousness must itself surrender to or be held captive by the other – that (white) consciousness is nothing without this captivity called "otherness." In both cases, however, what remains constant is the belief that we are not them, and that white is not other. This belief, which can be further encapsulated as "we are not other," is fascism *par excellence*.

Emerging in postcoloniality, the new "desire for our others" displays the same positive, projectional symptoms of fascism that I discussed in the preceding pages – a rebelliousness and a monstrous aesthetic, but most of all a longing for a transparent, idealized image and an identifying submission to such an image. Like the masses' embrace of a Hitler or a Mussolini, this fascism seeks empowerment through a surrender to the other as film – as the film that overcomes me in the spell of an unmediated "experience." The indiscriminate embrace of the peoples of colour as "correct" regardless of their differences and histories is ultimately the desire for a pure-other-ness-in-pristine-luminosity that is as dangerous as the fascism of hateful discrimination from which we all suppose we are safely distanced. The genealogical affinity of these two fascisms is perhaps best exemplified by the art of a Leni Riefenstahl, who progressed from embracing Nazi racism to embracing the beautiful Nuba men of the southern Sudan.

If the controversial label "fascism" is indeed useful, as I think it is, for a radical critique of the contemporary intellectual culture in the West, it is because it helps us identify and problematize the good conscience and noble obligations of the new liberal fascism with its multiculturalist modes and its sophisticated enterprises of visibility. Some will no doubt want to disavow such ongoing fascist longings in our midst; others, hopefully, will not.

Notes

1 Many people must be acknowledged for having contributed to the final shape of this essay. Nancy Armstrong, Chris Cullens, Prabhakara Jha, Kwai-cheung Lo, Austin Meredith, and Dorothea von Mücke were readers who responded with constructive comments to the first draft when it was completed in December 1992. Members of the Critical Theory Institute at the University of California, Irvine devoted a session to a subsequent version of the essay in Fall 1993, and I thank in particular Lindon Barrett, Alexander Gelley, and John Rowe for their extended remarks. I am also grateful to Iain Chambers, Chris Connery, Hal Foster, and Kathleen Woodward for their assistance at various stages. To Livia Monnet, who gave me her indefatigable enthusiasm and support, I owe a special debt of friendship.

2 For an informative analysis of some of the well-known and/or widely adopted interpretations of fascism in Germany, see Schulte-Sasse. For some of the more recent discussions of fascism in Europe and European writers, see the essays in Golsan, which also contains a useful "Selective Bibliography" of recent works in English on fascism.

3 The argument that ideology is the history that has been "naturalized" or "disguised" is a predominant way of understanding fascism; accordingly, fascism is construed as a matter of *lies*. As will become clear in the course of this essay, my argument differs from this major view of ideology in that I do not see fascism simply as lying.

4 It is well-known that even today members of the Japanese Parliament attempt to deny their country's war atrocities. *Magee's Testament* shows one such MP, Shintaro Ishihara, declaring

in an interview with *Playboy* that the atrocities did not happen and then changing his mind in a subsequent interview with *Time*. In the second interview, Ishihara proclaimed that merely 20,000, rather than 300,000, Chinese were killed in the Nanjing Massacre – as if a smaller number would make the massacre of less concern. This denial is so determined that the Japanese government ensured that Emperor Akihito's visit to China in 1992 would not be used as the occasion for an apology. "There was an unfortunate period in which my country inflicted great sufferings on the people of China," Akihito said, speaking in Japanese. "I feel deep sorrow about this." Meanwhile, the Japanese Education Ministry exercised its constitutional right to dictate the contents of schoolbooks by censoring descriptions of the Japanese army's germ warfare experiments on prisoners and of episodes such as the Rape of Nanjing. According to a Reuters report in March 1993, Japan's Supreme Court upheld this censorship and rejected the lawsuit by Saburo Ienaga, a retired history professor, who had waged a thirty-year battle against the whitewashing of wartime history ("Japanese Court OKs Censoring of Schoolbooks"). Ienaga finally won his battle in May 1994 ("Scholar Wins Ruling on Nanjing Massacre"). As Claude Lanzman writes in *Shoah: An Oral History of the Holocaust*, for the invention of genocide no one wants "copyright." Lanzman is quoted by Michael Lestz in a review essay on holocaust literature, "Lishi de mingji." For discussions of Japanese war atrocities in China published in Chinese, see for instance Xu Zhigeng, and also Gao Xingzu. For a recent overview of Sino-Japanese political and cultural relations since the Second World War, see Dirlik.

5   "The subject attributes tendencies, desires, etc., to others that he refuses to recognize in himself: the racist, for instance, projects his own faults and unacknowledged inclinations on to the group he reviles. This type of projection [...] seems to come closest to the Freudian sense of the term" (Laplanche and Pontalis, 351. See also the entire entry under "Projection," 349–56).

6   For instance, in an essay on the 1932 Exhibition of the Fascist Revolution in Rome, Jeffrey T. Schnapp describes "the structural undergirding of fascist ideology" as a "taut but hollow frame over which a canvas must be stretched in order for the illusion of fullness to spring forth." Fascism "required an aesthetic *overproduction* – a surfeit of fascist signs, images, slogans, books, and buildings – to compensate for, fill in, and cover up its forever unstable ideological core" (3). As I go on to argue in this essay, the twin components of lack and compensation are crucial to Freud's concept of projection.

7   Albert Memmi associates fascism with colonialism: "every colonial nation carries the seeds of fascist temptation in its bosom. [...] What is fascism, if not a regime of oppression for the benefit of a few? [...] colonialism is one variety of fascism" (62). Wilhelm Reich associates fascism with authoritarianism and mysticism; Ernesto Laclau analyzes fascism as a kind of populism or failed socialism; Alice Yaeger Kaplan studies fascism from the point of view of the banal and the everyday.

8   Quoting from Nietzsche's *On the Genealogy of Morals*, Deleuze and Guattari write: "In the latency system of terror, what is no longer active, en-acted, or reacted to, 'this *instinct for freedom* forcibly made latent [...] pushed back and repressed, incarcerated within and finally able to discharge and vent itself only on itself,' – that very thing is now *ressenti* [...]" (214; italics in the original).

9   By reading novels, autobiographies, and letters of the Freikorps officers, as well as illustrating his readings ironically with cartoons, posters, advertisements, and other graphic materials, Klaus Theweleit's work on fascism shares with Kaplan's a methodological focus on the obvious and everyday as the place to look for fascist aesthetics.

10 Elsaesser emphasizes throughout his essay the historicity of fascism and the historicity of film theory's privileged ability to explain processes of specularization.

11 Having said this, I should add, however, that the imagistic or projectional implications of fascism go well beyond the medium of film itself.

12 In the passage from which my title is taken, Sontag writes: "Riefenstahl's current de-Nazification and vindication as indomitable priestess of the beautiful – as a film maker and now, as a photographer – do not augur well for the keenness of current abilities to detect the fascist longings in our midst. The force of her work is precisely in the continuity of its political

and aesthetic ideas. What is interesting is that this was once seen so much more clearly than it seems to be now" (43).

13 Sontag's argument here is comparable to that of Georges Bataille, who describes fascist authority in terms of a "double character" in which "cruel tendencies" co-exist with "the need, characteristic of all domination, to realize and idealize order" (146).

14 Unlike orthodox Marxism, which reduces spiritual and artistic phenomena to economics, the fascism of the 1920s and 1930s had a great appeal to artists and intellectuals because it gave the potentially creative role of beliefs – of mythmaking – a central place in social life. This was especially so in the case of Italian fascism, which was, unlike German fascism, aesthetically compatible with the avant-garde tenets of modernism. For an informative argument, see Dasenbrock, 229–41.

15 See Kaplan's very interesting discussion of the "slogan text" in chapter 3 of her book. For Kaplan, the slogan is a form of encapsulation with the performative aura of the "self-evident," luminous, transparent speech act, which appeals through the clarity of refrain rather than through thought and discourse. Both visual and aural in effect, a slogan is a brief string of words that tells and makes history at the same time, and "a kind of self-fulfilling prophecy" (68).

16 For a similar critique of the positivistic manner in which some non-white feminists turn to 'lived experience' as "an alternative mode of radical subjectivity," see Suleri ("Woman").

17 This environment can in part be described in terms of what Paul A. Bové calls "the facile professionalization of the U.S. academy" (xv). However, the ramifications involved go far beyond the U.S. academy.

18 I want to emphasize once again that my point is not to defend Western imperialism or Eurocentrism per se, but rather to mobilize criticism of the trends of uninformed and unanalytical claims about "cultural pluralism" that are being made in the name of anti-imperialism and anti-Eurocentrism. By implication, it is also to criticize those who are kind and lenient whenever it comes to dealing with non-Western scholars – those, in other words, who base their judgements on the sole basis of skin colour.

19 The situation here is comparable, though not identical, to Slavoj Žižek's analysis of the popular support for Kurt Waldheim in the 1986 Austrian presidential campaign. The Austrian people, to put the matter in the form of a joke of the time, wanted to have "Waldheimer's Disease," the disease of not being able to remember that one has been a Nazi, but this is precisely what Waldheim's opponents missed. As Žižek writes:

> Starting from the assumption that Waldheim was attracting voters because of his great-statesman image, leftists put the emphasis of their campaign on proving to the public that not only is Waldheim a man with a dubious past (probably involved in war crimes) but also a man who is not prepared to confront his past, a man who evades crucial questions concerning it – in short, a man whose basic feature is a refusal to "work through" the traumatic past. What they overlooked was that it was precisely this feature with which the majority of centrist voters identified. Post-war Austria is a country whose very existence is based on a refusal to "work through" its Nazi past – proving that Waldheim evad[ed] confrontation with his past emphasized the exact trait-of-identification of the majority of voters.

The theoretical lesson to be learned from the campaign, Žižek continues, "is that the trait-of-identification can also be a certain failure, weakness, guilt of the other, so that by pointing out the failure we can unwittingly reinforce the identification" (105–06). Žižek's book is entirely relevant to the critique of idealism in fascist and totalitarian operations. See my discussion in "Ethics after Idealism."

20 Spivak refers to the current constructions of the Third World and marginality in the academy as a "new orientalism" (56). See also Sara Suleri's critique of what she calls "alterism," which is characterized by an indiscriminate reliance on the centrality of otherness and tends to replicate the familiar category of the exotic in imperialist discourse: "alterism enters the interpretive scene to insist on the conceptual centrality of an untouchable intransigence. Much like the

category of the exotic in the colonial narratives of the prior century, contemporary critical theory names the other in order that it need not be further known" (*The Rhetoric of English India* 13).

21 For a discussion of this epochal change from the viewpoint of the "Others," see Chow, "Against the Lures of Diaspora: Minority Discourse, Chinese Women, and Intellectual Hegemony."

22 Among other things, Armstrong and Tennenhouse's *The Imaginary Puritan: Literature, Intellectual Labor, and the Origins of Private Life* is a significant contribution to the vast project of deconstructing and thus provincializing Western European culture, in particular that of England.

Works Cited

Althusser, Louis. "Ideology and Ideological State Apparatuses (Notes towards an Investigation)." *Lenin and Philosophy and Other Essays*. Trans. Ben Brewster. New York: Monthly Review, 1971. 127–86.

Armstrong, Nancy, and Leonard Tennenhouse. *The Imaginary Puritan: Literature, Intellectual Labor, and the Origins of Private Life*. Berkeley: University of California Press, 1992.

Barthes, Roland. *Leçon*. Paris: Seuil, 1977. Qtd. in Jean Baudrillard. *For a Critique of the Political Economy of the Sign*. Trans. Charles Levin. St. Louis: Telos Press, 1981. 26.

———. *Mythologies*. Comp. and trans. Annette Lavers. London: Paladin, 1973.

Bataille, George. "The Psychological Structure of Fascism." *Visions of Excess: Selected Writings 1927–1939*. Vol. 14 of *Theory and History of Literature*. Ed. Allan Stoekl. Trans. Allan Stoekl, Carl R. Lovitt, and Donald M. Leslie, Jr. Minneapolis: University of Minnesota Press, 1985. 137–60.

Bazin, André. "The Stalin Myth in Soviet Cinema." 1950. Trans. Georgia Gurrieri. *Movies and Methods*. Ed. Bill Nichols. Vol. 2. Berkeley: University of California Press, 1985. 29–40.

Bové, Paul A. *In the Wake of Theory*. Hanover: Wesleyan University Press & University Press of New England, 1992.

Chow, Rey. "Against the Lures of Diaspora: Minority Discourse, Chinese Women, and Intellectual Hegemony." *Writing Diaspora: Tactics of Intervention in Contemporary Cultural Studies*. Bloomington: Indiana University Press, 1993. 99–119.

———. "Ethics after Idealism." *diacritics* 23 (1993): 3–22.

Dasenbrock, Reed Way. "Paul de Man: The Modernist as Fascist." Golsan 229–41.

Dirlik, Arif. "'Past Experience, If Not Forgotten, Is a Guide to the Future'; or, What Is in a Text? The Politics of History in Chinese-Japanese Relations." *boundary 2* 18 (1991): 29–58.

Elsaesser, Thomas. "Primary Identification and the Historical Subject: Fassbinder and Germany." *Narrative, Apparatus, Ideology: A Film Theory Reader*. Ed. Philip Rosen. New York: Columbia University Press, 1986. 535–49.

Foucault, Michel. Preface. *Anti-Oedipus: Capitalism and Schizophrenia*. Ed. Gilles Deleuze and Félix Guattari. Trans. Robert Hurley, Mark Seem, and Helen R. Lane. Minneapolis: University of Minnesota Press, 1983. xi–xiv.

———. "Power and Strategies." *Power/Knowledge: Selected Interviews and Other Writings 1972–1977*. Ed. Colin Gordon. Trans. Colin Gordon, Leo Marshall, John Mepham, and Kate Soper. New York: Pantheon, 1980. 134–45.

Gao, Xingzu. *Rijun qin hua baoxing – Nanjing da tusha*. Shanghai: Shanghai renmin chubanshe, 1985.

Golsan, Richard J., ed. *Fascism, Aesthetics, and Culture*. Hanover: University Press of New England, 1992.

"Japanese Court OKs Censoring of Schoolbooks." *Los Angeles Times* 17 Mar. 1993: A7.

Kaplan, Alice Yaeger. *Reproductions of Banality: Fascism, Literature, and French Intellectual Life*. Minneapolis: University of Minnesota Press, 1986.

Laclau, Ernesto. *Politics and Ideology in Marxist Theory: Capitalism, Fascism, Populism*. London: New Left Books, 1977.

Lanzman, Claude. *Shoah: An Oral History of the Holocaust*. New York: Pantheon, 1985.

Laplanche, J. and J.-B. Pontalis, *The Language of Psychoanalysis*. Trans. Donald Nicholson-Smith. New York: Norton, 1973.

Lestz, Michael. "Lishi de mingji (The unforgettable memory of history)." Trans. Lin Zhiling and Xie Zhengguang. *Jiuzhou xuekan* (*Chinese Culture Quarterly*) 1 (1987): 97–106.

Magee, John. *Magee's Testament*. Home movie camera film exposed by the Reverend Magee during and immediately after the rape of Nanking, edited and transferred to commercial stock by the filmmaker Peter Wang, and produced and distributed by the Alliance in Memory of the Victims of the Nanking Massacre, 1991.

Memmi, Albert. *The Colonizer and the Colonized*. Trans. Howard Greenfeld. Expanded ed. Boston: Beacon Press, 1991.

Mitscherlich, Alexander. *Society without the Father: A Contribution to Social Psychology* (*Auf dem Weg zur Vaterlosen Gesellschaft*). 1963. Trans. Eric Mosbacher. New York: Harcourt, Brace and World, 1969.

Pascal, Blaise. *Thoughts of Blaise Pascal*. London: Kegan Paul, 1888.

Poulantzas, Nicos. *Fascism and Dictatorship: The Third International and the Problem of Fascism*. London: New Left Books, 1974.

Reich, Wilhelm. *The Mass Psychology of Fascism*. Trans. Vincent R. Carfagno. New York: Farrar, 1970.

Schnapp, Jeffrey T. "Epic Demonstrations: Fascist Modernity and the 1932 Exhibition of the Fascist Revolution." Golsan 1–37.

"Scholar Wins Ruling on Nanjing Massacre." *New York Times* 13 May 1994: A3.

Schulte-Sasse, Linda. "National Socialism in Theory and Fiction: A Sampling of German Perspectives, 1923–1980." *Fascismo y Experiencia Literaria: Reflexiones para Una Recanonización*. Ed. Hernán Vidal. Edina, MN: Society for the Study of Contemporary Hispanic and Lusophone Revolutionary Literatures, 1985. 64–91.

Scott, Joan. "The Evidence of Experience." *Critical Inquiry* 17 (1991): 773–97.

Sontag, Susan. "Fascinating Fascism." 1975. *Movies and Methods*. Ed. Bill Nichols. Vol. 1. Berkeley: University of California Press, 1976. 31–43.

Spivak, Gayatri. "Marginality in the Teaching Machine." *Outside in the Teaching Machine*. New York: Routledge, 1993. 53–76.

Suleri, Sara. *The Rhetoric of English India*. Chicago: University of Chicago Press, 1992.

———. "Woman Skin Deep: Feminism and the Postcolonial Condition." *Critical Inquiry* 18 (1992): 756–69.

Theweleit, Klaus. *Male Fantasies*. 2 vols. Trans. Stephen Conway in collaboration with Erica Carter and Chris Turner. Minneapolis: University of Minnesota Press, 1987, 1989.

Virilio, Paul. *War and Cinema: The Logistics of Perception*. Trans. Patrick Camiller. London: Verso, 1989.

Xu Zhigeng. *Najing da tusha*. Hong Kong: Luzhou chuban gongsi; Beijing: Kunlun chubanshe, 1987.

Žižek, Slavoj. *The Sublime Object of Ideology*. London: Verso, 1989.

Introduction: The Linked Histories of the Globalized World   The Fascist Longings in our Midst

Cross-Mirrorings of Alterity: The Colonial Scenario and Its Psychological Legacy   Mythologies of Migrancy: Post-colonialism, Postmodernism, and the Politics of (Dis)location   Postcolonial DefferendDifferend: Diasporic Narratives of Salman Rushdie   At the Margins of Postcolonial Studies   Keeping History at Wind River and Acoma   Modernity's First Born: Latin America and Postcolonial Transformation   Towards Articulation: Postcolonial Theory and Demotic Resistance   Postcolonial Theory and the "Decolonization" of Chinese Culture

Queer with Class:

Absence of Third World Sweatshop
in Lesbian/Gay Discourse
and a Rearticulation of
Materialist Queer Theory

ROB COVER

Queer theory has been criticized recently by several academic authors for
its seeming inability to address postcolonial and class issues. It has been
described as non-materialist, as focusing on desire over needs. As a theory for
the exploration and analysis of constructed sexualities, it ignores a number
of obvious and non-obvious "absences" both within its own theoretical
focus and in its failure to address absence in the sites it attempts to explore.
For the purposes of this paper, I make use of two instances of absence: the
invisibility of the sweatshop and Third World labour in lesbian/gay discourse
despite the way this practice is used to prop up bourgeois production in the
West, and – through this spotlighting of closeted lesbian/gay skeletons – the
absence of "class" and the Third World from queer theory.

Queer Theory

There is not the space here to explore the many strands and trends of queer theory other than to point out some of the basic tenets that can be drawn from the body of academic work on sexuality and sexuality constructionism that labels itself "queer." As a form of textual reading and sexual politics, and reliant on post-structuralist/postmodernist theories derived chiefly from Foucault, Derrida, and Lacan, queer theory permits perspectives from which to challenge the normative, including those sexualities that have been normalized in contemporary discourse: lesbian, gay, straight. It opens a space for exploring diverse discourses that challenge hetero-normativity while prompting examination of the constructionism of non-heterosexual sexual positions. A prominent target of queer theory is identity, which, as is often asserted through the anti-foundationalist work of Judith Butler (*Gender Trouble, Bodies That Matter*), is performatively articulated as the *effect* of regulatory regimes – a constraint queer theory attempts to transgress, subvert, and disrupt.[1]

"Queer," as it appears in lesbian/gay discourse through lesbian/gay media publications, is not equivalent to the queer of "queer theory"[2] and frequently fails to stress the disruptive potential of the non-normative. It is used instead as a signifier for a grouping of non-heteronormative sexualities and genders (gay, lesbian, bisexual, transgendered), with an ultimate effect of stabilizing and regimenting those sexualities in opposition to the construct, hetero-sexuality. Criticism of the constructionist trends of queer theory is found in much lesbian/gay (or "umbrella queer") discourse that most frequently asserts an essentialist identity.

Queer Theory and Class/Race

Queer theory is subjected to more viable criticisms from within the academy. Much of this tension comes from non- (or anti-) poststructuralist theorists and researchers working within Marxist and neo-Marxist frameworks. Their criticisms of queer theory are based in a reading of the theory as inadequate for the exploration of class as an axis of differentiation and oppression. Donald Morton divides queer theorists into those who base their work in desire theory and those who look more closely at the issue of needs, finding that needs theory is almost completely absent from queer theory as a result of the theory's basis in continental poststructuralist philosophy (Morton, "Class Politics"). He suggests that queer theory's notion of "queering the planet" – derived from the title of Michael Warner's anthology *Fear of a Queer Planet* – is part of a project of establishing Baudrillardian desire over any investigation of need, and that this erasure of need obscures worldwide social responsibilities in places as diversely located as Bosnia, Somalia, and the South American and Asian Third World, as well as the non-privileged sites and subjects of Western cities (Morton, *Material Queer* 29). For Morton, needs theory makes possible a globalizing explanation of social injustice not just throughout diverse geographic localities but through local Western social problems such as disease (including HIV/AIDS), poverty, and sexual harassment in a pattern of determinate economic and class relations (Morton, "Class Politics" 474). He suggests that the liberal state – and by implication the concentration on desire – is a mask that covers over economic and racial exploitation (475–76), and that this is evidenced, as we shall see, by the pro-lesbian/gay strategies of transnational corporations.

At the same time, there has been some criticism of queer theory as overly universalizing. Leo Bersani sees Michael Warner's definition of the subjects of queer theory being those resistant to "regimes of the normal" as an obscuring of sexual distinctiveness (71–72). The assumption that worldwide sexual subjects transgressing heteronormativity operate in the same way is a chief failing of much queer theory; it ignores the different inflections class and postcolonial ethnicity perform on the sexual subject. Class theory and nation theory are, according to Omi and Winant, the identifiable primary paradigms of critical work on race (cited in Phelan 77), whereby race is understood in terms of the social allocation of advantage and disadvantage; queer theory has not been conflated with those theories that enable an understanding of class, exploitation, and sexuality on a broad transnational level. This failing stifles the ability of queer theoretical analysis to examine the way the construction of sexual identities has occurred within and through the discourses that *maintain* late capitalism.

The vast majority of queer theoretical analysis has concentrated not on broad notions of sexual constructionism but on close examination of the bourgeois constructs of lesbian and gay in the West. It has explored how subjectivities are constructed in terms of lifestyle, taste, and culture (Hennessy, "Queer Theory" 107–08) without an appropriate exploration of the way social class and geographic location (West/Third World) might inflect and add to the knowledge on sexual constructionism. In other words, queer theory focuses on texts produced in the West and, generally, by those well-positioned in the bourgeois class. I am arguing here that part of the reason for such a focus has been the inability of theorists to seek out the non-Western, non-bourgeois evidences of non-heteronormative sexualities, to see how the non-West is responsible for propping up the discourses of lesbian/gay sexualities, and to admit to the relative scarcity of research on non-Western desire, class, need, and position.

Materialist Queer Theory

What is necessary in order to extend the analytical potential of queer theory is its rearticulation through materialist theory,[3] with a return of class and globalism including global exploitation as basic tenets within the theory. In the critique he makes of queer theory through positing a dichotomy of desire versus needs, what Morton misses is the way needs can (or should) be focussed upon while maintaining explorations of desire (through semiotics, through text, through spectacle, through *jouissance*) as the means that uphold or obscure those who are (or should be) the subjects of needs theorizing and analysis. A materialist queer theory would allow such a multiple zoning of exploration and retain an ability to blur those two zones of analysis.

Needs have not, as Morton mistakenly suggests, been absent from queer theory, as it was the exploration of the manner in which various Western discourses privileged some over others in terms of AIDS treatments in the 1980s that prompted the developmental exploration of difference and contributed to what we now call queer theory. The beginning of the AIDS epidemic in the early 1980s caused a series of crises both in the lesbian/gay community and subsequently in the academy in lesbian and gay studies. There was an urgency and a necessity in addressing the *needs* of a community being quickly infected with – as much as affected by – a "killer disease"; this required the attention of lesbian/gay scholarship. Attempts in the mid- to later 1980s to educate the lesbian/gay community about safer sex methods caused awareness of the limitations and inadequate attention given to differences among those categorically labeled homosexual (Jagose 95). Considerations of difference in terms of sexual practice are apparent in the spotlight HIV/AIDS casts on sexuality, and, of course, necessitate further thought on the roles, placement, and situations of non-white, non-English-speaking lesbians and gay men. The fact that AIDS could no longer be defined a gay disease – despite continuing belief in this myth by certain groups (Sedgwick 5n8) – caused a necessary rethinking of the construction of the homo/hetero binarism. Tasmin Wilton posits the idea that AIDS creates a new binarism, at-risk and not-at-risk, in which heterosexual comes to be discursively equated with not-at-risk (Wilton 129). HIV/AIDS discourse is one of needs – and it is through the queer theoretical analysis of the lack of attention given to the needs of those affected subjects outside the bourgeois-white construction of non-heteronormative sexuality that queer theory has a basis (albeit small) in exploring needs along with desire (and sometimes both together). But need in terms of Western sexuality remains and goes beyond HIV/AIDS discourse into issues of lesbian/gay political practice and community formation. A materialist queer theory allows us to see the fact that sexuality is organized along community lines rather than class demarcations; this has the unfortunate effect of obscuring class status as an issue inflecting sexuality.

Through the exploration of needs and desires with globally enhanced perspectives (without losing the site of the local), construction of sexualities would be understood as partly determined by the rate of distribution of resources of all kinds throughout the West and non-West. The different rates of capitalist development in different regions of the planet would be a useful starting place for understanding the vastly different constructions of sexuality between the Third and First Worlds. John D'Emilio points out in "Capitalism and Gay Identity" that the free-labour system of the West broke down the need for family units as basic economic units, permitting a very specific social/sexual freedom to emerge (5).[4] The capitalist labour system of the non-West is markedly different, particularly in regions where sweatshop labour is extensive, and this, as well as cultural and discursive differences of the region, prompts us to see that non-heteronormative sexual identities can, and will, develop in markedly different ways in those regions. In other words, and as Morton points out, the increasing visibility of lesbian/gay subjects in liberal capitalist democracies is not the result of self-liberatory efforts but of the "reformative modifications undertaken by the system of capitalism." The interests of capitalism and the interests of heteronormative patriarchy no longer coincide in the West (Morton, *Material Queer* 275). The different emphases, positions, and styles of, say, religious/medical/legal discourses and of transnational marketing strategies in the non-West cause different conceptions and constructions of sexualities from the Western model and are a useful pointer for queer theory to promote effectively its anti-essentialist stance. But as a result of the differing uses that transnational corporate capitalism makes of subjects between the West and the Third World (primarily consumers and primarily labour force, respectively), the focus of queer theory in terms of desires/needs must differ. In other words, that branch of queer theory that we might foresee as materialist queer theory *must* retain the conceptual ability to analyze need in the Third World to the same degree that desire as sexual motivation is analyzed in the West.[5]

The recent evidence of transnational corporate behaviour in the Third World suggests an increasing necessity for a materialist queer theory that focuses on the needs of Third World subjects. As Rosemary Hennessy points out, the expanding network of the multinational industrial complex through exploitative relations of production and consumption has brought about violence against women in the Third World by corporate research, the increasing sexualization of women internationally by a commodity aesthetics, and the intensified contestation over women's bodies as the site of reproduction in the First World and as commodity production in the Third World (Hennessy, *Materialist Feminism* xii). Hennessy finds that a materialist queer theory can put forward a critique of heterosexuality "that stresses relations among divisions of labour while not shrinking from the examination of sensual pleasure" ("Queer Theory" 108–09). While it is not an easy task to incorporate theories of labour and exploitation into a desire-based queer theory, the dialogue that such an attempt can create will lead to further dynamic strengthening of two sets of (to date, seemingly incompatible) theories. The urgency of exploring needs can be suggested by articulating Morton's humanist/romantic conception of the difference: desire corresponds (following poststructuralism) to the unnameable yearnings of the unconscious, whereas need corresponds "to food, clothing, shelter, health care, education – the confrontational relation of these two modes of thought can be clarified by posing the question: What kind of subject can afford to explain politics and the social world strictly in terms of 'desire' except the subject whose 'needs' are already met?" ("Class Politics" 474–75). While this point seems strategically under-theorized and requires much further analysis of the potential intersections of need and desire, it is a useful platform from which we can launch an articulation of materialist queer theory that enables explorations of lesbian/gay discourse and the political implications of its bases.

The task that remains here – for now – is first, to examine the lack of class analysis in the lesbian/gay discourse as posited through lesbian/gay media publications, and second, to discuss the way that discourse posits a global, essentialist non-heterosexual subject without due attention to class, economic, and labour differences between the West and the Third World. I will continue from there by opening the site of the Third World sweatshop as the anomalous category *absent* from lesbian/gay media – an irony since the transnational corporations that fund those media publications are known to operate sweatshop labour. I will close with a brief look at how absence in lesbian/gay discourse can be accounted for within both political-economic and conceptual frameworks.

Gay/Lesbian Capitalist World and the Global Diaspora

Capitalism as economic structure and the emergence of the lesbian or gay (or queer) identity have intricately linked histories. As John D'Emilio points out, it is the free-labour system of capitalist societies that has allowed large numbers of men and women in the late twentieth century to be less dependent on the family as economic unit and to express non-heterosexual sexual identity away from that basic social model (5–6). Materially, capitalism weakens the economic bonds that once kept families together, but at the same time it enshrines the family as the chief symbolic source of affection and emotional security (11–12). Further, the possibility of establishing a community and organizing politically on the basis of sexuality is related to the liberalist system necessary for laissez-faire capitalism to flourish. The ability to organize on the basis of community rather than class is a key notion of liberal politics and society and underpins the discourses that keep the working-class poor appropriately subjected (Altman, *Homosexualization* ix). It is ironic that as non-heteronormative sexualities have become more free in the Western world, they have become more reliant on business institutions to provide the means to express this freedom, most particularly as places to make contact with other sexually interested persons (85), but also for the dissemination of (symbolic) lesbian/gay discourse. Without the social discourses of liberalist society that are inextricably linked with the promotion of capitalist organization, the possibility of economic survival outside the basic structure of the family would have been impossible. Likewise, the expression of a lesbian or gay or queer identity would not have been viable, nor would the organization of a community around business interests.

The promotion of a gay minority as a definable consumer market is, in some ways, a step toward tolerance and acceptance of non-heterosexual sexualities in America, Europe, and Australia. However, the dependence on consumerism and capitalist organization is, as Dennis Altman has pointed out, "a new form of social control more subtle and less violent than the old, but real nonetheless" (*Homosexualization* 102–03). Capitalist society and corporate enterprises are perfectly happy to allow lesbians, gay men, and queer persons to flourish with freedom to express sexualities, but only as long as we obey the rules of reciprocal promotion of a fixed, coherent sexual identity and of solid, devoted consumption. There is freedom to express sexuality, but only as long as queer groups are a market, only as long as they are sold to corporate enterprise by lesbian/gay media publications as affluent consumers with ready cash. That is a constraint I find oppressive, with the effect of marginalizing those non-heterosexual persons who are not in a position to contribute by freely spending and buying. Many non-heterosexual students and youth fall into this category.

Many corporations prey on queer people with disposable incomes. As Carrie Moyer recently discovered (443), an American advertising agency, Mulruan/Nash, focussing exclusively on the gay and lesbian market, noted that since many non-heterosexual people are geographically or emotionally separated from their homophobic families, the buying patterns normally learned from parents are not in place. When a company therefore reaches out to the queer consumer, it can expect a certain amount of brand loyalty. In Moyer's words, "Mom and Dad might not like me, but I know Absolut Vodka does!" (443) In the case of Australia, a significant number of working-class people are not in a position to be members of a supposedly diverse community. Lesbian/gay activities are centred on available cash. Drinking, drug use, patronage at clubs and dance parties, and coffee in queer cafés exclude the non-affluent and the working-class poor from participating in the established institutional practices of being queer. Such non-heterosexual members of the working class are invisible: their particular class-cultural identifications and images are absent in lesbian/gay media publications. They are not represented by queer lobby groups and organizations,[6] nor do such people make it into *OutRage* magazine's top 150 "powergays" in its December 1997 issue.[7]

In ways that are seemingly less specific but relevant to lesbian/gay persons and communities, capitalist society is responsible for a series of injustices, discriminations, alienations, and marginalizations. Most important is the way in which women have been treated in capitalistic societies built on patriarchal origins. As the free-labour system evolved over this century, capitalism drew more men than women from the home into the paid labour force, and the result is still evident today with the imbalance in wage rates for women (D'Emilio 76). This inequity, along with male control of urban public space (76), results in a lower profile for female non-heterosexuals, the relative poverty of many non-heterosexual women (Hennessy, "Queer Visibility"), and the exclusion of lesbians and queer women from the gay market and gay community. At the same time, the relative poverty of many persons of non-white ethnicities, migrants, the disabled, and indigenous populations in Australia results in exclusion from the queer community due to a similar lack of buying power and available disposable income.

The freedoms that capitalist society has brought about for the expression of lesbian/gay desire apply only to white, middle-class males. The discourses of law, economy, and identity maintain non-white, indigenous, disabled, and female non-heterosexual persons in marginalized positions and, frequently, relative poverty. While lesbian and gay organizations have been busy battling it out with right-wing politicians on the misguided notion that affecting legal discourse will change the culture of sexually non-normative lives, major corporations sign deals with prominent community members and media owners,[8] prompting the pink dollar strategy and permitting the marginalization of all non-heteronormative people who are not easy targets for a collusive marketing plan.

Early lesbian/gay discourse (in a period in which there was no definable queer academic discourse in competition with community-level minoritarian politics) was strongly marked by an awareness of capitalist structure and class difference. Dennis Altman's important work, *Homosexual Oppression and Liberation* (1971), focussed its analysis of the early gay protests through a Marcusean class/psychoanalytic theory and made strong suggestions that the growing evidence of gay existence would drastically disrupt the system of patriarchal capitalism in the West. D'Emilio's work was similarly marked by a class awareness, as were the many newsletters, periodicals, writings, pamphlets, and publications of the Gay Liberation Front and other lesbian/gay organizations of that first decade after "Stonewall69." It could be argued that the growing professionalization of lesbian/gay political organizations, community institutions, and media publications, combined with a shift in political focus from gay revolution to an assimilationism/gay nationalism dynamic, as well as the increasing and seemingly positive tolerance extended by liberal democratic societies, has resulted in the wholesale acceptance of the liberal-capitalist discourse as the essential and natural social system.

In terms of the non-West, lesbian/gay media discourse – with much reiteration – posits the notion of the global lesbian/gay essentialist identity, one that has always existed and crosses all axes of difference and locational/regional/cultural boundaries (D'Emilio 5). In the words of the subtitle of Dennis Altman's 1982 analysis of lesbian/gay culture, there has been an "Americanization of the homosexual." While communication technology and postcolonial economic colonization of the Third World are the driving forces behind the promotion of Euro-American culture systems on a global scale, increasing economic globalization is having the side effect of prompting the cultural globalization of queer sexualities in the style of the American; this exporting of a Euro-American lesbian/gay sexual identity has two distinct negative effects. The first is that the discourse of lesbian/gay identity – with its rhetoric of "Come Out! Be queer! Be happy! Pride!" – puts Third World individuals practising non-heterosexual sexualities in a position of danger within a cultural and political context that may be incapable of conceiving of sexualities and sexual freedom along American and European models. The second is that the distinctive cultural ways of representing and understanding sexuality and non-heterosexuality in the non-Western regions of the world, such as through the *banci kathoey* in Indonesia, are wiped out and sexuality is subsumed within the Western definition of gay – similar, but clearly not the same (Altman, "On Global Queering" 2). Much Euro-American cultural domination of the discourses of sexuality in the Third World is the result of American and European AIDS-related promotional material being funded for distribution in the non-West; equally so, the blame lies with the proliferation of more general cultural codes exported from the West. This destruction of unique and culturally specific sexualities is part of a new colonial enterprise in the non-West, and, as I shall later discuss, the buying power of so-called queer communities in America, Australia, and Europe are indirectly responsible.

This global essentialist lesbian/gay identity, which is so strongly posited in lesbian/gay discourse, has most recently been theorized as a cultural condition of diaspora – the suggestion is that a symbolic homeland (frequently, ancient Greece) and a shared history of oppression and alienation on the basis of sexuality permit lesbian/gay self-identifying persons (and, by implication, those yet to identify or come out) to see themselves as part of a global, universal family, as destined eventually to return to a togetherness (Buchbinder). This symbolic togetherness through which an essentialist notion of identity is posited is one of the several conceptual structures within lesbian/gay discourse that obscures difference on the basis of regional situation or position in the labour market of the non-West. It is contemporary lesbian/gay discourse that (not necessarily deliberately) obscures the notions of class, ethnicity, and the postcolonial subject in favour of the simplistic essentialist identity and the notion of progress (along liberal-democratic or humanist lines) through coming out and via support of the capitalist enterprises supposedly catering to the needs (read desires) of Western bourgeois lesbian/gay communities.

Sweatshop

In the corporate search for new markets and through the cultural hegemony of the United States, capitalism as economic and social organization has manifested itself in the non-West, or the Third World. With the continuing globalization of Western orders of knowledge (Foucault, *Power/Knowledge* 69) it is important for Western thinkers in every field to consider the implications for Third World peoples of the very corporate structures that have, in part, prompted the queer freedoms in the West. I want to talk briefly about sweatshops, which are the factory systems used by many corporate organizations for ridiculously cheap labour (often paying as little as ten cents an hour and providing few safety or health measures) to provide massive profit margins. Sweatshops breach standards of human rights in many countries, but they exist and flourish. They can be seen as the greatest, most disgraceful scourge of capitalism, with several major sweatshop factories known to make use of corporal punishment, child labour, and imprisonment as standard employment practices.

What does this have to do with sexuality and queer people? At first glance, not a lot – it seems to be a different problem for a different struggle at a different time. However, there is a very clear and direct connection between the way corporate organizations market to queer middle-class people in the West and the way Third World people are subjected to the cruelest, most humiliating, and most depriving means of existence. Many of the corporate organizations that market directly to gay and lesbian persons and advertise in queer newspapers and magazines produce their commodities under sweatshop labour conditions – Guess clothing, Gap clothing, Levi Strauss clothing, and, to a lesser extent, Hyundai car manufacturing, McDonalds, Disney Productions, and Nike shoes (*Campaign for Labor Rights* 1997).

The ways in which these corporations frequently operate in terms of lesbian and gay marketing is astounding. To take one example, Levi Strauss provides health insurance benefits to the partners of lesbian and gay employees; the company creates a supportive environment for employees who test HIV+, and it funds a Lesbian and Gay Employees association. Furthermore, it boasts about this commitment in its marketing strategies directed to lesbian and gay consumers (Hennessy, "Queer Visibility" 173). However, the workers in its sweatshops of Spain earn as little as US$2.15 an hour and live in inhumanely cramped and crowded barracks. By operating with a window-dressing strategy of supporting lesbian/gay/queer rights and community, corporations such as Levi Strauss suppress the issues of class and perpetuate an unjust division of labour. It is a common corporate strategy: Nike, which employs a largely female workforce in Asian sweatshop factories and uses severe corporal punishment for those who do not work hard enough, hypocritically advertises with female athletes in the West, asserting that women will be healthier, stronger, and more independent if they play sports and wear Nike shoes (Greenhouse; see also Alexander).[9] By ignoring the underprivileged classes while publicly promoting queer rights, profit-motivated corporations like Levi Strauss are responsible for keeping Third World working-class lives from view and for stemming deliberation on the ways in which sexual identities are complicated by priorities imposed by impoverishment (Hennessy, "Queer Visibility" 176).

While middle-class lesbian/gay consumers are busy buying commodities from these corporations, they are subjecting a very large group of people to cruel and unfair work conditions. The affluence of middle-class lesbian/gay people rests heavily on the shoulders of an international/global working class. Part of the responsibility lies with media that unashamedly attract corporate advertising without questioning either the motives or the labour record of those companies and that fail to link issues that have interest and implications for their queer readership. While these media publications, international corporations, HIV/AIDS organizations, and lesbian and gay political organizations are promoting the notion of a global queer identity, they are all failing to give attention to the people most in need of anti-corporate combat.

Finally, the greatest achievement of this corporate strategy is to break down the possibilities of large-scale progressive coalitionism, whereby queer issues can be understood, discussed, and fought alongside issues of class and transnational corporatism, where the underprivileged – whether economically or culturally – are pitted equally against the reigning power-bloc (Fiske 45) and where the discourses that maintain corporate capitalism are put in a position of material and cultural dominance.

While it can be argued that much middle-class affluence relies on the labour exploitation of the Third World, the case of Levi Strauss and lesbian/gay advertising (and purchasing) opens a space for the discussion of ethics in lesbian/gay discourse. The use of minoritarian language and politics and the positing of a sense of shared oppression (not just with other lesbian/gay persons, but with *all* the socially oppressed) obscures the global class demarcation of the visible Western lesbian/gay community and permits a certain self-righteousness among lesbian/gay persons as having suffered the ills of homophobia, thereby having become aware of other worldly injustices. The dissemination of this myth, the positing of lesbian/gay persons as apart from other middle-class consumers, and the obscuration of the Third World factor in lesbian/gay spending patterns are iteratively circulated by lesbian/gay media publications as part of their marketing process. My finding here is that there is no such right to a lesbian/gay self-image as ethical – in fact, the lesbian/gay reliance on the Third World working class is politically more unethical than general bourgeois exploitation on the basis of that self-righteous sense of shared oppression. The acceptance of corporate target marketing is the moment in which the ethics of shared oppression are lost.

Materialist Queer Theory and Absence (political economy)

Despite the connections drawn between the Third World sweatshop and the operations of lesbian/gay discourse and lesbian/gay media, I am led to ask how we can understand the absence of the sweatshop in that discourse. At the level of political economy, material queer theory can assist us through briefly exploring the production of lesbian/gay media – which sees itself as the central arbiter and police(man) of lesbian/gay identity, community, and politics. Lesbian/gay media is almost always locally or nationally based. In Australia, many publications cater to audiences residing in inner-city regions, and the two magazines – *Campaign* and *OutRage* – are both national Australian publications; they promote a certain Australian nationalism even as they posit a queer or gay nationalism and draw frequently on North American sources for news and lifestyle features. Being positioned within a liberal-democratic society that upholds transnational corporate activity and a national focus in terms of providing for needs/desires of the regional inhabitants, these media publications fail to subvert those national goals, even as much as they might subvert the nationally preferred heteronormatively constructed sexualities. At the same time, these publications are directly reliant on selling an audience (as commodity) to large corporate bidders in order to maintain finances for ongoing publication. While it might seem an outrage that these publications do not scrutinize their advertisers in terms of their exploitative operations, this lack of scrutiny draws attention to the simple fact that lesbian/gay media publications do not service anti-capitalist activism but exist for the generation of profits. In other words, the publication owners are implicated in the extraction of surplus value from Third World sweatshop workers. They are able to justify their position through the promotion of the "pink dollar" – the attraction of large corporate interest in a lesbian/gay audience and lesbian/gay market, positing the idea that this is a form of (however temporary) progress in the liberal-democratic political struggle for tolerance of non-heteronormative sexualities. In other words, it would not be financially useful for the publications to name these silent sufferers, no matter what recognizable sexual identities might be discovered in the dark corners of the sweatshop. As Butler points out, the absent is such because it is, or has to be, unnamed ("Critically Queer" 12).

Materialist Queer Theory and Absence (the competing spectacle)

While political-economic factors might be an underlying reason for the absence of the sweatshop (and the Third World) from lesbian/gay discourse, materialist queer theory is able to draw attention to the conceptual framework through which this absence can be understood and to the ways in which the absence is reinforced and stabilized. Within lesbian/gay discourse, the hetero/homo binarism is central to the establishment of the essentialist lesbian/gay identity,[10] and the repetitive promotion in lesbian/gay media of that binarism distracts from the possibility of any other binarial representations: hence the frequent exclusion of non-white ethnicities in the dominant publications (except, perhaps, as a highly irregular special interest issue); hence the nil interest in class (as anything more than style from which stylistic appropriations can take place); hence the absence of women or lesbian women from many of the pages of the publications. The Third World cannot appear in lesbian/gay media because that positing of a West/non-West binarism would draw focus from the hetero/homo binarism.[11]

A secondary reason for the sweatshop workers' absence, which queer theory might provide some clues about, involves the notion of the body. Rosemary Hennessy draws attention to the differences in the role of the female body between West and non-West: in the latter it is primarily for labour, for production; in the First World, the body exists for *re*production (*Materialist Feminism* xii). In a similar (though not exact) way, the queer body operates with parallel constraints between the two worlds: in the West the queer body is about desiring (and, in many ways, about purchasing that which is desired), whereas in the Third World the body exists once again for the production of commodities for the West.[12] The Western labour system's comparatively easier working day (which includes technology, safety, and often household after-work comfort) means that the body is, even at a practical level, free for the expression of desire for at least some part of time, even if that desire must be performed through genital activity (though often the rest of the body remains at the disposal of the purchasers of labour). In the Third World sweatshop there is no time even for sexualized body parts. The understanding, and often the reality, of the sweatshop world is that workers are operating for ridiculously low pay during most hours of the day. The body cannot be used for the purposes of desire (sexual or otherwise) when, as Morton points out, the needs of survival are overriding ("Class Politics" 474–75).

Another way to make sense of that absence is through the notion of the spectacle. While contemporary liberal discourses exoticize non-heteronormative identities with a precedented fascination, it remains for lesbian/gay discourse to maintain that spectacle – partly for the small political gains that the economic interests of corporations permit. The lesbian or gay must continue, in the lesbian/gay press, to be performed with glamour and flair. Part of that glamour has been dictated through the notion of shared oppression, through the hardship of the bourgeois white lesbian/gay life. By not concentrating on Third World sweatshop workers, by not naming and not even Othering them, the bourgeois lesbian/gay literally steals the limelight, refusing to permit a more exotic, more spectacular, more suffering subject to be posited. In this case the spectacle that is the lesbian/gay carnivalesque portrayal of itself is used not for Othering, for distancing itself from something grotesque (Stallybrass and White 290), but for establishing and reinforcing the boundaries that normalize the bourgeois white male as *the* non-heteronormative spectacle, as the *only* queer within the lesbian/gay discourse.

Notes

1 See Butler, *Gender Trouble* and *Bodies That Matter*; Sedgwick, *Epistemology of the Closet*; Foucault, *Power/Knowledge* and *The History of Sexuality*, Vol. 1., and for a good summary of the contentions and stresses within queer theory, see Jagose.

2 And, in fact, it has a somewhat different origin. See de Lauretis.

3 A currently popular term for Marxian or neo-Marxian class analysis.

4 Religious, legal, medical, and moral discourses, however, have operated from time to time to counter the freedom from family that economic conditions have permitted, thus shifting the basis by which family is maintained and regimented from one discourse into another.

5 A dynamic of need/desire might also play a role in a queer theoretical analysis of the sexuality of prostitution in Western urban centres, a matter that needs further exploration and one that might start with John Rechy's *The Sexual Outlaw*.

6 Among the agenda items addressed by the Gay and Lesbian Rights Lobby (Sydney) are legislative protection of superannuation and the right for same-sex marriage – both, arguably, are bourgeois institutions.

7 *OutRage* magazine is the top-selling Australian national gay magazine, directed to a gay-male and ostensibly upper middle-class audience. The top twenty-five of their 150 "powergays" included eight politicians/judges, six high profile personality artists, six major businesspeople and investors, two senior academics, one high profile sportsperson, and one fashion designer – the majority of the categories here are wealth-attracting positions promoted as important within contemporary bourgeois discourse.

8 Note particularly the role played by Australian gay press company Bluestone Media and its co-director Danny Vadasz in securing telephone corporation *Telstra* advertising for the magazine chain that includes the glossy *OutRage*.

9 Likewise, Guess clothing, which once operated a Los Angeles sweatshop, attempted to buy off student protests by advertising their involvement in the sponsoring of a campus film festival (*Campaign for Labor Rights* 1997).

10 Although bisexuality, which from time to time is alluded to in lesbian/gay discourse, disrupts that hetero/homo binary, the new umbrella term of "queer" has provided the answer to maintaining the binary while including bisexuality in lesbian/gay discourse – "all-of-us-nonheteronormative-sexualities" versus "the straights."

11 There is, of course, some evidence of the eroticization of the black male and Asian transsexual Other in lesbian/gay imagery – a matter for which there is no room for discussion at present (see Mercer). It should be noted, though, that this eroticization is both a Westernization of the Asian Other, and one that – in the imagery – divorces (and obscures) that Other from notions of Third World sweatshop work.

12 And for the desire of the West, see note 11 above, bearing in mind prostitution, sex tours, and so on.

Works Cited

Alexander, Nick. "Sweatshop Activism: Missing Pieces." *Z Magazine* Sept. 1997: 14–17.

Altman, Dennis. *The Homosexualization of America, The Americanization of the Homosexual.* New York: St. Martin's, 1982.

———. "On Global Queering." *Australian Humanities Review* 2 (1996): 1–7.

Bersani, Leo. *Homos.* Cambridge, MA: Harvard University Press, 1995.

Bigelow, Bill. "The Human Lives Behind the Labels: The Global Sweatshop, Nike, and the Race to the Bottom." *Phi Delta Kappan* 79.2 (1997): 112–20.

Buchbinder, David. "Queer Diasporas." Unpublished paper given at Postmodernism in Practice Conference, Adelaide, South Australia. Feb./Mar. 1998.

Butler, Judith. *Bodies That Matter: On the Discursive Limits of "Sex."* New York: Routledge, 1993.

——. "Critically Queer." *Playing with Fire: Queer Politics, Queer Theories.* Ed. Shane Phelan. London: Routledge, 1997. 11–29.

——. *Gender Trouble:Feminism and the Subversion of Identity.* New York: Routledge, 1990.

Campaign for Labor Rights (CLR): *Select Documents.* Washington, DC, 1997, 1998.

de Lauretis, Teresa. "Queer Theory: Lesbian and Gay Sexualities: An Introduction." *Differences* 3.2 (1989): iii–xvii.

D'Emilio, John. "Capitalism and Gay Identity." *Making Trouble: Essays on Gay History, Politics and the University.* New York: Routledge, 1992. 3–16.

Fiske, John. "Popularity and the Politics of Information." *Journalism and Popular Culture.* Ed. Peter Dahlgren and Colin Sparks. London: Sage, 1992. 45–63.

Foucault, Michel. *Power/Knowledge: Selected Interviews and Other Writings 1972–1977.* Ed. Colin Gordon. New York: Pantheon, 1980.

——. *An Introduction.* Vol. 1 of *The History of Sexuality.* 3 vols. 1976. Trans. Robert Hurley. London: Penguin, 1981.

Greenhouse, Steven. "Nike Supports Women in Its Ads but not Its Factories, Groups Say." *New York Times* 26 Oct.1997: C12.

Hennessy, Rosemary. *Materialist Feminism and the Politics of Discourse.* London: Routledge, 1993.

——. "Queer Theory, Left Politics." *Rethinking Marxism* 7.3 (1994): 142–83.

——. "Queer Visibility in Commodity Culture." *Social Postmodernism: Beyond Identity Politics.* Ed. Linda Nicholson and Steven Seidman. Cambridge, UK: Cambridge University Press, 1995. 142–85.

Jagose, Annamarie. *Queer Theory.* Melbourne: University of Melbourne Press, 1996.

Mercer, K. "Just Looking for Trouble: Robert Mapplethorpe and Fantasies of Race." *Sex Exposed: Sexuality and the Pornography Debate.* Ed. Lynne Segal and Mary McIntosh. London: Virago, 1992. 127–41.

Morton, Donald. "The Class Politics of Queer Theory." *College English* 58.4 (1996): 471–82.

——, ed. *The Material Queer: A LesBiGay Cultural Studies Reader.* Boulder, CO: Westview Press, 1996.

Moyer, Carrie, *et al.* "Do You Love the Dyke in Your Face." *Queers in Space: Communities/ Public Places/Sites of Resistance.* Ed. Gordon Brent Ingram, Anne-Marie Bouthillette, and Yolanda Retter. Seattle: Bay Press, 1997. 439–46.

Rechy, John. *The Sexual Outlaw.* New York: Grove, 1977.

Sedgwick, Eve Kosofsky. 1990. *Epistemology of the Closet.* London: Penguin, 1994.

Stallybrass, Peter, and Allon White. "Bourgeois Hysteria and the Carnivalesque." *The Cultural Studies Reader.* Ed. S. During. London: Routledge, 1993. 284–92.

Warner, Michael, ed. *Fear of a Queer Planet: Queer Politics and Social Theory.* Minneapolis: University of Minnesota Press, 1993.

Wilton, Tasmin. "Which One's the Man? The Heterosexualization of Lesbian Sex." *Theorising Heterosexuality: Telling It Straight.* Ed. Diane Richardson. Buckingham: Open University Press (1996): 125–42.

Introduction: The Linked Histories of the Globalized World   The Fascist Longings in our Midst   Queer with Class: Absence of Third World Sweatshop in Lesbian/ Gay Discourse and a Rearticulation of Materialist Queer Theory

Mythologies of Migrancy: Post-colonialism, Postmodernism, and the Politics of (Dis)location   Postcolonial DefferendDifferend: Diasporic Narratives of Salman Rushdie   At the Margins of Postcolonial Studies   Keeping History at Wind River and Acoma   Modernity's First Born: Latin America and Postcolonial Transformation   Towards Articulation: Postcolonial Theory and Demotic Resistance   Postcolonial Theory and the "Decolonization" of Chinese Culture

I have lived that moment of the scattering of the people that in other times and other places, in the nations of others, becomes a time of gathering. Gatherings of exiles and émigrés and refugees; gathering at the edge of "foreign cultures"; gathering at the frontiers; gathering in the ghettos or cafés of city centres; gathering in the half-life, half-light of foreign tongues, or in the uncanny fluency of another's language; gathering the signs of approval and acceptance, degrees, discourse, disciplines; gathering the memories of underdevelopment, of other worlds lived retroactively; gathering the past in a ritual of revival; gathering the present. Also the gathering of people in the diaspora: indentured, migrant, interned; the gathering of incriminatory statistics, educational performance, legal statutes, immigration status.

—Homi Bhabha,
THE LOCATION OF CULTURE

Cross-Mirrorings of Alterity:
The Colonial Scenario
and Its Psychological Legacy

MONIKA FLUDERNIK

Although postcolonial issues and terminology form the frame of my analysis, I am concerned in this article with defining transferential projections of stereotypes within a fairly traditional imagological framework.[1] Imagological research has for the most part concentrated on the portrayal of foreigners: the image of the German in English literature, the image of the Englishman in national European literatures. These heterostereotypes traced in the various national literatures of Europe are part of a long imagological tradition,[2] in which several key characteristics of the national character have become attached to the national stereotype: the drunken German, the proud Spaniard, the stingy Scotsman.[3] Autostereotypes, by contrast, are rarely discussed, and the complex transfer between projections that one finds under the conditions of colonial oppression or, more complicated still, in the circumstances of migration, exile, and cultural hybridity has not had much attention from the discipline of imagology.[4] It is no coincidence that poststructuralist approaches have flourished in postcolonial studies that deal precisely with this murky realm of dislocated and displaced identities, whether in the area of racially tinged colonialism (as portrayed in Frantz Fanon's *Black Skin, White Masks*[5]), the gender-oriented inflection of colonial oppression (Spivak 197–221, 241–68), or the state of intercultural homelessness,[6] a situation that is portrayed in numerous texts by expatriate Indian writers.

If my analysis initially skirts some of the famous recent studies in postcolonial theory, such as Homi Bhabha's *The Location of Culture* (1994), the reason for this temporary neglect is not hostility but a strategic bracketing of the poststructuralist framework. By putting Lacanian and Derridean formulations of the circulation and displacement of transferential images under erasure, I want to ensure that the more traditional imagological toolbox is exhausted for its full conceptual potential before turning to different methodological frameworks. Rather than, as yet, indulging in "reading between the lines" (Bhabha, *Location* 188) or employing "catachrestic gesture[s] of interpretation" (184), I will map out the iteration and circulation of autostereotypes and heterostereotypes in the double bind of colonial and postcolonial constitutions of the self and discuss the social displacements that these projections of alterity regularly undergo. My examples come from a small number of fairly well-known works by Indian expatriates, among which Anita Desai's *Bye-Bye Blackbird* (1985) will receive the most detailed attention since it covers nearly the full range of possible combinations of image projections. I present five scenarios that define typical constellations of image transfer: colony, exoticism/orientalism, exile, globalization/cosmopolitanism, and third party. Each of these has specific parameters that are relevant to the scenario. As I will show, the last three categories deploy parameters from the first two in strategic ways to serve their own political ends.

The Colonial Scenario

The colonial scenario is characterized by the appropriation on the part of the colonial subject of the negative heterostereotype imposed on him[7] as his very own autostereotype. This goes hand in hand with the wish to become white, to exchange places with the colonizer and therefore induce a positive heterostereotype projected on the colonizer (which corresponds with the colonizer's flattering autostereotype). The colonial scenario lends itself to psychoanalytic analyses such as those proffered by Frantz Fanon and Albert Memmi. The colonized subject flounders in self-hatred, whereas – despite the native's admiration for the colonizer – the colonizer in turn feels threatened by the glance of the oppressed. Fanon's and Memmi's delineation of the deliberately inculcated inferiority complex that afflicts blacks is as much part of the colonial scenario as the sweeper Bakha's adoration of things British in Mulk Raj Anand's novel *Untouchable* (1935). This lethal acceptance of white superiority as portrayed in the Indian texts I will be looking at could be extended in its application to other contexts of discrimination in which the deprived connive at their own victimization by the system. Much of the nineteenth-century discourse about the working-class poor reiterates the structures that Fanon, and more radically still, Bhabha have outlined for colonial discourse; indeed the same stereotypes of laziness, stupidity, and sly servility were projected on the working class, with a corresponding attempt to create the worker in one's own (middle-class) image[8] (the "Educate our masters" slogan), and the same emergence of the fear of retaliation from the workers can be observed.[9] The scenario can be traced additionally in contemporary discourses that marginalize the poor, whether in the American social security debates (invariably recipients of welfare are blamed for their social ineptitude) or in the patronizing First World attitudes about Third World economic disabilities.

Not only is there a consistent strategy of blaming the victims, with a familiar set of derogatory stereotypes that also show up in anti-foreigner discourse (see Essed); there also exists the quite evident fear of aggression that is projected from the bad conscience of those who "have," thereby legitimating repressive measures against the have-nots that are meant to ensure the preservation of the unequal status quo. Here, too, the poor, the homeless, and the marginalized frequently cooperate with the strategies designed to contain the threat that they represent to the privileged classes. Having internalized the contempt directed at them (which is but an exaggerated image of the fear their just demands inspire), they in fact behave as the deserving poor by blaming themselves, by aspiring to the idealized status of the moneyed, and by seriously making way for those whom they believe to be "better." (Sympathy for, and rescue at the hands of, potentially dangerous "low elements" is also a recurring theme in Victorian literature.)

In the West, this scenario is increasingly played out in the daily confrontation with the homeless in the streets, whereas in Third World countries one encounters ghosts of the Victorian scene. Thus, in Ngugi wa Thiong'o's notorious play *Ngaahika Ndeenda* (*I Will Marry When I Want*), the "good" worker, Kiguunda, has much sympathy for his exploitative superiors, and they in turn deride the stupidity of those like him but are really afraid of the workers' retaliation. In a scene of Sunetra Gupta's *Memories of Rain* (1992), the female protagonist Moni remembers train rides with her parents and outlines the perpetual bad conscience of middle-class Indians toward their social inferiors:

> [T]he rancid layers of the child's rags bit into her senses, she refused
> food, her mother shrugged and doled out puffed bread and potato curry
> to her brother and her father, she watched the family eat, their gaze
> fastened upon their food to avoid the million hungry eyes [...] and so it
> had been and would ever be, on every journey, except those they took
> in the insulated comfort of air-conditioned sleepers, famished eyes
> would fall upon them, the food would turn to cinder in her mouth, she
> would shrink from the diseased hands that stretched in through the train
> window [...] she would watch the hungry eyes pass, empty cups would
> be flung out of the window, crash against the rail tracks, ashes to ashes,
> dust to dust. (86)

It is therefore quite intriguing to trace the interpenetration of economic deprivation and political discrimination on the basis of the specifically colonial make-up of the primal scene in Fanon or Bhabha. The colonial scenario seems to intensify the interplay of transferential images because the political and economic oppression is part of a calculated strategy of the instrumentalization and disciplining of the oriental and racial Other. Bhabha's formulations indeed are more pertinent to the African scene: Indian self-derogation never reached the abysses sounded by the black man; in India, adulation of things British was excessive with a wide segment of the population.[10]

Another aspect of internalized colonialism can be located in the conspicuous presence of Foucault in postcolonial studies. (Bhabha, for instance, frequently resorts to Foucauldian formulations.) The connection between the workings of colonial power and the general archaeology of the imperial age (automatization, normalization, depersonalization, disciplining) suggests itself as a matter of course. It should be noted, however, that the structures of the colonial scenario are not replicated in the relationship between prisoners and their wardens. Significantly, Foucault's prototypical emblem for the strategies of disciplining, the panopticon, forbids incorporation into postcolonial parameters. Although the colonial subject is "known" and "surveyed" (Bhabha, "Difference" 199), this surveillance is not panoptic in terms of Bentham's model penitentiary because the colonial subject turns his look back on the colonizer and thereby retains access to subversive counter-colonial agency. Bentham's prisoners, by contrast, are entrapped within a gaze they cannot return. The psychological consequences of Bentham's carceral scheme is debilitating to the point of annihilating prisoners' self-determination. Scarry's descriptions of the complex bond tying victims to their torturers are much more appropriate to the panoptic scenario than the colonial landscape of manipulation and strategic insurgency.[11] The colonial subject may come to love the master, but jailers or torturers never thus endear themselves to their victims. Moreover, penal intimacy and immediacy are to be contrasted with colonialism's mediacy through discourse and through institutional delegation. Bhabha's point about the conspicuous presence of British colonial institutions (the barracks next to the church and the bazaar)[12] can therefore be fruitfully contrasted with the secrecy of penitentiary surveillance and disciplining that are shielded from the public gaze. In the colonies, it is only the government that remains invisible, behind the scenes, in Delhi or in England; the tools of colonial subjugation are in clear view of all and sundry. It is this comparative relaxation of the colonial apparatus of power that, according to Bhabha, facilitates the enactment of contestual claims and affects the colonial discourse with splitting and differencing.

In addition to the autostereotypes and heterostereotypes in the prototypical colonial scenario, there are two complementary scenes located, so to speak, on the other side of the colonial medal. In the first of these, the colonial scenario is attacked and inverted in nationalistic counter-colonial discourse. In the second, effects of hybridity are produced in the subject who comes to situate himself between the colonial scenario and its nativist inversion, or finds himself implicated with both.

Nationalist counter-colonial discourse is a reaction to the effects of colonization, not an *original* "natural" state of affairs. Since indigenous cultures have for the most part not been of the colonizing type, they have not themselves participated in a colonial scenario as colonizers and have therefore failed to engage in the discriminating processes of knowledge and power toward their political enemies. They have therefore tended to have a pragmatic or even positive attitude toward Europeans, rather than an attitude of typical colonial superiority with its attendant psychological effects (blaming the victim, exaggerating the objection or the magic powers of the Other). This was no doubt due to the actual military superiority of the Europeans, which at once induced respect and a desire to be like the conqueror – a desire motivated also by the wish to oust eventually the colonial regime from its seat of power.[13]

The nationalist scenario is therefore no mere instantiation of a negative heterostereotype for the Other, this time the invader; both the colonial scenario and the nationalist reaction to it are qualitatively different from the imagological framework underlying the image of the Englishman in German literature. The main reason for that disparity between colonial and non-colonial images lies in the operations of power exercised over the colonial subject (but not over, or by, the individual Englishman entering Germany during his Grand Tour),[14] a power that is again qualitatively different from social discrimination, as we have seen. The poststructuralist approaches in postcolonial studies are therefore correct in pointing to the secondariness of transferential processes in the colonial scenario, and we can now extend this insight to apply also to the reactive nature of nationalist inversions of the already inverted image structure of the colonial situation.

Besides a characteristic celebration of native culture as a political move against the potent colonial adversary, one can additionally posit a recurring scenario of hybridity attaching to the state of colonial subjugation. I am here using the term *hybridity* to denote both an intermingling of cultures – as in the irredeemably compromised native culture propagated by nationalist counterforce[15] – and in the more specifically psychoanalytic sense in which Bhabha defines the term: the colonial subject becomes hybridized as a consequence of the confrontation with the psychological effects of the colonial scenario and so does the retaliatory but inevitably secondary nationalistic counterculture. Bhabha's recurring use of the term *ambivalence*[16] relates precisely to this complex interplay of transferential images that cannot be resolved in the plenitude of a subjective identification but constrains the colonial subject to hover between exchangeable positions of stereotypes whose fixations prove difficult to escape.

The trajectory traced here from colonial to anti-colonial to hybrid identifications emerges both from Mulk Raj Anand's *Untouchable* (1935) and from R.K. Narayan's *The Guide* (1958). In *Untouchable*, Bakha starts out with an unmitigated admiration for the British (and also a qualified respect for the Brahmins),[17] only to lapse into a rejection of the Western model (the failed conversion) and a brief nationalistic enthusiasm (the Gandhi interlude), ending up with the hope for the introduction of the Western contraption of the toilet. That invention, in its social consequences for Untouchables, constitutes a typical site of cultural hybridity. Likewise, in Narayan's *The Guide*, Raju's erstwhile adoption of Western forms of enterprise (Raju as tourist guide, Raju as manager) and of subservience (Raju as a model prisoner of "sly civility") gives way to a spurious self-immersion in the native tradition of the holy man, an enactment of holy ways that – from mimicry and simulation – turns into deadly seriousness. The hybridity attaching to the final moments of the novel relates to the unintended refunctionalization of Raju's publicity stunt – rescuing the village from drought by his sacrificial fast – in terms of both the traditional culture (the open ending makes it possible to read as prophetic Raju's final words) and of the foreign media culture in which Raju's craving for respect from his fellow villagers is cruelly displaced in the glare of the sensationalist requirements of television reporting.[18]

The colonial scenario describes the effects of colonialism on the colonized; the second scenario – the exoticist/orientalist scenario – defines the same situation from the perspective of the colonizer. Before dealing with the issue of exoticism, however, I want to introduce briefly a topic that strongly affects exoticist discourse, the parameter of gender. The prototypical colonial subject is male, and so is the colonizer – another proof of the imaginary[19] relationship subsisting between the two. In the exoticist scenario, on the other hand, the colonized territory is frequently pictured as female, to be conquered and penetrated. Moreover, the colonial woman with her characteristic allure plays a prominent role in the cultural imaginary, symbolizing both the attractions of the colonized land and the treachery and danger of its seductive charm. (This of course echoes stereotypical views about women prevalent in the West.)

It is also quite significant to observe the types of women who *do* get inscribed into the colonial discourse. Fascination with the Hindu practice of *suttee*, for instance, betokens a clearly sensationalist and voyeuristic attitude on the part of the witnessing Englishmen, as the recent literature on *suttee* amply illustrates (see Mani; Fludernik, "Suttee Revisited"), and the topos of the blood-thirsty princess – another recurrent figure in the colonial novel – likewise caters to the seamy side of the colonizers' fantasies. In portrayals of British womanhood, too, the "primal scene" is that of a gang rape of British wives and daughters by rioting Indian barbarians (Sharpe), and the inverse negative image of Western women emerges in the prototype of feminine cruelty, the *memsahib* (Ghose). In typical orientalist fashion, one therefore has two complementary (and contradictory) stereotypes about women – the victim and the monster – and these are applied to both Indian and British subjects.[20]

The implication of womenfolk in the colonial economy of power is always present on the sidelines in the recent theoretical discussion but is rarely thematized in the classic texts. Spivak, of course, started a trend in the opposite direction (see also Minh-ha; Mani; and Mohanty). For example, Bhabha treats two "primal" scenes in Fanon's *Black Skin, White Masks* as constitutive of hybridization and splitting, and both crucially implicate women in the colonial system. In the first scene the black man is pointed at by the child[21] who says "Look, a Negro [...] Mama, see the Negro. I'm frightened!" (111–12) – a confrontation in which the discrimination of the black man is enacted by means of verbal execration by mother and daughter. In the continuation of this encounter (Fanon's second scene), a little boy identifies this fear of the black man as the primeval trauma that the black man is going to eat him up:

> The Negro is an animal, the Negro is bad, the Negro is mean, the Negro
> is ugly; look, a nigger, it's cold, the nigger is shivering, the nigger is
> shivering because he is cold, the little boy [!] is trembling because he is
> afraid of the nigger, the nigger is shivering with cold, that cold that goes

through your bones, the handsome little boy [!] is trembling because he thinks that the nigger is quivering with rage, the little white boy [!] throws himself into his mother's arms: Mama, the nigger's going to eat me up. (113–14)

Again, the child seeks refuge with the mother, fleeing from the black man.

Two observations suggest themselves in connection with these scenes. One concerns Fanon's situating of the white woman within the colonial and racial power structure; the other, Bhabha's complete silence about the issue of gender in his two key citations from Fanon. In Fanon's text, the story continues by relating how the black man fights back:[22] "'Kiss the handsome Negro's ass, Madame!' says the black man. Shame flooded her face. At last I was set free from any rumination. At the same time I accomplished two things: I identified my enemies and I made a scene. A grand slam. No one would be able to laugh" (114).

What exactly are the implications of Fanon's tale? By locating racism in the triangle between mother, child, and black man, he not only draws the production of racist stereotypes into the sphere of the family at its most intimate core; he also makes women responsible for the racist education of their offspring. In both cases the woman provides a bulwark of whiteness, a refuge for the frightened child. The enemy of the black man, the story implies, is not the white man but the white woman. By shaming the white woman into admitting her sexual interest in him, the black man turns the colonial rhetoric back on her: the colonial system had reduced the black man to an animal precisely because he was said to desire white women. And that attribution of guilt to the black man, Fanon implies, is a projection of the white man's knowledge (or fear) of (white) women's lust for the "Negro," a desire that whites consider to be animalistic and therefore has to be denied, projected on the black man, and traced to the black man's mythically exaggerated sexual prowess. The inferiority complex inculcated into black men is thus the projection of white males' feeling of sexual inferiority (Fanon 41–69). Fanon's analysis therefore shifts the entire blame of racial discrimination onto white women, "blaspheming" against the so-called civilizing powers of womanhood *qua* motherhood and thereby transgressing against one of the most cherished myths of colonial society.

To present-day ears, Fanon's entire schema sounds entirely gynophobic and fixated on the male perspective. Whereas Fanon is perfectly capable of recognizing that ascriptions of abnormal sexual prowess are constructions designed to reduce the black man to a conceptual position of sheer animality, the ascription to white women of sexual desire for the black man, which is as much of a construct – motivated by a sexual inferiority complex and sexual jealousy[23] (with a good measure of misogyny on the part of white males) – is swallowed by him as the truth pure and simple. Here are two of the most scandalous passages:

> I understand this extra-fragile woman: At bottom what she wants most is to have the powerful Negro bruise her frail shoulders. (167)

and,

> Are we not now observing a complete inversion? Basically, does this fear of rape not itself cry out for rape? Just as there are faces that ask to be slapped, can one not speak of women who ask to be raped? (156)

Of course, Fanon tries to "rescue" these lamentably misogynistic statements by linking them to psychoanalytic theories about women's sexuality (178–79), thereby subscribing to the view that masochism is natural to the female psychic development.[24] In fact, he ends up explaining women's rape fantasies as the displacement of an unconscious wish for aggression that they turn back on themselves by locating it in the aggressive male. As Vergès explains,

> The fantasy "A Negro is raping me" is thus the conjunction of two desires: to disembowel the mother and to be beaten/penetrated by the father's penis. Both desires are fulfilled through the fantasy of being raped by the Negro. The Negro occupies both the position of the father fulfilling the wish to be hurt and the wish to attack the mother. There is a conflation between the little girl (*i.e.,* Marie Bonaparte's/Freud's little girl from their "A Child is Being Beaten" essays) and the Negro, and the latter becomes the aggressor of the female/maternal body. The Negro can occupy this place because culture has constructed him as violent and murderous. In the Freudian fantasy, beating also means to the child an affirmation of the father's love. The Negro capitalized would then give the white woman a masochistic affirmation of love. ("Creole Skin" 592)

Since the black man's threat has been fixated on his genitals (Fanon 162–63), he comes to serve as the primal phantom of the aggressive male.[25] This is tantamount to blaming women for evoking justified sexual jealousy in their husbands and therefore making them responsible for the subsequent discriminatory treatment of black men at the hands of white men.

Indeed, one can easily turn the tables on Fanon. For instance, it can be noted that he is quite willing to leave Freudian psychoanalysis behind if this serves his own purposes. Thus, in Mozambique, dreams about cruel black men are no longer to be explained in terms of Freudian neuroses; they simply relate to the massacres and torture of one in five of every Malagasy by the Sengalese troops conquering Mozambique (100–04). One is therefore perfectly justified to start with Fanon's own admission of the black man's desire for white women, a desire that is ultimately not sexual but symbolic of the wish to become purely white, an after-effect of the black man's constitutive abandonment neurosis under colonialism (76–79). Since in this hypothetical scenario the black man wants to be loved by the white woman, it is therefore only logical that he should fantasize about white women's sexual desires for black men.

Such fantasies, however, refuse any real understanding of women and their sexual vulnerability. This is the more shameful on Fanon's part because he is quite clearly aware of black men's vulnerability in their sexual organs, pointing out that blacks have traditionally been threatened with castration (162). It should therefore have been possible for him to acknowledge the fact that for women too the site of their greatest intimacy is precisely the space that is maximally vulnerable to aggressive invasion, and that such penetration threatens to destroy their very ego. Fanon not only refuses to engage with the female experience of vulnerability but also implicitly subscribes to a version of Freudian psychoanalysis that defines women's sexual pleasure as synonymous with a masochistic desire for aggressive penetration – a male fantasy *par excellence* since this projects the very parameters of male sexual pleasure onto female desire.

The screw can in fact be turned further on Fanon by noting that his text in general gives ample evidence of misogyny, and that it particularly focusses on his hatred of black women who spurned him for white(r) men. Black women are accused of social climbing, snobbery, and downright cruelty. Fanon's most egregious case is the mulatto who nearly has her dark black lover prosecuted for his impertinence of writing her a letter (56–57). A very personal touch to this criticism of black women enters the picture in the chapter "The Fact of Blackness":

> Shame. Shame and self-contempt. Nausea. When people like me, they tell me it is in spite of my color. When they dislike me, they point out that it is not because of my color. Either way, I am locked into the infernal circle.
>
> I turn away from these inspectors of the Ark before the Flood and I attach myself to my brothers, Negroes like myself. To my horror, they too reject me. They are almost white. And besides they are about to marry white women. They will have children faintly tinged with brown: Who knows, perhaps little by little... (116–17)

There is also the woman who jumps at him for calling her a Negress and the black "girl" who keeps a list of dance halls "Where-there-was-no-chance-of-running-into-niggers" (50). This should be read against an earlier passage:

> It is always essential to avoid falling back into the pit of niggerhood, and
> every woman in the Antilles [...] is determined to select the least black of
> the men. [...] I know a great number of girls from Martinique, students in
> France, who admitted to me with complete candor [...] that they would find
> it impossible to marry black men. (Get out of that and then deliberately go
> back to it? Thank you, no.) (47–48)

One can therefore, reading between the lines, uncover a great hurt, the
wound of hurt pride, the wound of rejection by women black or white and a
subsequent unconscious need for revenge by means of projection. Suitably
so for someone whose vision of love is articulated in terms of ego rather than
the giving or receiving of tenderness and respect: "The person I love will
strengthen me by endorsing my assumption of my manhood" (41).

To return from Fanon's text to Bhabha's creative reading of Fanon, Bhabha's
silence on the gender factor in Fanon is extremely odd because his theory of
splitting literally and explicitly bases itself on a correlation between power
and desire ("Difference" 194), the combination of which is crucial to Bhabha's
explication of differencing in the field of colonial oppression and rebellion.
Surely, it is significant that the Law of the Father is here represented by the
mother, and that Bhabha, remarking on the self-assurance of the "white
girl" (76) by an exchange of glances with the mother, never points out that
this would need to be read as the girl's reassurance of her *gender status*,
whereas in Fanon it is precisely the *difference* in gender that produces racial
tension.

Bhabha's unconcern for gender becomes, indeed, even more disquieting
when one looks at Fanon's text to establish the precise quality of this exchange
of glances between the "white girl" and her mother. Neither the English
translation nor the French original bear any trace of femininity. No gender
indication is provided the first time we read "Look a Negro! [...] Mama, see
the Negro! I'm frightened!" (111–12). Nor can such genderization be detected
in the second passage a page and a half later ("Look at the nigger! [...] Mama,
a Negro!" [113]), except in the sentence "Take no notice, sir, he does not
know that you are as civilized as we," which needs to be interpreted as the
mother's address to Fanon-the-character and hence the "he" must refer to
the "handsome little boy" of the next page. If there is explicit gendering, it is
therefore male. Since in the original "I'm frightened" reads as "J'ai peur" (*Peau
noire* 115), a gender-nonspecific formula,[26] no "girl" can be said to show up in
Fanon's text.[27] Bhabha's odd and incorrect imposition of female gender on
Fanon's child protagonist therefore betrays a blind spot in his own analysis
and constitutes an unconscious projection of Fanon's misogyny onto the
critical postcolonial discourse.

As a consequence of Bhabha's gender blindness, he also fails to discuss the crucial psychoanalytic significance of the little boy. Surely, the scenario reverberates with the boy's relationship to the mother – in Freudian terms, he must by now have noted her lack of the male organ. In this line of interpretation, the black man's penis acquires more than symbolic overtones since the black man comes to embody the threat of replacing the absent father – the white man – in *pars pro toto* fashion. In this implicit scenario the small boy comes to compete with the black man (instead of his real father) for the desire of the mother (in both readings of the genitive).[28] In this symbolic contest, the "handsome little boy" seems to have an advantage over the "Negro," since his competitor has been discredited by the set of contemptuous attributes applied to him in the text. As Bergner notes perceptively, Fanon's earlier self experiences the abasement of a "'feminine' position" (80), that of being subjected to scopic determination by the colonizers. This humiliation is aggravated by the fact that scopic violence is performed by a woman since in the traditional scopic regimes women end up being subjected to the male gaze (79–80). Since the black man's insult to the woman exposes the mother's supposed desire for the "Negro," however, the little boy in fact loses the competition in proper Oedipal fashion.

Beyond Bhabha's silence on the gender issue and beyond the curious absence of the white man from Fanon's primal scene, the gendering of the colonial scenario remains of crucial importance elsewhere. Memmi's description of the master/slave typology of the colonial bond(ing) carries remarkably explicit homosocial tones: the identification of the colonial subject with the colonizer is quite openly one with his virility – the desire to "become" the colonizer being tantamount to a desire to regain one's virility lost in the emasculating defeat by the white man.[29] In other contexts, too, it is always the sly servant, the peasant, the warrior, the oriental prince in his harem who confronts the Western government: power relations are by definition between men. Subaltern studies, by foregrounding the family and the village community, have contributed significantly to the colonial debate since they have helped to revise the classic gender-blind analyses of colonial history. That traditional scenario, by viewing women as mere appendages to the men, denied them political agency. As Fanon's anecdote shows, however, even within postcolonial theory, gender issues are indeed constitutive of the colonial situation, and women are still unwittingly forced to function as the neuralgic point in a system of racial discrimination. The historical implication of women in the colonial power structure thus leaves traces in the cultural episteme whose reverberations, as we have seen, re-emerge in odd moments of Bhabha's poststructuralist discourse.

The Exoticist Scenario

India has been an exceptionally fruitful ground for exoticist discourses. A number of typically exotic elements combine in Indian experience, echoing topoi with which the English have been familiar since William Beckford's *Vathek* (1786). There is, first of all, the sublimity of the Indian landscape in an ideal combination of the Himalayas (the sublime mountain scenery) with the deserts and the majestic course of the River Ganga, examples of the oriental sublime. Among stereotypes of the sublime, only the arctic regions cannot be supplied by India. Other features of Indian society also lend themselves to orientalist stereotyping: the harem, *suttee*, and Mogul valour in warfare are all welcome extensions of the exoticist fantasy. (It is particularly interesting to observe, incidentally, how the orientalist typing of India concentrates on the Mogul empire, with otherwise peaceful Hindus coming in for consideration only when *suttee* or the "monstrosities"[30] of the Hindu plastic arts are being noted.)

These fairly alluring pictures of India are flanked by a depiction of the Indian landscape as hell, with an emphasis on the oppressive heat, the hordes of vermin,[31] hellish religious rites (*suttee*), and the monstrosity of its architecture. Since these descriptions centre on the very elements that lend themselves to an exotic reading, the exotic can be argued to be intrinsically ambivalent. The sensual allure of the sublime has an inherent dark undercurrent, with sexual connotations given prominence in the imagery.

This exoticist scenario needs to be considered alongside its inverse counterpart, the set of stereotypes describing Indians' views of England. Here, on the positive side, England's green valleys with their Wordsworthian echoes are contrasted with the negative features of England's coldness and dreariness, its continual rainfall and lack of human warmth. Whereas the positive features correspond to a picturesque view of the English landscape that the British themselves used to articulate with relief, contrasting India's excessive heat, drought, and expansiveness with their own country of homely and manageable proportions, the negative stereotypes of the British Isles are of external (Indian) origin – with the exception of the rain, perhaps: the one point that the English themselves would concede to be rather a nuisance. All these views of England are thematized at great length in Nirad Chaudhuri's voluble and cliché-ridden account of his trip to England. In stereotypical fashion, Chaudhuri contrasts the picturesqueness of the English landscape in its harmony, moderation, and benignity with the Indian scenario in its disparity, excessivity, and monstrosity. In Anita Desai's *Bye-Bye Blackbird* (1985), it is Dev's epiphany in the countryside in which he experiences the "real" Wordsworthian England (168–72) that aptly illustrates these correlations. Dev has been imbued with English poetry, and this is what he wants to find in England. Adit, who has been much more realistic in his attitude towards England (no Wordsworthian illusions for him when he observes the discontent of Sarah's parents – Dev's in-laws – in their country home), by contrast succumbs to exoticist fantasies about his home country, thereby enacting a typical reaction to his prolonged exile from home.

> When he had leaned over the bridge and gazed down at the River Test and laughed at the downy cygnets following their regal parent under the silver-leaved willows, the insane spectacles on his eyes had actually shown him the rivers of India – the shameful little Jumna, so unworthy of its mythical glory; the mud and slush of the Ganges with its temples and yogis, its jackals and alligators lining the banks; the murderous Mahanadi, each year going berserk like an elephant, trampling those who sought to pacify it, in riverside temples, with marigolds and oil lamps; the uncivilised, mosquito ridden Brahmaputra swirling through the jungles; the fine silver fingers of Punjab's rivers raking the scorched earth. [...]
>
> The long, lingering twilight of the English summer trembling over the garden had seemed to him like an invalid stricken with anaemia, had aroused in him a sudden clamour, like a child's tantrum, to see again an Indian sunset, its wild conflagration, rose and orange, flamingo pink and lemon, scattering into a million sparks in the night sky. (177–78)

Adit's nostalgia for India does not start out with a craving for the sublime. His initial view of Indian rivers concentrates not on their grandeur (which is in fact explicitly rejected as a mythical mystification of an inglorious reality), but on the messiness and squalor of Indian watercourses in contrast to the idyllic neatness of English river scenes. By the end of the cited passage, however, Adit has managed to transform the Wordsworthian pastoral into an emotional desert and has acceded to his violent longings for Indian sunsets with their aggressive onslaught of colours. Such a "wild conflagration," like the earlier depiction of Indian riverscapes in terms of contemptible squalor, ironically mirrors *English* attitudes toward the oriental sublime and its uncivilized counterpart, the abject.

The exoticist paradigm, one can therefore conclude, constitutes an escapist fantasy, with Westerners thrilling to the allure of the sublime and Indians basking in the neatness and picturesqueness of the English scene – for which they have acquired a taste from reading English pastoral romantic poetry where that landscape served the escapist fantasy of frustrated city dwellers.

The Exile: Criticism of Self and Other

The condition of exile combines a number of recurring features: a nostalgia for the home country that results in an idealization of India's positive features and an indulgence in fond memories that tend to acquire gilded overtones; an attempt to create a genuine replica of home in the foreign environment, thereby producing a false imitation that resembles exoticist simulacra of Indian culture; an increasing distance from the host culture, with a tendency to move from open criticism of the colonial past and of Britain's current patronizing stance toward Indian immigrants to fantasies of counter-colonization and the assumption of national superiority over the British. In addition to these parameters, one can observe a tendency to displace the experience of racial discrimination in England onto other immigrant groups, transposing racial epithets into descriptors of class membership or religious affiliation.

This last point has to do with the Indians' self-image in London rather than with their views about India or England. British racism against coloured immigrants is experienced by both Dev and Adit in Desai's novel. Adit has simply stopped paying attention, whereas Dev is deeply bothered by the inscriptions of "Wog" slogans on the underground and by racist remarks in general (16). Both Dev and Adit, however, immediately agree to label the Sikh family in the same house as low-class, and to look down upon them because they live in overcrowded lodgings and are supposedly dirty (28). The matriarch once corners Dev, who has caught a cold, and tends to his medical needs, even offering to get a job and a wife for him. As becomes evident from her remarks, her sons have not shied away from the most menial jobs and are now engaged in profitable business, whereas Dev, who is looking for a white-collar job only, has been unemployed since his arrival in England. Dev's feelings of disgust toward the Sikhs, therefore, disguise a good measure of guilty conscience and they help disguise his concern over his own inferiority in relation to his neighbours' success story. Such a displacement of the racial stereotype onto lower-class Indians serves a double function: it deflects the feelings of inferiority generated by racial remarks onto the already despised Sikhs, and it pretends that British racist clichés are class-related, that they do (correctly) apply to the lower-class Sikhs but are inappropriate to the upper-class Hindus. By means of this double strategy, respect for the English and a positive (class-related) self-image can be preserved, circumventing serious puncturing of Brahmin self-respect.

In connection with the class issue, it also becomes apparent that the colonial inferiority complex is still at work in these Indian exiles. Dev, it is claimed, would be more than lucky to marry the shop girl whom he woos at the end of the story, and Adit has of course taken a huge step up the social ladder by marrying Sarah. Neither man would ever have dreamed of taking a wife from the working class in India,[32] and Sarah's own choice of an Indian husband is conspicuously fraught with family scandal, rejection, and loneliness. Sarah is ashamed of her husband (ch. 2) and has lost all her friends as a consequence of the marriage, her relationship to her parents has suffered, and she refuses to address these problems, repressing them carefully. Her forlorn look as Adit happens to observe her getting down from the bus (31) tells of the emotional price she is paying for her mixed marriage, and it can even be argued that her headlong plunge into motherhood and expatriation to India is yet another futile attempt to suppress the British side of herself.

The condition of exile is characterized first and foremost, as I have noted, by nostalgia for the home country. Indian food in retrospect acquires a lusciousness much exaggerated – as Dev notes when Adit enthuses about *halwa*, which one merely takes for granted in India (15–16). This attitude is part of a complex immersion in nostalgia. The thing to do is to go out to an Indian restaurant that evokes the Raj period in its decor, a kind of museum of times past:

> Here [at Veeraswamy's] you have the real thing – the very essence of the Raj, of the role of the *sahib log* – in its fullest bloom.
>
> Sarah, listening to a rather drunken Dev's flamboyant words, looked about her again and thought she saw what he meant. Through his eyes, she saw that essence, that living bloom in these halls – brilliant, exotic, gold-dusted, rose-tinted. Here were the tiger skins and the gold leaf elephants, the chandeliers and rainbow-coloured Jaipur furniture, the crimson carpets and the starched turbans of another age, another world – all a bit outsize, more brilliant than they had been in real life, in India, for here there was no clammy tropical heat, no insidious dust, no insecurity, no shadow of history to shake or darken or wilt them. Here was only that essence, that rose bloom, transported to a climate that touched more gently on human dreams; here it could flower and shed its perfume in the safety of mirror-lined, carpet-laid hallucination. Even the grace and good manners of the Indian servants were a little more theatrical than they would have been in India. Everyone seemed to be playing a part in a technicoloured film about the East – even I, thought Sarah, fingering the gold chain at her neck. (195)

Nostalgia for the home country therefore apparently evokes artificial re-creations of a past that never existed in such an idealized form, a nativeness born of postcoloniality. Likewise, at another point in the novel, bad music comes to be accepted for a good performance (96) simply because rarity and nostalgia combine to make the fake article precious, to value it as the real thing. These simulacra of India (which correspond to Western imports from India – particularly in the case of the decor of the restaurant, a collection of colonialist plunder from the subcontinent) are appropriated by expatriate Indians as their own heritage.

Negative images of India are either completely repressed or subjected to nostalgic interpretation. Adit, as we have seen, feels affection for the Indian rivers although they are much less grand than in the mythical shape in which they have loomed in his mind (177–78), and he enthuses over the glorious Indian sunsets and the Indian landscape in terms of its "wild, wide grandeur, its supreme grandeur, its loneliness and black, glittering enchantment" (180). This exotic picture, too, is a cliché of Western provenance, as is its negative underside, which Adit has to face later, again in a film. Adit and Sarah are watching videos of Indian movies set in Indian landscapes, "feeling Bengal, feeling India sweep into their room like a flooded river, drowning it all and replacing it with the emptiness and sorrow, the despair and rage, the flat grey melancholy and the black glamour of India" (224). In all of these instances, the exotic orientalist cliché of India comes to serve as a substitute for expatriates' real experience of their home country, memories of which have become warped by nostalgia and desire. It is only when Adit thinks of taking Sarah back with the baby that he recalls with a pang the poverty, crowding and lack of sanitary facilities and what this might mean to his wife. Adit bases his appreciation of England on his material living standard in London (the appliances he can afford, the freedom, the privacy) – a view that is manifestly imbricated with British attitudes of superiority and condescension – and he is realistic in his description of the Indian situation: not only would he have been unable to get a job there had he remained, but he also would have had to live on the brink of destitution (17–18).

Expatriates are therefore caught in a web of false images of India since the experience of the source has been lost to them. Moreover, they become embroiled in an orientalist discourse about their home country and are unable to extricate themselves from the West and the categories it imposes on them and their culture. This leads to a schizophrenia of sorts, such as the one Dev experiences soon after his arrival in England when he tries to decide whether to stay or not:

> There are days in which the life of an alien appears enthrallingly rich and beautiful to him, and that of a homebody too dull, too stale to return to ever. Then he hears a word in the tube or notices an expression on an English face that overturns his latest decision and, drawing himself together, he feels he can never bear to be the unwanted immigrant but must return to his own land, however abject or dull, where he has, at least, a place in the sun, security, status and freedom. (86)

England appears to him as either exotically attractive ("enthrallingly rich and beautiful") or as hostile, and India has been turned into a familiar but unloved bogeyman.

To extricate oneself from these colonial bonds, one has to strike back. The exile scenario therefore includes criticism of the British colonialist past as a typical reaction of the expatriate: Dev, for instance, refuses to like St. Paul's Cathedral because it symbolizes Britain's imperial grandeur (67–68). There is also the attempt at aggressive retaliation under the aegis of a cultural and economic counter-colonization of England. Thus, Dev is delighted to find an Indian bazaar in London that evokes in him fantasies of an Indian takeover of the British Isles (thereby, one can note bemusedly, realizing the worst Western fears of "Balkanization"):

> "It seems to me the East India Company has come to take over England now."
> Dev is delighted with the idea. He is exhilarated by the rowdy, libertine Indian atmosphere about him. His guard is lowered and "Topping!" he shouts, remembering the phrase from some schoolboy comic and finding it appropriate. "Let history turn the tables now. Let the Indian traders come to England – the Sikhs and Sindhis with their brass elephants and boxes of spice and tea. Let them take over the City, to begin with – let them move into Cheapside and Leadenhall and Cornhill. Let them move into Threadneedle Street and take over the Bank, the Royal Exchange and Guildhall. Then let them spread over the country – the Sikhs with their turbans and swords and the Sindhis with their gold bars and bangles. Let them build their forts along the coast, in Brighton and Bristol and Bath. Then let our army come across, our Gurkhas and our Rajputs with the camel corps and elephants of Rajasthan." (11)

This rather carnivalesque scenario is complemented by Adit's and Dev's talk about Indian ambassadorship in England. Indian hospitality and "gentlemanliness" are cited by Adit in order to reject accusations of Indian inferiority. Adit wants to "[show] the English what a gentleman an Indian can be [...] dazzling everyone with [his] Oriental wit and fluency" (154). This rather half-hearted attempt – Adit has to prove Indian worth against Western allegations of unworthiness – contrasts with Dev's markedly more combative attitude:

> I am showing these damn imperialists with their lost colonies complex that we are free people now, with our own personalities that this veneer of an English education has not obscured, and not afraid to match ours with theirs. I am here, he proselytized, to interpret my country to them, to conquer England as they once conquered India, to show them, to show them... (123)

Such a turning of the tables, however, remains sheer fantasy. Nobody is going to take either Dev or Adit seriously, so even their attempts to break through the inhibiting straitjacket of Western stereotyping founders on their hopeless enmeshment with orientalist discourse: the subaltern can never speak but in the language of the oppressor. The two options outlined above parallel the nationalist reactions within the colonial scenario. In the colonial context, however, agency is a distinct opportunity; in the context of diasporic homelessness, aggressive discourse peters out in ineffective posturing and utopian wish-fulfillment.

The scenario of expatriate self-definition most clearly illustrates the cross-mirrorings of alterity apostrophized in my title: exile is a condition of inherent and ineluctable inauthenticity in which several types of Western stereotyping are adopted in the attempt to constitute a sort of Indian self-identification even if at second remove. There is no attempt to *become*, simply, British. Such a project would not merely founder on the patent impossibility of a visible minority becoming invisible (like Ellison's invisible man), but it additionally presupposes the utopian scenario of a complete elimination of one's past. Thus Bharati Mukherjee's claim of an American identity (much more convincing in the melting pot scenario of American immigration) has elicited a vigorous antagonism within the Indian expatriate community. Her claim to be "American" is seen as a treachery to inherited cultural values.[33] There is, however, more than one way in which to become "British." One such option is delineated in the following discussion of globalization.

Globalization

In the scenario of globalization, the emigré is part of a cosmopolitan "scene" in a major cultural centre in the West. He or she participates in, say, British culture at the upper level, has a professional – usually academic – job, and has the privilege to choose eclectically between cultures and between identities. On the negative side, this position frequently entails an inability to feel at home anywhere at all, a cultural rootlessness: one is part of the global elite but no longer Indian or fully British. On the positive side, the class privilege afforded by the status within a global professional elite allows expatriates to avoid both racial discrimination and contact with their poorer country-folk who suffer from it. It is this role of a cosmopolitan subject that is frequently celebrated in postcolonial work on migrancy and hybridity (Krishnaswamy), a role that no doubt yields quite noticeable advantages to those able to claim it, despite the fact that exile itself, even in the best of conditions, induces nostalgia, homesickness, or a loss of orientation.

The scenario of globalization becomes particularly important in the handling of cultural clichés. We noted earlier that travelling Indians project romanticized visions of England (imported into India by means of British education) on their exotic "occidental" other, thereby inverting the orientalist gaze and subjecting England to an inauthentic stereotyping. This inversion of the colonial paradigm is, however, still rooted in colonial education and does not significantly escape the clutches of Western discourse. In a globalized context, however, clichés of Britain lose their counter-colonial specificity since they now come to be situated on the same level as clichés about France, the U.S., Japan, or India itself. From a cosmopolitan vantage point, these different countries and their cultural products become exchangeable within an economy of tourism and international migrancy. Moreover, these symbolic nationalist simulacra allow the cosmopolitan subject to exercise power over the image-making process by selecting, combining, and exploiting the clichés for his or her own purposes.

These processes of appropriation and exploitation can be illustrated by a passage from Sunetra Gupta's *The Glassblower's Breath*:

> Turning for a last farewell glance, he [Avishek] had been hit by the pastry texture of the snow-dusted spires, and this gentle vision had resurrected his desire to craft in cake flesh the spires of Oxford, his first dream, his last dream, his one enduring fantasy, Balliol in bakemeat, a gingerbread Christchurch. (59)

Avishek the baker not only fantasizes about the architecture of colleges but he also exploits these clichés for his own industry, producing simulacra of Christchurch and Balliol in the shape of quite literally consumable bakery. Avishek therefore commodifies British culture for his own profit in the same way as souvenir factories bank on the popularity of cultural symbols like the Taj Mahal, the Eiffel Tower, or Big Ben. Avishek's commodification of Christchurch and Balliol is therefore situated within a global culture of tourism and trade that converts any marketable symbol into simulacra, which are then distributed in the global consumer culture.

The ascendancy of the global elite over the native culture of the host country can be signalled in a different manner too. In Gupta's novels the Indian expatriates frequently have a higher social status than the British characters, and some of the Westerners can even be said to possess the traits typically ascribed to the native from the arrogant colonial perspective. Thus, in *The Glassblower's Breath*, Daniel the butcher is the one Englishman among the major protagonists of the novel, and he is inferior to the Indian and Persian expatriates in terms of education, intelligence, elegance, and of course social status. (Besides Daniel, the only other memorable British character is a pervert who organizes alphabetical dinners.) The American good-for-nothing Sparrow, on the other hand, epitomizes the figure of the *shlemiel*. He is a lazy, drifting character, a promiscuous, carnivalesque figure, whose actions are haphazard and therefore indeterminable and who engages in all sorts of tricks (pretending to be the butler simply because he is intrigued with the purloined diary of the gourmet fanatic). In this manner, it could be argued, Sparrow instantiates precisely those characteristics of laziness, inefficiency, and slyness typically projected on the colonial subject. Indeed, the parallel can be extended to Daniel the butcher who evokes images of the native devil; by enticing the passions of the female protagonist, he eventually is responsible for her death. Allusions to death prevail in the novel and are particularly centred on Daniel. Daniel's coitus with the female protagonist also inverts the colonial pattern as regards the sexual parameters of colonialism: here it is the expatriate Indian woman who sleeps with the white male native, and not the other way round. That intercourse in *The Glassblower's Breath* is linked with death – a fairly standard male topos – can moreover be treated as yet another inversion on the gender line: this time female passion is figured as loss and transcendence, relegating the male lover to a position of passivity and lack of articulation. We never get an insight into Daniel's mind, so the woman's "penetration" of him in the sexual act corresponds precisely to the epistemological metaphor of penetrating to the truth with which we are so familiar from the Western male tradition.

In Gupta's novel, the suppressed national and cultural origins of the protagonist return, however, with a vengeance. In the final scene of the book, the protagonist's husband, Alexander, (who is of Persian background) kills all three lovers and suitors of his wife. Whatever freedom from her gender-related cultural anchorings the protagonist may have enjoyed, this freedom is abruptly nullified by the eruption of patriarchal jealousy and "Eastern" cruelty. Since most of the novel renders the perceptions of the unnamed heroine through the eyes of her husband and three suitors, the text moreover fails to liberate the female figure from the male gaze and ultimately, through the actions of her husband, ends up catching and entrapping her in traditional marital possessiveness.

Globalization, it could therefore be suggested, provides a measure of relief from the colonial trauma, but one must also reckon with one's nationalist tradition, which may be equally lethal to the subject's free development. Whereas the colonial subject used to be always in the position of a victim of external forces, in the globalization scenario expatriates have begun to participate in the processes of cultural dominance – a constellation that is elsewhere described only in relation to the Third World elite's implication with neo-colonial regimes.[34] When the native culture, in its nationalist (and patriarchal) excrescences, catches up with those who have removed themselves from their victimization, guilt is expiated in a bloodbath of major proportions.[35]

The Third Party

There is one other blind spot in many studies of imagological relevance: the complication of the scenario by means of a third term in the image/counter-image relation. I do not mean a Lacanian third term in the sense in which both Fanon and Bhabha utilize it, but – in a more pedestrian way – the deflection and doubling of images through a third party that functions as a catalyst or point of comparison with the basic scenario of the self and the other in their multi-level mirrorings.

The third party, in most texts, is a figure or group of people that contrast with the Indian self or the British other. In Desai's *Bye-Bye Blackbird*, for instance, the Sikhs function as a third party, and their treatment by Dev and Adit significantly affects the extent of Indian self-identification in the novel. In Desai's *Baumgartner's Bombay* (1988), Jews, Germans, and Indians are contrasted, and the Germans certainly fare the worst in this comparison. In Gupta's *The Glassblower's Breath*, the scenario is complicated by the globetrotter Sparrow from the U.S., the Russian Vladimir Jovanovitch, and the Persian husband, Alexander. In comparison with these, Daniel, the British protagonist, pales into insignificance.

Baumgartner's Bombay is particularly sophisticated in complicating the Indian relationship to the West by means of the vantage point of a third party or a third term. For instance, this is not a simple situation of Jewish Baumgartner coming to Bombay, the city of the exotic East. On his way to Bombay, he passes through Venice, which he experiences in all its exotic splendour and allure. India, where he finally settles down, turns out to be a home much like the Germany he has left – a country torn by civil war, a country that allows him only an existence among the masses of the poor, and a country in which he is finally killed by a German after all, even though this does not happen in a concentration camp. In his own experiences in India, Baumgartner thus repeats the decline of his family's fortunes and victimization by the Nazis. His possessions are as little worth robbing as were his family's by the time they were killed in the camps. Although the German tourist turned robber represents "white trash" at its most despicable, the book leaves no doubt that for the Indian pub owner, himself certainly not well off, Baumgartner and his girlfriend, Lotte, are the dregs of Western society. Yet that evaluation needs to be measured against the pub owner's (but also Baumgartner's) inevitable callousness toward the homeless squatter family on the pavement outside Baumgartner's execrable hole of a flat.

Stereotypes about the colonized are therefore, in the final analysis, stereotypes about the downtrodden, and the introduction of third and fourth positions into the central binary constellation of colonizer versus colonized helps to foreground precisely the class-related underpinnings of recurrent cultural clichés. These resurrect colonial epithets for the bad native in order to recirculate them as racist or classist language against the poor, the marginal, or the disadvantaged. Very little "national" content is transported in these stereotypes and attitudes against immigrants, a new set of others who are not conveniently housed far away in India but encroach upon the very centre of the (Westerners') home country. Thinking through the functions of the third party, therefore, reveals this textual ploy as a strategy to outline the dark underside of the globalization scenario. Some former victims of marginalization and (cultural) oppression have been enabled to turn the tables on the West, but they thus become implicated in a general Western economy that continues to exclude and discriminate. The move to the global elite is a move to domination, and domination in turn inevitably produces discrimination against the lower social classes. The cross-mirrorings of alterity have shifted from a colonial to a postcolonial scenario and from the safe distance of the empire's furthest reaches to the immediate vicinity of Western urban environment. Likewise, the former colonial subject has either sunk to the low level of a postcolonial subject in a neo-colonial state or to the uneasy position of an unwanted immigrant. In both places, he or she must face not merely the continuing presence of the former colonial master but also the new faces of the neo-colonial and cosmopolitan elites, those among his own who have "made" it to the enviable position of postmodernity. Yet the guilt-ridden vision of their native alter egos continues to haunt these lucky ones in the very web of cultural hybridity that both sustains them and ultimately threatens to give way, to drop them back into the abyss from which they escaped with such heroic endeavour. The assumption of Western superiority remains an unstable and risky, even hazardous, achievement that compounds the miseries of the colonial inferiority complex with the acquisition of the guilt suffered by the rich. Indeed, the expatriate elite re-enacts the colonial scenario with a vengeance, clinging to the proven colonial strategies of marginalization of the other as a means of exorcizing their own selves in the place of that other. After all, the colonizer always felt superior or pretended to feel superior against manifest evidence of his physical and moral degeneration in the colonies.[36] The former colonial subject, by contrast, has to repress the knowledge of his (erstwhile) inferiority and therefore needs to re-enact colonialist strategies of discrimination, expropriation, and victimization to secure the still shaky new position at the top of the social or global scale. Cross-mirrorings of alterity, one can conclude, constitute unending processes of projection that apparently never get resolved;[37] they merely intensify the doubling by yet one more turn of the screw.

Notes

1 This paper, in its original shorter version, was first read at the GNEL conference at Konstanz in September 1996. The research is part of a larger project on expatriate Indian writing funded by the Deutsche Forschungsgemeinschaft (DFG) in the context of an interdisciplinary study group (Sonderforschungsbereich 541) on "Identities and Alterities" at Freiburg University.

2 See "maps" of national stereotypes such as, for example, the one referred to in Stanzel ("National Character"; *Europäer*). See also the essays in Zacharasiewicz. Perhaps the best two contributions to imagology are Bleicher and Dyserinck.

3 It is mainly the *male* representative of a European culture that is thus figured.

4 A laudable exception is Godzich in his article "Emergent Literature," in which he applies imagological research to a South African context.

5 Fanon's text from 1952 (*Peau noire, masques blancs*) is used strategically in Bhabha's post- or para-Lacanian readings in the colonial deployment of the economy of desire and power. See Bhabha ("Difference" and *Location*).

6 This condition of cultural hybridity, in the theoretical literature, is frequently portrayed in celebratory terms, ignoring the plight of exiles in the contexts of forced emigration and refugee existence, or that of bonded labourers belonging to a migrant workforce. (For a criticism of the "sweet sorrows of exile" suffered by the self-exiled intellectual, see Krishnaswamy's "Mythologies of Migrancy.")

7 See below for a problematization of the gender issue which remains off limits in most "classic" accounts.

8 The figure of Stephen Blackpool in Dickens's *Hard Times* (1854) is a typical example of the meek and self-deprecatory ideal from the factory owners' point of view.

9 See Isaac for a discussion of the representation of the working class in political writings of the period. Middle-class conceptualizations of the poor reach back to formulae about the deserving and undeserving poor, the lazy apprentice, and wholesome beer versus debilitating gin (Hogarth), all of which had been in currency since the Renaissance vagrancy laws.

10 One can still measure this excessive admiration for British culture in Chaudhuri's aptly named *A Passage to England* (1971). Responsible for Indian anglophilia was, of course, the thorough indoctrination of Indians with British culture in the colonial educational system, whose influence did not affect to the same extent either the African colonies or the Caribbean.

11 I am thinking of Bhabha's sly natives in "Signs Taken for Wonders" (*Location* 102–22).

12 See Bhabha's "Difference": "Such visibility of the institutions and apparatuses of power is possible because the exercise of colonial power makes their relationship obscure, produces them as fetishes, spectacles of a 'natural'/racial pre-eminence. Only the seat of government is always elsewhere – alien and separate by that distance upon which surveillance depends for its strategies of objectification, normalization and discipline" (209).

13 See Fanon (*Black Skin* 99) on the natives' welcoming even shipwrecked Europeans as "honorable stranger[s]." The white man is either "deified or devoured" (92; qtd. in Mannoni).

14 Note that the typical scenes of imagological study treat the experience of the tourist abroad, in both directions: the tourist in a strange environment being judged by the natives, or the tourist judging the indigenous culture in its natural habitat. The situation becomes more "colonial," however, in the study of anti-Semitic clichés and, even more so, in the analysis of Anglo-Irish relationships in Ireland.

15 Note too that all nationalistic propaganda *constructs* an image of a nativist culture that was never in existence in such a form, first, because native culture never tended to see itself as a unitary field of reference before its confrontation with the colonizer's Other, and, second, because by the time of the national countermovement, native culture has already been irremediably changed: some practices have been lost, some have become modified through the contact with the colonizer, some have acquired new functions, and foreign ways have been adopted in other areas. (Cf. Appiah's apt remarks on African art in *Critical Inquiry*.)

16 Bhabha's commitment to never defining his terminology in a consistent manner – no doubt a deliberate poststructuralist ploy – makes this somewhat frustrating to pin down in precise terms. The term *ambivalence* of course originally refers to Freud's theories, where it denotes a simultaneous presence of contradictory effects (love and hate, trust and distrust) toward the object of desire.

17 Note also that Bakha's treatment by the Brahmins is charged by the same protocolonial effects that we earlier observed to apply in nineteenth-century attitudes toward the working-class poor.

18 For a much more extensive analysis of hybridity in these novels and for a distinction between different kinds of hybridity, see my "Colonial vs. Cosmopolitan Hybridity," in *Hybridity and Postcolonialism*.

19 This, naturally, is here used in a Lacanian sense, and is so used by Bhabha. Cf. also Fanon (*Black Skin* 161 n25).

20 I am of course aware of the fact that the heroism of the *sati or suttee* does not entirely "fit" the role of the victim, but female heroism also sometimes occurs on the British side in the colonial novel – so the parallelism does hold true.

21 I come back to the fact that Bhabha later calls this child "the girl."

22 Bhabha never mentions this conclusion to the trauma.

23 Cf. "Projecting his own desires onto the Negro, the white man behaves 'as if' the Negro really had them [*i.e.*, the white women]" (Fanon *Black Skin* 165).

24 Fanon's problematic gynophobic discourse has recently been the subject of work by Diana Fuss, Gwen Bergner, and Lola Young (89–97); and Françoise Vergès ("Heritage" and "Creole Skin"). See, for example, Bergner's critique of this line of argument: "Bhabha's ostensibly ameliorative observation that Fanon, in a later chapter, 'attempts a somewhat more complex reading of masochism' leaves disturbingly intact *Black Skin, White Masks*'s equation of (white) women's sexuality with masochism" (85).

25 As Fuss notes, it "is, however, important to recall at this juncture that Fanon elaborates his reading of this particular fantasy during a period when fabricated charges of rape were used as powerful colonial instruments of fear and intimidation against black men. Fanon's deeply troubling comments on white women and rape are formulated within a historical context in which the phobically charged stereotype of the violent, lawless, and oversexed Negro put all black men at perpetual risk. What we might call Fanon's myth of white women's rape fantasies is offered as a counter narrative to 'the myth of the black rapist'" (31).

26 Other syntagms might have enforced obligatory gender agreement (*e.g.*, je suis epouvantée).

27 The oddity of this mistranslation has been noted by Bergner (86, n.4): "In discussing this scene Rhabha makes a telling slip. He writes that 'a white girl fixes Fanon in a look and word as she turns to *identify with her mother.*' [...] But nowhere does Fanon say that the child is a girl. Moreover, he seems to refer to the child's gender on the next page: 'the handsome little *boy* [...] le beau petit *garçon.*' [...] Bhabha's slip suggests that preconceptions of how race, gender, and sexuality intersect run deep."

28 Cf. also Chow's claim about Fanon's Oedipal construction of the native: "The native (the black man) is thus imagined to be an angry son who wants to displace the white man, the father" (125).

29 Thus, Suleri, in *The Rhetoric of English India*, traces strong homoerotic reverberations in key Anglo-Indian texts.

30 See Mitter for a history of Western representations of Indian sculpture.

31 See, for instance, the travel accounts that Ghose quotes.

32 Dev teases Adit for trying "to show Sarah what a sahib a *babu* can be" (28). Compare Adit's words to Dev, "I predict that in six months – no, three months from now, it will be Dev himself who will be rolling in the grass in Hyde Park with some blonde landlady's daughter" (66).

33 Recently Mukherjee has thrown further oil on the firebrand by repeating her unpopular standpoint in an article in *Mother Jones*.

34 This theme is of course particularly prominent in the African novel (for example, in Ngugi's

Petals of Blood or Armah's *The Beautyful Ones Are Not Yet Born*), but can also be observed in the Indian novel, particularly in the work of Nayantara Sahgal.

35 Gupta's work is the only example of celebratory globalization. All the other texts about cosmopolitan migrants that I am aware of are fraught with ambivalence, nostalgia for the home country, unhappiness, the problems of expatriation and exile. Adib Khan's superb novel *Seasonal Adjustments* (1994) provides particularly subtle delineations of these problems.

36 See Orwell's clear-headed delineation of this process in *Burmese Days* (1934).

37 For a similar argument in relation to the deadlock in which postcolonial criticism finds itself in its dependence on the colonial scenario, see my "The Hybridity of Discourses about Hybridity."

Works Cited

Anand, Mulk Raj. *Untouchable*. 1935. London: Penguin, 1940.

Appiah, Kwame. "Is the Post- in Postmodernism the Post- in Postcolonialism?" *Critical Inquiry* 17.2 (1990–91): 336–57.

Armah, Ayi Kwei. *The Beautyful Ones Are Not Yet Born*. London: Heinemann, 1975.

Bentham, Jeremy. *Panopticon; or The Inspection-House*. Dublin: T. Payne, 1791.

Bergner, Gwen. "Who Is that Masked Woman? or, The Role of Gender in Fanon's *Black Skin, White Masks*." *PMLA* 110.1 (1995): 75–88.

Bhabha, Homi. "Difference, Discrimination and the Discourse of Colonialism." *The Politics of Theory: Proceedings of the Essex Conference on the Sociology of Literature, July 1982*. Ed. Francis Barker, *et al*. Colchester: University of Essex Press, 1983. 194–211.

———. *The Location of Culture*. London: Routledge, 1994.

Bleicher, Thomas. "Elemente einer komparatistischen Imagologie." *Komparatistische Hefte* 2 (1980): 12–24.

Chaudhuri, Nirad C. *A Passage to England*. 1959. New Delhi: Orient Paperbacks, 1994.

Chow, Rey. "Where Have All the Natives Gone?" 1993. *Contemporary Postcolonial Theory*. Ed. Padmini Mongia. London: Arnold, 1996. 122–46.

Desai, Anita. *Baumgartner's Bombay*. 1988. London: Penguin, 1990.

———. *Bye-Bye Blackbird*. 1985. New Delhi: Orient Paperbacks, 1991.

Dickens, Charles. *Hard Times*. 1854. Oxford: Oxford University Press, 1989.

Dyserinck, Hugo. "'Komparatistische Imagologie': Zur Politischen Tragweite einer europäischen Wissenschaft von der Literatur." *Europa und das Nationale Selbstverständnis: Imagologische Probleme in Literatur, Kunst und Kultur Des 19. und 20. Jahrhunderts*. Ed. Hugo Dyserinck and Karl-Ulrich Syndram. Bonn: Bouvier, 1988. 13–37.

Essed, Philomela. *Everyday Racism: Reports from Women of Two Cultures*. Claremont, CA: Hunter House, 1990.

Fanon, Frantz. *Black Skin, White Masks*. 1952. Trans. Charles Lam Markmann. New York: Grove, 1967.

———. *Peau noire, masques blancs*. Paris: Seuil, 1952.

Fludernik, Monika. "Colonial vs. Cosmopolitan Hybridity: A Comparison of Mulk Raj Anand and R.K. Narayan with Recent British and North American Expatriate Writing." *Hybridity and Postcolonialism: Twentieth-Century Indian Literature*. Ed. Monika Fludernik. Tübingen: Stauffenburg, 1998. 261–90.

———. "The Hybridity of Discourses about Hybridity." *Crossover: Ethnicity, Gender and Ethics in Literary and Visual Worlds*. Ed. Therese Steffen. Tübingen: Stauffenburg, 1999.

———. "Suttee Revisited: From the Iconography of Martyrdom to the Burkean Sublime." *New Literary History* 30.2 (1999): 411–37.

Foucault, Michel. *Discipline and Punish: The Birth of the Prison.* 1975. New York: Vintage, 1979.

Fuss, Diana. "Interior Colonies: Frantz Fanon and the Politics of Identification." *Diacritics* 24 (1994): 20–42.

Ghose, Indira. "Der Memsahib-Mythos: Frauen und Kolonialismus in Indien." *Feministische Studien* 2 (1995): 34–45.

Godzich, Wlad. "Emergent Literature and the Field of Comparative Literature." *The Comparative Perspective on Literature: Approaches to Theory and Practice.* Ed. Clayton Koelb and Susan Noakes. Ithaca: Cornell University Press, 1998. 18–36.

Gupta, Sunetra. *The Glassblower's Breath.* 1993. London: Penguin, 1994.

———. *Memories of Rain.* 1992. London: Phoenix House, 1993.

Isaac, Judith. "The Working Class in Early Victorian Novels." *DAI* 33 (1973): 12A.

Khan, Adib. *Seasonal Adjustments.* St. Leonards, NSW: Allen & Unwin, 1994.

Krishnaswamy, Revathi. "Mythologies of Migrancy: Postcolonialism, Postmodernism and the Politics of (Dis) location." *ARIEL* 26.1 (1995): 125–46.

Mani, Lata. "Contentious Traditions: The Debate on Sati in Colonial India." *The Nature and Context of Minority Discourse.* Ed. Abdul R. JanMohamed and David Llovd. Oxford: Oxford University Press, 1990. 319–56.

Mannoni, o. *Prospero and Caliban: The Psychology of Colonization.* Paris: Seuil, 1950.

Memmi, Albert. *Der Kolonisator und der Kolonisierte [Portrait du colonisé précédé du Portrait du colonisateur].* 1957. Hamburg: Europäische Verlagsanstalt, 1994.

———. *The Colonizer and the Colonized.* New York: Orion Press, 1965.

Minh-ha, Trinh T. *Woman, Native, Other: Writing Postcoloniality and Feminism.* Bloomington, IN: Indiana University Press, 1989.

Mitter, Partha. *Much Maligned Monsters: A History of European Reactions to Indian Art.* Oxford: Clarendon Press, 1977.

Mohanty, Chandra. "Under Western Eyes: Feminist Scholarship and Colonial Discourses." *Feminist Review 30* (1988): 60–88.

Mukherjee, Bharati. "American Dreamer." *Mother Jones* Jan.-Feb. 1997: 32–35.

Narayan, R.K. *The Guide.* 1958. London: Penguin, 1988.

Ngugi wa Thiong'o. *Ngaahika Ndeenda (I Will Marry When I Want).* London: Heinemann, 1982.

———. *Petals of Blood.* 1977. London: Heinemann, 1993.

Orwell, George. *Burmese Days.* New York: Harper, 1934.

Scarry, Elaine. *The Body in Pain: The Making and Unmaking of the World.* Oxford: Oxford University Press, 1985.

Sharma, Arvind, ed. *Sati: Historical and Phenomenological Essays.* Delhi: Motilal, 1988.

Sharpe, Jenny. *Allegories of Empire: The Figure of Woman in the Colonial Text.* Minneapolis: University of Minnesota Press, 1993.

Spivak, Gayatri Chakravorty. *In Other Worlds: Essays in Cultural Politics.* New York: Routledge, 1988.

Stanzel, Franz K. *Eurpoäer: Ein imagologischer Essay.* Heidelberg: Winter, 1997.

———. "National Character as Literary Stereotype: An Analysis of the Image of the German in English Literature before 1806." *London German Studies* 1 (1980): 101–15.

Suleri, Sara. *The Rhetoric of English India.* Chicago: Chicago University Press, 1992.

Vergès, Françoise. "The Heritage of Frantz Fanon." *The European Legacy* 1.3 (1996): 994–98.

———. "Creole Skin, Black Mask: Fanon and Disavowal." *Critical Inquiry* 23.3 (1997): 578–95.

Young, Lola. "Missingpersons: Fantasising Black Women in *Black Skin, White Masks.*" *The Fact of Blackness: Frantz Fanon and Visual Representation.* Ed. Alan Read. London: Institute of Contemporary Arts, 1996. 86–101.

Zacharasiewicz, Waldemar, ed. *Images of Central Europe in Travelogues and Fiction by North American Writers. Transatlantic Perspectives 6.* Tübingen: Stauffenburg Verlag, 1995.

Introduction: The Linked Histories of the Globalized World   The Fascist Longings in our Midst   Queer with Class: Absence of Third World Sweatshop in Lesbian/Gay Discourse and a Rearticulation of Materialist Queer Theory   Cross-Mirrorings of Alterity: The Colonial Scenario and Its Psychological Legacy

Postcolonial DefferendDifferend: Diasporic Narratives of Salman Rushdie   At the Margins of Postcolonial Studies   Keeping History at Wind River and Acoma   Modernity's First Born: Latin America and Postcolonial Transformation   Towards Articulation: Postcolonial Theory and Demotic Resistance   Postcolonial Theory and the "Decolonization" of Chinese Culture

Mythologies of Migrancy:

Postcolonialism, Postmodernism,
and the Politics of (Dis)location

REVATHI KRISHNASWAMY

A new type of "Third World"[1] intellectual, cross-pollinated by postmodernism and postcolonialism, has arrived: a migrant who, having dispensed with
territorial affiliations, travels unencumbered through the cultures of the
world bearing only the burden of a unique yet representative sensibility that
refracts the fragmented and contingent condition of both postmodernity
and postcoloniality. Journeying from the "peripheries" to the metropolitan
"centre," this itinerant intellectual becomes an international figure who at
once feels at home nowhere and everywhere. No longer disempowered by
cultural schizophrenia or confined within collectivities such as race, class,
or nation, the nomadic postcolonial intellectual is said to "write back" to the
empire in the name of all displaced and dispossessed peoples, denouncing
both colonialism and nationalism as equally coercive constructs.

91

The ideological lineage of this itinerant postcolonial intellectual is typically hybrid because postcoloniality, as Kwame Anthony Appiah observes, "is the condition of what we might ungenerously call a comprador intelligentsia: a relatively small, Western-style, Western-trained group of writers and thinkers, who mediate the trade in cultural commodities of world capitalism at the periphery" (348). These cultural mediators are invariably dependent on and inevitably influenced by Euro-American publishers and readers, Western universities, and Westernized elite educational institutions in Asia or Africa. Not surprisingly, then, the first generation of postcolonial novels largely reflected the belief held by both "Third World" intellectuals and the high culture of Europe – that new literatures in new nations should be anti-colonial and nationalistic. For instance, Indian subcontinental as well as African novels of the 1950s and 1960s frequently are represented as the imaginative re-creations of a common historical/cultural past crafted into a shared tradition by the writer in the manner of Walter Scott: "they are thus realist legitimations of nationalism: they authorize a 'return to traditions' while at the same time recognizing the demands of a Weberian rationalized modernity" (Appiah 349).

Since the late 1960s, however, such celebratory novels have gradually faded away.[2] Their place has been taken by novels that aimed to expose corrupt national bourgeoisies that had championed the cause of rationalization, industrialization, and bureaucratization in the name of nationalism and nativism, only to keep the national bourgeoisies of other nations in check. In addition to stridently opposing nationalism and nativism, the novels of the 1970s and 1980s strongly repudiated the realist novel because it naturalized a failed nationalism. Appiah observes:

> Far from being a celebration of the nation, the novels of the second postcolonial stage are novels of delegitimation: they reject not only the Western imperium but also the nationalist project of the national bourgeoisie. The basis for that delegitimation does not derive from a postmodernist relativism; rather it is grounded in an appeal to an ethical universal, a fundamental revolt against oppression and human suffering. (353)

It is precisely as spokespersons for the dislocated and the disenfranchised that postcolonial immigrant intellectuals have gained legitimacy in the international media-market.

Thus, from his distinct (dis)location within the metropolis, Salman Rushdie declares that "to be a migrant is, perhaps, to be the only species of human being free of the shackles of nationalism (to say nothing of its ugly sister, patriotism). It is a burdensome freedom" ("Location" 124). A whole mythology of migrancy and a concomitant oppositional politics, of course, has been formulated by Rushdie, who sees the development of the "migrant sensibility" to be "one of the central themes of this century of displaced persons" (124). Not only does Rushdie endow the migrant sensibility with the freedom and facility to construct its own (contingent) truths, but he also makes it a singular repository of experience and resistance. Like the Afghan refugee in Bharati Mukherjee's story "Orbiting" (in her collection *The Middleman and Other Stories*) who is forced to circle the world, camping only in airport transit lounges, Rushdie's migrant is a fractured yet autonomous individual, segregated from the collective sites of history.

By focussing attention on Rushdie, I do not mean to imply that he is somehow unproblematically paradigmatic of the postcolonial (exilic) writer. However, it cannot be denied that he stands foremost among those "spokespersons for a kind of permanent immigration" (Brennan 33) who have been elevated by global media-markets and metropolitan academies as the pre-eminent interpreters of postcolonial realities to postmodern audiences. With the cultural productions of "cosmopolitan celebrities" (Brennan 26) such as Rushdie increasingly forming the critical archival material of alternative canons in the metropolitan academy, the language of migrancy has gained wide currency among today's theorists of identity and authority. Thus, for instance, Edward Said's essay "Third World Intellectuals and Metropolitan Culture" foregrounds the "exile figure" as the most authentic embodiment of the postcolonial intellectual. In a more recent essay entitled "Identity, Authority and Freedom: The Potentate and the Traveler," Said has suggested that "our model for academic freedom" should be "the migrant or traveller" (17). James Clifford's travelling theory goes a step further, metaphorizing postcoloniality into a restructured relationship between anthropologist and informant and casting the theorist in the role of "traveller."

The critical centrality migrancy has acquired in contemporary cultural discourse raises important questions about the nature of postcolonial "diaspora," the role of "Third World" immigrants, and the function of metropolitan academic institutions. How has the uprooting of postcolonial populations helped to generate a vocabulary of migrancy? What part has the "cosmopolitan," "Third World" intellectual played in the manufacture of "diasporic consciousness"? How have metropolitan discourses framed contemporary conceptions of hybridity and migrancy? Has the mythology of migrancy provided a productive site for postcolonial resistance or has it willy-nilly become complicit with hegemonic postmodern theorizations of power and identity? To answer these questions, we must consider the nexus of historical, political, economic, cultural, and ideological forces affecting the construction and consumption of postcolonial realities and representations.

93

The figure of migrancy indeed has proved quite useful in drawing attention to the marginalized, in problematizing conceptions of borders, and in critiquing the politics of power. However, it also appears to have acquired an excessive figurative flexibility that threatens to undermine severely the oppositional force of postcolonial politics. The metaphorization of postcolonial migrancy is becoming so overblown, overdetermined, and amorphous as to repudiate any meaningful specificity of historical location or interpretation. Politically charged words such as "diaspora" and "exile" are being emptied of their histories of pain and suffering and are being deployed promiscuously to designate a wide array of cross-cultural phenomena. For instance, the editor of a recent collection of essays subtitled *The Literature of the Indian Diaspora* argues that the term *diaspora* can be used legitimately to describe not only "those Indian indentured workers who braved long voyages on ill-equipped ships to Mauritius, Trinidad, and Fiji during the nineteenth century" but also "young subcontinental scientists, professors, surgeons, and architects who now emigrate" to the West as part of the brain-drain (Nelson x). Refugees of any brand take the wind out of the sails of even those intellectuals who have been forced to become real political exiles; what then can be said for the inflated claims of upper-class professionals whose emigration fundamentally has been a voluntary and personal choice?

The compulsions behind such claims are not only enormous but actually symptomatic of the discursive space in which many "Third World" intellectuals who choose to live in the "First World" function. The entry of postcolonialism into the metropolitan academy under the hegemonic theoretical rubric of postmodernism obviously has been a powerful factor in determining how the "Third World" is conceived and consumed. All too frequently, the postcolonial text is approached as a localized embellishment of a universal narrative, an object of knowledge that may be known through a postmodern critical discourse. Analytical attention is focussed primarily on the formal similarities between postmodern and postcolonial texts, while the radical historical and political differences between the two are erased (Sangari 264–69). The complex "local" histories and culture-specific knowledges inscribed in postcolonial narratives get neutralized into versions of postmodern diversity, allowing "others" to be seen, but shorn of their dense specificity. Class, gender, and intellectual hierarchies within other cultures, which happen to be at least as elaborate as those in the West, are frequently ignored. Thus Fredric Jameson's paradigm of postcolonial literature as national allegory uniformly constitutes all "Third World" intellectuals, regardless of their gender or class, as marginalized insurgents or as nationalists struggling against a monolithic Western imperialism. Difference is reduced to equivalence, interchangeability, syncretism, and diversity, as a levelling subversive subalternity indiscriminately gets attributed to any and all.

Given that metropolitan attitudes toward the postcolonial are caught between Orientalism and nativism, between unmitigated condemnation and uncritical celebration of Otherness, identification with subalternity and commodification of the "Third World" often seem the only assured means to authority for many "Third World" intellectuals. The very modes of access to power are thus rife with the risk of reification and subordination under such currently popular theoretical categories as cultural diversity, hybridity, syncretism, and migrancy. However, if postcolonial politics is to retain its radical cutting edge, what "Third World" intellectuals must confront is not our "subalternity" or even our "subalternity-in-solidarity-with-the-oppressed," but the comparative power and privilege that ironically accumulate from our "oppositional" stance, and the upward mobility we gain from our semantics of subalternity. As Arif Dirlik points out, to challenge successfully culturalist hegemony, it is not enough to concentrate exclusively on the unequal relations between nations, such as those between the "First" and the "Third" worlds, but to include an investigation of the unequal relations *within* societies as well (37). We therefore must face up to the fact that any mythology of migrancy that fails to differentiate rigorously between diverse modalities of postcolonial diaspora, such as migrant intellect, migrant labour, economic refugees, political exiles, and self-exiles, exploits the subordinate position of the "Third World," suppresses the class/gender-differentiated histories of immigration, robs the oppressed of the vocabulary of protest, and blunts the edges of much-needed oppositional discourse.

A myopic focus on migrancy also may potentially shut out alternative figurations of postcoloniality by marginalizing the visions of those who may not be (dis)located within the metropolis or who may be dislocated in ways not recognized in metropolitan circles. Thus to argue that "the ability to see at once from inside and out is a great thing, a piece of good fortune which the indigenous writer cannot enjoy" (Rushdie, "Dangerous Art Form" 4) or to declare that "the contest over decolonization has moved from the peripheries to the center" (Said, "Third World Intellectuals" 30) seems to militate against postcolonial struggles for greater inclusiveness by reinscribing the binary opposition between centre and periphery in the very discourse that seeks to contest such a dichotomy.

The problematic discourse of diaspora and exile in contemporary critical discourse clearly calls for a systematic examination of the material conditions and ideological contexts within which migrancy has emerged as the privileged paradigmatic trope of postcolonialism in the metropolis.

95

Attempting such an examination, this essay considers such factors as the circulation of "Third World" populations, the peripheral position of the "Third World," the pedagogic presence of the metropolitan academy, and the influence of its poststructuralist/postmodern theories. The first section traces the historical patterns of immigration from the Indian subcontinent in order to bring out the heterogeneous and uneven nature of that diaspora – a fact that, as I try to show, is strategically marginalized or neutralized by Salman Rushdie. Based on a critical review of Rushdie's formulation of migrancy, the second section explores the ideological intersection between postcolonialism and postmodernism. My discussion reveals that the rhetoric of migrancy in postcolonial discourse is not only accessible and acceptable but also assimilable to dominant postmodernist theories. The irony of this exchange becomes evident in the simultaneous elevation and subordination of the immigrant intellectual in the metropolis. Throughout the discussion, I draw very selectively from Rushdie's writings, for I intend my comments less as exhaustive interpretations of this individual author's works and more as symptomatic pointers toward a larger ideological field. The essay concludes by arguing that the overblown rhetoric of diaspora and exile in vogue today calls for a vigilance over the excesses marginal discourses accrue in the very process of theorizing the obsolescence of marginality. In addressing the issue of migrancy from a location within the circuits of metropolitan power and knowledge, I take up Gayatri Spivak's contention that "even as we join in the struggle to establish the institutional study of marginality we must still go on saying 'And yet...'" (154).

The rhetoric of migrancy, exile, and diaspora in contemporary post-colonial discourse owes much of its credibility to the massive and uneven uprooting of "Third World" peoples in recent decades, particularly after large-scale decolonization in the 1960s. As the euphoria of independence and the great expectations of nationalism gave way to disillusionment and oppression, emigration increasingly became the supreme reward for citizens of impoverished or repressive ex-colonies. Millions of people dream of becoming exiles at any cost, and many government officials make a living helping or hindering the fulfillment of this mass fantasy.

The rhetoric of migrancy in contemporary postcolonial discourse, however, does not stress the economic and political forces behind immigration. Salman Rushdie thus observes:

> [T]he effect of mass migrations has been the creation of radically new types of human being: people who root themselves in ideas rather than places, in memories as much as in material things; people who have been obliged to define themselves – because they are so defined by others

– by their otherness; people in whose deepest selves strange fusions occur, unprecedented unions between what they were and where they find themselves. ("Location" 124)

This passage employs an almost spiritual or mystic vocabulary to describe the formation of the "migrant sensibility." By emphasizing mental or psychological processes over sociological or political forces, Rushdie dematerializes the migrant into an abstract idea. The insistent and pervasive use of such psychological terminology tends to obscure or at least minimize the material and historical contexts of "Third World" immigration. It fails to account for two fundamental factors that fracture immigrant experience: the exigencies of neo-colonial global capitalism determining the dispersal of "Third World" peoples, and the distinctly class- and gender-differentiated nature of immigrant experience.

The historic pattern of Indian emigration since the 1960s alone is quite revealing. Until the last decade, women formed but a small percentage of immigrant populations and often subsisted in conditions of complete dependency, if not abuse and exploitation.[3] In addition, there is a distinct class character to the current pattern of Indian emigration. The vast majority of Indians emigrating to the United States and, secondarily, to Britain are members of the commercial or professional bourgeoisie and typically have little to do with the working class inside or outside India. By contrast, the oil-rich countries of the Persian Gulf, and to a lesser degree Britain, attract a predominantly working-class population (the trade to the Gulf being as much a traffic in female flesh as in cheap labour). Lured by unscrupulous job-recruitment agencies and victimized by greedy travel agents, these working-class immigrants frequently end up as little more than indentured labourers subsisting on the margins of alien(ating) societies. Their dehumanized condition casts an inescapable shadow upon the exuberance that characterizes metropolitan perceptions of migrancy. Clearly, the grim realities of migrant labour inflect the notion of migrancy in ways that make it difficult to link consistently freedom and liberation with movement and displacement.

By contrast, what takes place for many postcolonial intellectuals is a transition to an industrially advanced capitalist society with the latest word on individual liberty on its lips. Taking this route is in many ways like going home because it brings one closer to a world that one had imagined all along. As Rushdie observes, "In common with many Bombay-raised middle-class children of my generation, I grew up with an intimate knowledge of, and even sense of friendship with, a certain kind of England: a dream-England. [...] I wanted to come to England. I couldn't wait" ("Imaginary Homelands" 18). Edward Said, therefore, is quite correct in describing the migration of the superior scholar from the non-Western "periphery" to the Western "centre" as a "voyage in" ("Third World Intellectuals" 31).

Once they find themselves within the belly of the metropolitan beast, immigrant intellectuals do indeed face the grim facts of racism and Eurocentrism. For most, however, what Bharati Mukherjee calls "loss-of-face meltdown" ("Prophet and Loss" 11) rarely involves floundering around among disempowered minorities. In fact, Mukherjee's fiction typically casts immigrant aspirations in terms of class expectations: "Great privilege had been conferred upon me; my struggle was to work hard enough to deserve it. And I did. This bred confidence, but not conceit. [...] Calcutta equipped me to survive theft or even assault; it did not equip me to accept proof of my unworthiness" ("Invisible Woman" 36, 38). Indeed, class origins and professional affiliations open up an adversarial kind of assimilation into metropolitan institutions. Thus Rushdie is able to actually use his class privilege as a platform to chastise English society for failing to live up to its promise of "tolerance and fair play":

> England has done all right by me; but I find it difficult to be properly grateful. I can't escape the view that my relatively easy ride is not the result of the dream-England's famous sense of tolerance and fair play, but of my social class, my freak fair skin and my "English" English accent. Take away any of these, and the story would have been very different. Because of course the dream-England is no more than a dream. ("Imaginary Homelands" 18)

In this passage, an acknowledgment of class privilege is countered neatly by an indictment of England's racist/classist attitudes. The author's refusal to be "properly grateful" for the advantages he has derived from his class position rhetorically aligns him with the less privileged members of the immigrant population and thereby helps to legitimize him as an authentic spokesman for whole groups of dispossessed migrants.

Self-conscious contextualizations of class privilege through parody or irony are not difficult to find in the writings of such astute writers as Mukherjee and Rushdie. However, these rhetorical gestures rarely add up to anything more than momentary indulgences in self-pleasuring destabilization. Ultimately, they offer little radical challenge to metropolitan methods of thematizing diversity in ways that make "difference" a mere matter of adding new labels or categories to an ever-expanding pluralist horizon. As such, they can neither form a firm basis for historical awareness nor constitute an adequate confrontation of the heterogeneity of postcolonial/immigrant experience.

Rushdie's self-fashioned public persona, of course, is intertwined inextricably with his own ambiguous status as a migrant postcolonial intellectual writing for a predominantly metropolitan readership. It therefore may be necessary to remind ourselves that, like Rushdie, most immigrant intellectuals, especially those from the Indian subcontinent, are not forced exiles but voluntary self-exiles. (Rushdie's status, of course, has been transformed into a grimly real exile by the Ayatollah Khomeini's ominous *fatwa*.) Unlike the prolonged pain of exile, the anguish of self-exile is usually more accommodating. Often no more than a longing for the imaginary homeland's sensuous characteristics, it is easy to summon up, especially if emigration has turned out to be a financial and professional success. Words such as "exile" or "diaspora" barely describe the moment of departure; what follows is both too comfortable and too autonomous to be called by these names, which suggest so strongly a comprehensible and sustained grief.

It is not my intention to question the motives of any "Third World" immigrant – motives that are always heterogeneous and personal, ranging from political persecution and economic desperation to professional ambition and cultural preference. Nor do I mean to imply that class privilege alone necessarily delegitimizes one's testimony against the injustices of bourgeois racism, colonialism, or nationalism. What I wish to do, however, is to draw attention to the complex historical and material context within which a highly charged mythology of migrancy is being fabricated to legitimize a particular public (literary) persona. Clearly, if "diasporic consciousness" is fundamentally "an intellectualization of [the] existential condition" of dispersal from the homeland (Safran 87), then we must acknowledge the fact that this consciousness has been shaped not so much by the haphazard accidents of history as by the material and ideological realities of immigrant intellectuals.

The image of the postcolonial writer as migrant is, of course, central to Salman Rushdie's politico-aesthetics, which regard the experience of multiple dislocation – temporal, spatial, and linguistic – to be crucial, even necessary, for artistic development:

> It may be argued that the past is a country from which we have all emigrated, that its loss is part of our common humanity. Which seems to me self-evidently true; but I suggest that the writer who is out-of-country and even out-of-language may experience this loss in an intensified form. It is made more concrete for him by the physical fact of discontinuity, of his present being in a different place from his past, of his being "elsewhere." This may enable him to speak properly and concretely on a subject of universal significance and appeal. ("Imaginary Homelands" 12)

The passage, which begins by presenting immigration as a metaphor for a common human experience, quickly proceeds to privilege the geographically/

culturally displaced writer as someone uniquely equipped to at once reclaim the faded contours of a specific lost homeland and to speak of things that have "universal" significance. In contemporary corporate parlance, we might say the migrant writer combines "local touch with global reach."

The experience of dislocation apparently gives the writer an enhanced ability to self-consciously reflect on the constructedness of reality: "The migrant suspects reality: having experienced several ways of being, he understands their illusory nature" (Rushdie, "Location" 125). Yet, if "to see things plainly, you have to cross a frontier" (125), for Rushdie, the frontier seems to be a movable line going wherever the writer goes:

> I mean there're all kinds of dislocations. [...] First of all as you say, I live in England and I've written about India. That's one dislocation. Secondly, my family went to Pakistan so that's three countries anyway. [...] Then Bombay is not like the rest of India. People who come from Bombay anyway feel different from the rest of India and quite rightly. On top of that, my family comes from Kashmir and Kashmir is not like the rest of India. So that's four or five separate dislocations. ("Interview" 353)

Moving geographic borders around with dexterity, Rushdie makes his dislocation from the Indian subcontinent appear to be a mere extension of his many dislocations within the subcontinent itself. What he erases with one hand, he redraws with the other, for the notion of border, after all, is critical to Rushdie's literary persona/project.

Indeed, it is precisely along the border that Rushdie, in an explicit gesture of exclusion, opposes the migrant to the non-migrant, privileging the former over the latter: "the ability to see at once from inside and out is a great thing, a piece of good fortune which the indigenous writer cannot enjoy" ("Dangerous Art Form" 4). Surely, however, such a binary distinction between "migrant" and "indigenous" is quite obsolete unless we allow for an excessively literal recuperation of the opposition between "inside" and "outside." If, on the other hand, we read the frontier as a metaphor for the margin, as Rushdie does when he wants to present migrancy as a shared existential condition, we could include "internal exiles" such as women living within patriarchy, minorities living on the margins of hegemonic cultures, or oppressed majorities living under occupation, thereby undermining the migrant's claim to an exclusive uniqueness. This discursive "contradiction" may be seen as a result of a strategic process of exclusion-inclusion through which Rushdie represents the migrant writer as atypical as well as representative, unique yet universal.

The proliferating and shifting definition of borders in Rushdie's writing is linked intimately to the ideological issue of control:

> It may be that writers in my position, exiles or emigrants or expatriates,
> are haunted by some sense of loss, some urge to reclaim, to look back,
> even at the risk of being mutated into pillars of salt. But if we do look
> back, we must also do so in the knowledge – which gives rise to profound
> uncertainties – that our physical alienation from India almost inevitably
> means that we will not be capable of reclaiming precisely the thing that
> was lost; that we will, in short, create fictions, not actual cities or villages,
> but invisible ones, imaginary homelands, Indias of the mind. ("Imaginary
> Homelands" 10)

Inscribed in this passage is a notion of margins waiting to be destroyed, replaced, expanded, and incorporated as new territorial acquisitions, as novel "fields" of inquiry. The migrant writer's project is defined as one of drawing new or imaginary borders, of re-creating and reclaiming new or imaginary territories. Although fractured, the migrant imagination is an imperializing consciousness imposing itself upon the world. As the narrator of Rushdie's *Shame* declares, "I too, like all migrants, am a fantasist. I build imaginary countries and try to impose them on the ones that exist" (92).

From this brief overview of Rushdie's formulation of migrancy, two variations on the theme may be detected: one invokes an existential condition of homelessness with a concomitant attitude of autonomy and detachment as the privileged locus of imaginative experience; the other validates multiplicity and hybridity of subject positions, generating a feeling of belonging to several, even too many, homes. These conceptions of migrancy, Aijaz Ahmad has pointed out, have much in common with the philosophical positions of poststructuralism/postmodernism and the literary traditions of modernism. The overlap is hardly surprising, since the discourses of European bourgeois humanism and anti-humanism are available to (and perhaps even constitutive of) the postcolonial writer. The image of the intellectual as an embattled figure of exile is not new; all the major icons of modernism – Conrad, Joyce, James, Pound, T.S. Eliot – embody and represent exile as a painful yet exquisitely enabling experience for the artistic consciousness (Ahmad 134). What is novel and decidedly postmodern, however, is the delinking of distress from dislocation and the attendant idea of belonging everywhere by belonging nowhere:

> What is new in the contemporary metropolitan philosophies and
> the literary ideologies which have arisen since the 1960s, in tandem
> with vastly novel restructurings of global capitalist investments,
> communication systems and information networks – not to speak of
> actual travelling facilities – is that the idea of belonging is itself

> being abandoned as antiquated false consciousness. The terrors of
> High Modernism at the prospect of inner fragmentation and social
> disconnection have now been stripped, in Derridean strands of
> postmodernism, of their tragic edge, pushing that experience of loss,
> instead, in a celebratory direction [...] (Ahmad 129)

In modernism, exile is an inexorable double-bind, signifying both loss and gain, deprivation and surplus, alienation and unity. Fragmentation is never quite disjoined from pain and terror. Postmodernism, rather than being terrorized by the fragment, celebrates the impossibility of totality and valorizes the partial, plural nature of human consciousness. Delegitimizing the self-privileging affirmations of bourgeois humanism through its ironic negations, postmodernism has transformed the world into a vast playful text and legitimized the pleasures of non-attachment and non-commitment.

The change from a comparatively modernist to a more postmodernist interpretation of exile may account, in part, for some of the differences between writers such as Salman Rushdie and V.S. Naipaul – a point implied in Bharati Mukherjee's assessment of the two authors: "one of Rushdie's most appealing notions (which I hope is not an unfounded flattery) is that immigration, despite losses and confusions, its sheer absurdities, is a net gain, a form of levitation, as opposed to Naipaul's loss and mimicry" ("Prophet and Loss" 11). Although it is the creative impulse of exile that generates novels such as *The Mimic Men* and *Mr. Stone and the Knights Companion*, exile, especially in Naipaul's early works, is often an experience of division and defilement, alienation and isolation, frustration and futility. Instead of discovering new and exciting worlds in the mode of the imperial explorer, Naipaul's postcolonial traveller frequently ends up in the same arid place from which he has been physically but not quite psychologically unmoored. In the end, Naipaul's apparently "objective" eye tends to leave the observer as maimed as the observed. A markedly different view is evident in *The Satanic Verses*, which offers a whole typology of postcolonial migrancy. Rushdie's narrative divides the postcolonial into two basic identities: the migrant and the national, as polarized most sharply in Saladin Chamcha and the Imam, respectively. While Saladin as postcolonial migrant seeks to assimilate into the metropolis, the Imam lives segregated from the metropolis within the metropolis. Although Saladin's definition of migrant as metropolitan is not endorsed unequivocally by the text, the novel's condemnation of the Imam's view of migrant as (fanatic) national is far more stinging and forthright: "Exile is a soulless country" (*Satanic Verses* 208).

If Naipaul's position may be characterized as one of eternal exile, Rushdie's may be defined as one of permanent migrancy. Unlike the painful condition of eternal exile, the state of permanent migrancy emanates an exuberance that dissipates the pain of multiple dislocation and translates migrancy into a positive and prolific idiom. Instead of disempowering the self, dislocation actually opens up an abundance of alternative locations, allowing the individual to own several different homes by first becoming homeless. Notwithstanding these differences, however, one feature is shared by both paradigms: a deterritorialized consciousness freed from such collectivities as race, class, gender, or nation, an unattached imagination that can conveniently become cosmopolitan and subaltern, alternately or simultaneously.

In emphasizing a deterritorialized postcolonial consciousness, the views of Indian immigrant writers such as Naipaul and Rushdie depart from the positions taken by many African writers who, in the wake of colonialism, have sought to reterritorialize rather than deterritorialize themselves. Comparing African with Indian postcolonial writing, Meenakshi Mukherjee observes:

> All the major writers in Africa today who write in English – including Chinua Achebe, Wole Soyinka, and Ngugi wa Thiong'o – have powerfully articulated their critical norms and defined their positions regarding life and literature, assuming the centrality of Africa to their experience. This is very different from the situation in India, where there is generally much more cultural acquiescence, a greater acceptance of literary and critical fiats issued from the Western metropolis and a wider separation between political engagement and literary or critical pursuits. (45)

The obdurate presence of the "local" seems to have made the territorialized narratives of African writers comparatively less compatible with hegemonic postmodern theories. Thus, for instance, the authors of *The Empire Writes Back* conclude that "nationalist and Black criticisms" fail to offer "a way out of the historical and philosophical impasse" of imperialism because they continue to assert a localized postcolonial identity based on essentialist notions of purity and difference (Ashcroft, Griffiths, and Tiffin 20–22, 36). Obviously, the practice of challenging imperialism by asserting and affirming a denied or alienated subjectivity does not accord with the postmodernist project of deconstructing the coherent, autonomous subject.

Notwithstanding the authors' avowed intention to avoid collapsing the postcolonial into the postmodern, the preferred model of postcolonialism in *The Empire Writes Back* is a decidedly postmodernist one: it provides "a framework of '*difference on equal terms*' within which multi-cultural theories, both within and between societies, may continue to be fruitfully explored" and offers a "hybridized and syncretic view of the modern world" (36–37; emphasis added).[4] Bracketed thus, the polyglot, multiracial world envisioned by a writer such as Salman Rushdie becomes increasingly visible as a veritable supermarket of identities in which difference, instead of being a complex codification of power, manifests itself as a plethora of alternatives jostling one another in entrancing fluidity. Such a postcoloniality indeed can seem seamlessly postmodernist.

The possibility of locking postcolonial practices into postmodern positions has made postcolonialism aesthetically and formally accessible to postmodern audiences. For instance, the fact that the postcolonial novel is in a way "post-realist," allowing the author to borrow, when needed, the techniques of modernism, which are often the techniques of postmodernism as well, frequently elides the very different motivations behind postcolonial post-realism and postmodernist post-realism (Appiah 350). In addition to such aesthetic or formal assimilation, postcolonial practices are ideologically and politically domesticated to dominant postmodernist theories. Postcolonial repudiations of fixity and purity, for instance, cease to be potent political strategies of subversion within specific historical contexts by being bracketed as playful postmodernist rejections of transcendental unities. Thus, many postmodernist defences of *The Satanic Verses* minimize, if not ignore, the destabilizing political arguments and culture-specific allusions in the text (such as the "420" reference) by invoking notions of postmodern parody, alterity, and multiplicity.[5]

Varying conceptions of marginality, lack, victimization, and subalternity are assimilated indiscriminately into the figure of migrancy without regard to the elaborate socio-political (class, gender, intellectual) hierarchies of postcolonial cultures. As a result, metropolitan readers continue to view Salman Rushdie primarily in monochromatic tones as a champion of the oppressed "Third World" (especially of "Third World" women), while the classist and sexist biases of his fictions remain inadequately problematized.[6] Thus Timothy Brennan accepts the overtly textualized "feminist" intent of *Shame* at face value, proclaiming women to be "*Shame's* only rebels" (Brennan 126). What Brennan's study overlooks, however, is the demeaning and offensive manner in which women are sexualized systematically in the text. Even in the comparatively more generous novel about India, *Midnight's Children*, Rushdie almost always links in overdetermined ways the women and the working class to sexual prowess, while connecting upper-class male impotence (as embodied in Saleem) to intellectual capability. Further, in *The Satanic Verses*, in which so much else is challenged or subverted, an unquestioned gendered sexual code continues to serve as the ground on which postcolonial male desire is played out. Ironically, the highly charged erotic register employed by Rushdie ultimately undermines his anxiety to write woman into postcolonial history.

Metropolitan perceptions of Rushdie are complicated further by the commodification of the immigrant writer as the ultimate authentic representor of subcontinental affairs. Of course, Rushdie himself has played an active role in promoting his public image as the itinerant insider-outsider endowed with a unique, although splintered, sensibility. Thus the narrator of *Shame* confesses he has "learned Pakistan in slices" and must therefore reconcile himself to "the inevitability of the missing bits" (70–71). What exactly are these "missing bits" to which the immigrant must reconcile himself? On what basis does a writer decide to include/exclude a particular "bit"? These questions do not trouble us when we frame Rushdie's reclamation project within the postmodernist epistemology of the fragment. We can then see the migrant's fractured vision as an affirmation of the partial nature of all perception, conveniently overlooking the ideological choices that determine what "bits" get included or excluded. Calling attention to dangers underlying such critical omissions, Aijaz Ahmad has pointed out that the "missing bits" in Rushdie's narratives are precisely those aspects of life that the immigrant's absence inevitably shuts out: the resilient texture of everyday life, the healing quality of ordinary friendships, and those commonly shared experiences that provide people with secret spaces of refuge or even subterraneous sites of resistance (139).

Rushdie's novels are most astute and insightful when the author uncovers the delusions and distortions of the paternal ruling class with which he is closely acquainted. Combined with the candid observations of an immigrant, his intimate knowledge of bourgeois society enables Rushdie to write alternative histories that offer many moving accounts of the frustrations and failures on the Indian subcontinent. Yet this field of vision inevitably is circumscribed by the material facts and ideological lures of migrancy. As a result, Rushdie's "imaginary homelands" are almost always wrapped in a miasmic atmosphere of guilt, complicity and folly in which individual resistance seems futile and collective resistance practically inconceivable. Belying the exorbitance of their fictional forms, India and Pakistan thus collapse with a frighteningly predictable finality at the end of *Midnight's Children* and *Shame*.

Immigrant writers gazing back at their "imaginary homelands" often seem unable to recognize or accept the healing balm from within that gradually fills up the wound left by their departure. I am reminded here of another immigrant, who wrote in another context – of Milan Kundera, who, upon deciding not to return to Prague, wrote an article in which he attempted to attract the attention of the West to the predicament of Czech culture in general and that of the Czech intellectual in particular. The article described Czechoslovakia as a cultural desert where everything had died and everyone was stifled. Kundera had only recently emigrated and was full of good intentions in writing such an article, but the response he got from Czecho-slovakia horrified him. He was taken to task for presuming to think that everybody had died just because he had left the country!

Immigrant postcolonial writers have indeed offered us some profound insights into culture and society, but unless we alert ourselves to the specific realities within which their works are manufactured and marketed, we are likely to grant their formulations much more than they can, or should, rightfully claim. The embarrassingly absolute, even exclusive, centrality currently commanded by "cosmopolitan celebrities" such as Rushdie in the emerging metropolitan counter-canon of postcolonial literature often obscures the material conditions and ideological contexts of their cultural production/consumption. Consequently, the public persona of the postcolonial writer as an autonomous and exuberant exile uniquely equipped to mediate "Third World" realities to "First World" readers has remained inadequately problematized.

Resisting the lures of diaspora, we must recognize that the mythology of migrancy decontextualizes "Third World" immigration in order to minimize or obscure differences of class and gender. The mythology also exploits the peripheral position of the "Third World" to conflate falsely personal convenience with political persecution. Moreover, by decontaminating the migrant of all territorial affiliations and social affinities, the mythology of migrancy ironically reinvents, in the very process of destabilizing subjectivity, a postmodernist avatar of the free-floating bourgeois subject. Once this autonomous and unattached individual, this migrant, exiled, or nomadic consciousness, is legitimized as the only true site of postcolonial resistance, all other forms of collective commitment automatically get devalued as coercive and corrupt.

Clearly, not all "Third World" literature is produced by immigrants, and as Kwame Anthony Appiah has pointed out, neither is all cultural production in the "Third World" postcolonial in ways recognized by the postmodern West (348). If both postmodernism and postcolonialism are, to an extent, space-clearing gestures that seek to reject and replace prior practices that claimed a certain exclusivity of vision (for example, modernism and colonialism, respectively), many areas of contemporary cultural productions in/from the "Third World" are not in this way self-consciously concerned with transcending or going beyond coloniality: "Indeed it might be said to be a mark of popular culture that its borrowings from international cultural forms are remarkably insensitive to, not so much dismissive of as blind to, the issue of neo-colonialism or 'cultural imperialism'" (Appiah 348). Yet in the international marketplace, such cultural commodities do not attract the kind of attention and respect currently reserved for the more "proper" postcolonial productions.

The uncritical privileging of immigrant writers prevents us from seriously considering figurations of postcoloniality that may be grounded in alternative strategies for change. If postcolonial politics is to retain its radical cutting edge in dismantling the dichotomy between margin and centre, we cannot afford to indulge in self-legitimizing mythologies and self-aggrandizing manoeuvres that dilute efforts toward decolonization.

Notes

1 The term/category "Third World" obviously has little theoretical validity. I therefore use quotation marks to indicate its political rather than sociological signification.

2 Neil Lazarus's *Resistance in Postcolonial Fiction* (especially 1–26) offers a useful periodization of African fiction in relation to the "great expectation" of the independence era and the "mourning after."

3 For instance, before the law finally was repealed in 1992, female Indian nationals did not have the right to pass on citizenship to children born overseas.

4 For an extensive critique of *The Empire Writes Back*, see Mishra and Hodge.

5 For examples of such readings, see McLaren; Watson-Williams; and Malak.

6 These attitudes continue to prevail despite the efforts of such immigrant scholars as Spivak, Suleri, Grewal, and Ahmad to focus on issues of class and gender in Rushdie's writing.

Works Cited

Ahmad, Aijaz. "Salman Rushdie's Shame: Postmodern Migrancy and the Representation of Women." *Theory: Classes, Nations, Literatures*. London: Verso, 1992. 123–58.

Appiah, Kwame Anthony. "Is the Post- in Postmodernism the Post- in Postcolonial?" *Critical Inquiry* 17 (Winter 1991): 336–57.

Ashcroft, Bill, Gareth Griffiths, and Helen Tiffin. *The Empire Writes Back: Theory and Practice in Post-Colonial Literatures*. London: Routledge, 1989.

Brennan, Timothy. *Salman Rushdie and the Third World*. New York: St. Martin's, 1989.

Clifford, James. "Travel and Identity in Twentieth-Century Interculture." The Henry Luce Seminar, Yale University, Fall 1990.

Dirlik, Arif. "Culturalism as Hegemonic Ideology and Liberating Practice." *Cultural Critique* 6 (Spring 1987): 13–50.

Grewal, Inderpal. "Salman Rushdie: Marginality, Women and Shame." *Genders* 3 (Fall 1988): 24–42.

Kundera, Milan. "The Tragedy of Central Europe." *New York Review of Books* 26 April 1984: 33–38.

Jameson, Fredric. "Third World Literature in the Era of Multinational Capitalism." *Social Text* 15 (Fall 1986): 65–88.

Lazarus Neil. *Resistance in Postcolonial Fiction*. New Haven, CT: Yale University Press, 1990.

Malak, Amin. "Reading the Crisis: The Polemics of Salman Rushdie's *The Satanic Verses*." *ARIEL* 20.4 (1989): 176–86.

McLaren, John. "The Power of the Word: Salman Rushdie and *The Satanic Verses.*" *Westerly* 1 (March 1990): 61–65.

Mishra, Vijay, and Bob Hodge. "What is post(-)colonialism?" *Textual Practice* 5 (1991): 399–414.

Mukherjee, Bharati. "An Invisible Woman." *Saturday Night* March 1981: 36–40.

———. *The Middleman and Other Stories.* New York: Viking Penguin, 1987.

———. "Prophet and Loss: Salman Rushdie's Migration of Souls." *Village Voice Literary Supplement* 72 (March 1989): 9–12.

Mukherjee, Meenakshi. "The Centre Cannot Hold: Two Views of the Periphery." *After Europe: Critical Theory and Post-Colonial Writing.* Ed. Stephen Slemon and Helen Tiffin. Sydney: Dangaroo, 1989. 41–49.

Nelson, Emmanuel S., ed. *Reworlding: The Literature of the Indian Diaspora.* New York: Greenwood Press, 1992.

Rushdie, Salman. "A Dangerous Art Form." *Third World Book Review* 1 (1984): 3–5.

———. "Imaginary Homelands." *Imaginary Homelands: Essays and Criticism. 1981–1991.* London: Granta & Viking, 1991. 9–21.

———. "An Interview with Salman Rushdie." By Rani Dharkar. *New Quest* 42 (Nov.–Dec. 1983): 351–60.

———. "The Location of *Brazil.*" *Imaginary Homelands: Essays and Criticism. 1981–1991.* London: Granta & Viking, 1991. 118–28.

———. *Midnight's Children.* New York: Avon, 1980.

———. *The Satanic Verses.* New York: Viking, 1989.

———. *Shame.* New York: Vintage, 1984.

Safran, William. "Diasporas in Modern Societies: Myths of Homeland and Return." *Diaspora* 1.1 (1991): 83–99.

Said, Edward. "Identity, Authority and Freedom: The Potentate and the Traveler." *Transitions* 54 (1991): 131–50.

———. "Third World Intellectuals and Metropolitan Culture." *Raritan* 9 (Winter 1990): 27–50.

Sangari, Kumkum. "The Politics of the Possible." *Interrogating Modernity: Culture and Colonialism in India.* Ed. Tejaswini Niranjana, P. Sudhir, and Vivek Dhareshwar. Calcutta: Seagull Books, 1993. 242–72.

Spivak, Gayatri. "Theory in the Margin." *Consequences of Theory.* Ed. Jonathan Arac and Barbara Johnson. Baltimore: Johns Hopkins University Press, 1991. 154–80.

Suleri, Sara. "Salman Rushdie: Embodiments of Blasphemy, Censorships of Shame." *The Rhetoric of English India.* Chicago: University of Chicago Press, 1992. 174–206.

Watson-Williams, Helen. "Finding a Father: A Reading of Salman Rushdie's *The Satanic Verses.*" *Westerly* 1 (March 1990): 66–71.

Introduction: The Linked Histories of the Globalized World   The Fascist Longings in our Midst   Queer with Class: Absence of Third World Sweatshop in Lesbian/Gay Discourse and a Rearticulation of Materialist Queer Theory   Cross-Mirrorings of Alterity: The Colonial Scenario and Its Psychological Legacy   Mythologies of Migrancy: Postcolonialism, Postmodernism, and the Politics of (Dis)location

At the Margins of Postcolonial Studies   Keeping History at Wind River and Acoma   Modernity's First Born: Latin America and Postcolonial Transformation   Towards Articulation: Postcolonial Theory and Demotic Resistance   Postcolonial Theory and the "Decolonization" of Chinese Culture

*"Home" has become such a
scattered, damaged, various
concept in our present travails.*

—Salman Rushdie
EAST, WEST (93)

Postcolonial Differend:

Diasporic Narratives
of Salman Rushdie

VIJAY MISHRA

For large groups of people around the world – Cubans and Mexicans in the
U.S.; Indians and Pakistanis in Britain, Canada, and the U.S.; Meghrebis
in France; Turks in Germany; Chinese in Southeast Asia; Greeks, Poles,
Armenians in various parts of the world; Chinese and Vietnamese in Australia,
Canada and the U.S.; Indians in Mauritius, Fiji, the Caribbean (the list can
go on and on) – the idea of "home" has indeed become a damaged concept.[1]
The word *damaged* forces us to face up to the scars and fractures, to the
blisters and sores, to the psychic traumas of bodies on the move. Indeed,
"home" (the *heimlich*) is the new epistemological logic of (post)modernity
as the condition of "living here and belonging elsewhere" begins to affect
people in an unprecedented fashion (Clifford 311). No longer is exile rendered
simply through an essentially aesthetic formulation (note the geographical
breaks, the "damaged" hyphens of Joyce [Dublin-Trieste], Pound [London-

Paris-Rome], or Eliot [New England-London], for instance); on the contrary, it is a travail/travel to which we are becoming inextricably linked as we get progressively dragged into a global village. "Home" now signals a shift away from homogeneous nation-states based on the ideology of assimilation to a much more fluid and contradictory definition of nations as a multiplicity of diasporic identities. The Indian shopkeeper in Vancouver who comes to Canada via Fiji already has held two previous passports; his (for he is a man) third, the Canadian passport, is one that gives him the greatest difficulty in reconciling his body with the idea of Canadian citizenry. He remains a negative yet to be processed, a penumbra in the new nation-state of Canada, his privileges as a Canadian citizen most obvious only when he is travelling overseas. Back at home his condition remains hyphenated because in Canada (as in Australia, Britain, and Europe, but not to the same degree in the U.S.), "home" is only available to those passport holders, those citizens whose bodies signify an unproblematic identity of selves with the nation-state. For Indian shopkeepers who are outside of this identity politics, whose corporealities fissure the logic of unproblematic identity of bodies with citizens, the new dogma of multiculturalism constructs the subject-in-hyphen forever negotiating and fashioning selves at once Indian and Canadian: *Canadian* Indian *and* Canadian *Indian*.

It is becoming increasingly obvious that the narrative of the damaged home thus takes its exemplary form in what may be called diasporas, and especially in diasporas of colour, those migrant communities that do not quite fit into the nation-state's barely concealed preference for the narrative of assimilation. Diasporas of colour, however, are a relatively recent phenomenon in the West and, as I have already suggested, perhaps the most important marker of late modernity. In the larger narrative of postcolonialism (which has been informed implicitly by a theory of diasporic identifications), the story of diasporas is both its cause and its effect. In the politics of transfer and migration, postcolonialism recovers its own justification as an academic site or as a legitimate object of knowledge. To write about damaged homes, to reimage the impact of migration in the age of late capital, requires us to enter into debates about diasporic theory. This is not my primary concern here, but a few words about it will not be out of place.

One of the overriding characteristics of diasporas is that they do not, as a general rule, return. This is not to be confused with the symbols of return or the invocations, largely through the sacred, of the homeland or the home-idea. The trouble with diasporas is that while the reference point is in the past, unreal as it may be, there is, in fact, no future, no sense of a teleological end. Diasporas cannot conceptualize the point toward which the community, the nation within a nation, is heading. The absence of teleologies in the diaspora is also linked to Walter Benjamin's understanding of the ever-present time of historical (messianic) redemption. In this lateral argument, an eventual homecoming is not projected into the future but introjected into the present, thereby both interrupting it and multiplying it. Diasporic history thus contests both the utopic and irreversible causality of history through heterotopic (Foucault) or subversive (Benjamin) readings. In these readings, time is turned back against itself in order that alternative readings, alternative histories, may be released.

In this "diverse scansion of temporality,"[2] in this active re-membering (as opposed to the mere recalling) of traces and fragments, a new space in language and time is opened up, and historical moments are sundered to reveal heterotopic paths not taken. The absence of teleologies, this intense meditation on synchronicity, thus opposes the tyranny of linear time and blasts open the continuum of history to reveal moments, fragments, traces that can be recaptured and transformed into another history. As Salman Rushdie writes:

> It may be that writers in my position, exiles or emigrants or expatriates, are haunted by some sense of loss, some urge to reclaim, to look back, even at the risk of being mutated into pillars of salt. But if we do look back, we must also do so in the knowledge – which gives rise to profound uncertainties – that our physical alienation from India almost inevitably means that we will not be capable of reclaiming precisely the thing that was lost; that we will, in short, create fictions, not actual cities or villages, but invisible ones, imaginary homelands, Indias of the mind. (*Imaginary Homelands* 10)

We cannot trace the growth of diasporas in any systematic form here. All we can do is refer very schematically to one particular diasporic development that has a direct bearing on the texts discussed in this paper. 1963, the year the Beatles exploded on the world scene, may also be chosen as the watershed year in global migration. Demand for labour in western Europe and Britain, and the collapse of the colonial empires of Britain, France, and Holland meant that millions of non-white migrants from the outposts of the Empire, as well as guest workers from Turkey, began to enter the European city on a scale unprecedented since the Moorish invasions. The contemporary European city, for instance, is now a very different demographic fact. It is no longer the centre out of which radiates imperial activity. Instead, European cities are no longer controlled by the logic of centre and periphery which was the traditional metaphor of empire. What we have, in Iain Chambers's words, is a new kind of demographic redistribution "along the spatio-temporal-information axes of a world economy" (*Migrancy, Culture, Identity* 108). He continues, "[T]he national, unilateral colonial model has been interrupted by the emergence of a transversal world that occupies a 'third space' (Bateson, Bhabha), a 'third culture' (Featherstone) beyond the confines of the nation state" (108). It is symptomatic of a greater awareness of the transnational nature of nation-states and the presence within them of degrees of difference that led Khachig Tölölyan, editor of the new journal *Diaspora*, to maintain that struggles from the margins for the centre and for definitions of the "national" subject are equally legitimate concerns for the constructions of identity or selfhood. Nevertheless, Tölölyan's cautious remarks toward the end of his editorial warn us of the difficult space occupied by diasporas and the dangers of displacing the centre (made up of the vast majority of citizens who do not define themselves in diasporic terms) totally by the margins. Tölölyan writes: "To affirm that diasporas are the exemplary communities of the transnational moment is not to write the premature obituary of the nation-state as in original, which remains a privileged form of polity" (5). This proviso is important.

Elsewhere I have spoken about this condition as the indeterminate, the contaminated condition of diaspora. Here I want to do something slightly different, something at once bold and fraught with difficulties. I want to examine the literary production of an author – Salman Rushdie – whose works exemplify the blasting open of agonistic politics in embattled ethnicities within nation-states that can no longer construct their nationalisms through a homogeneous and synchronous imagining of a body collective consensually reading its newspapers or responding to global events as a totality. Indeed, if we are to follow the hidden text of the previous sentence – Benedict Anderson's influential *Imagined Communities* – we begin to detect not so much the logic of capitalism at work here but the religious, millenarian dogma of an earlier age in which the issue was not necessarily that of imagining national identities but of participating, through sacred languages (Latin, Sanskrit, Pali, or Arabic) with communities across "nations." There is, then, a reverse scansion of history at work here, a desire for a lost unity within the ethnicized state that minorities continue to inhabit. In the cultural sphere, this leads to the end of consensual politics, the end of a community of speakers/thinkers that could be relied upon to arbitrate for the national good. In short, what is emerging is "the postcolonial differend." What I would like to offer in the following pages is an instance of this postcolonial differend with reference to the Indian-Pakistani diaspora in Britain.

The diaspora, however, stages a "difference" that can be accommodated only if consensual politics also takes into account the possibility of the diasporic subject itself initiating the consensus. In other words, the majority population has to concede that the diaspora's ground rules (what constitutes belief, what is a work of art, what is literary freedom) may be different from its own. It is here that postcolonial theory, through a careful study of diasporic archive(s), could address what Lyotard has called the differend. This is to anticipate my concluding remarks, however. What I would like to continue here is an examination of key texts of an author whose works have something of an exemplary status as proof-texts of diaspora as an intermediate, increasingly mobile idea. In the works of Salman Rushdie, the Indian-Pakistani diaspora in Britain is seen as a powerful source for the hermeneutics of the liminal, the borders of culture, the unassimilable, the margins, and so on. The critique of the centre through the kinds of hybrid, hyphenated identities occupied by this diaspora has been one of the more exciting and original theorizations of the project of modernity itself. As an ideological critique of, as well as a corrective to, established working-class British social histories, the payoff has been considerable: one remembers how historians of the working class consistently overlooked the diaspora as a significant formation in class histories. There are no people of colour in E. P. Thompson.

The Texts of Salman Rushdie

Few works of fiction have been the subject of debates as intense as those that have surrounded *The Satanic Verses* since its publication in 1988. Books have now been written on the Rushdie Affair, and a film made on the author's death (much-deserved, as portrayed in the film) by the Pakistani film industry, and Tehran continues to re-emphasize Khomeini's *fatwa* during any staged denunciation of the West. The author's life, meanwhile, is one of double exile in the company of his "protectors" in the Welsh countryside of "unafraid lambs," country houses, and farmers from whom he must "hide [his] face," as Rushdie describes it in his poem "Crusoe."[3] However, he still hankers after travel, the diasporic condition, even though this travel, like V.S. Naipaul's "arrival," is toward the Arthurian "once and future Avalon." The cause of Rushdie's second exile, of course, is a book about migrancy, dispossession, cultural hybridity, and the absence of centres in diasporic lives. To give these themes an intertext, a frame, or a narrative template, they are hoisted on another moment in history when "newness" enters the world. The entry of strange people into so many parts of the globe presents the older inhabitants with precisely the threat of the new, the threat of "ideas" no longer commensurable with its pre-existing epistemologies. In this retelling, Indian Islam (always contaminated by autochthonous gods, dervishes, the figure of the ascetic, and other borrowings from Hinduism) is seen as a hybrid, contradictory phenomenon that conjures strange dreams about the founding text and prophet of that religion. Indian Islam thus has a polytheistic splinter in the side of its monotheism in which the intercession of female gods in any act of worship is not excluded outright. Moreover, this kind of syncretism is truer still of Bombay, Rushdie's magical metropolis, *the* postcolonial city, which challenges the erstwhile metropolises of London and Paris. What is true of Indian Islam is also true of Indian narrative forms and culture generally. The Aryans, the Moguls, the British have all been invaders, leaving their traces behind as the nation gradually reabsorbs multiplicity into a totality. Thus the central themes of the book – how "newness" enters the world, how the many co-exist within the one, and why love remains the only organizing principle of our lives – get written in a hybrid discourse that is borrowed from the Bombay film industry, the idioms of Hobson-Jobson,[4] a colonial English curriculum, the *Katha-Sarit-Sagar* (342), the nativist jokes on the *ooparvala-neechayvala* (he who lives upstairs, he who lives downstairs), the narrative of the epic recast as the battle for the Mahavilayat (283), the populist narratives of Phoolan Devi,[5] the female dacoit, the fundamentalist world of the post-Ayodhya Hindus, the references to the Indian Penal Code section 420 (Gibreel sings Raj Kapoor's well-known song from *Shree 420*), as well as the Indian Civic Code section 125, and many more.

The Satanic Verses situates itself in the midst of these heterogeneous discourses. It is from the space of hybridity, of multiplicity, that many of the characters speak. Mimi Mamoulian, for instance, knows very well the meaning of the world as "pastiche: a 'flattened' world" (261), and the author's own, very postmodern intervention makes this clearer still:

> Gibreel [...] has wished to remain, to a large degree, *continuous* – that is, joined to and arising from his past; [...] whereas Saladin Chamcha is a creature of *selected* discontinuities, a *willing* re-invention; his *preferred* revolt against history being what makes him, in our chosen idiom, "false"? [Where Chamcha is therefore perceived as "evil"] Gibreel, to follow the logic of our established terminology, is to be considered "good" by virtue of *wishing to remain,* for all his vicissitudes, at bottom an untranslated man.
>
>   – But, and again but: this sounds, does it not, dangerously like an intentionalist fallacy? – Such distinctions, resting as they must on an idea of the self as being (ideally) homogeneous, non-hybrid, "pure," – an utterly fantastic notion – cannot, must not, suffice. (427)

Rushdie begins by offering the usual binarism between the continuous and the discontinuous, between tradition and modernity, between good and evil, only to undercut it through the intervention of the hybrid. Indeed, what this extended statement about the construction of the self indicates, in the context of the diaspora and margins, is that subjectivity is now formed through modes of translation and encoding because erstwhile distinctions "cannot, must not, suffice." This last phrase, in fact, sums up the agenda of the book as a whole: distinctions made through established cultural epistemologies (including the ubiquitous self-other distinction) will always fail. Yet, even as hybridity is celebrated, one gets the feeling that the disavowed leaves its traces behind because, as we shall see, *The Satanic Verses* itself failed to convince the diaspora that there is no such thing as an "untranslated man": large sections of the diaspora wish to retain this nostalgic definition of the self and cling to "millenarian" narratives of self-empowerment in which only the untranslated can recapture a lost harmony but, paradoxically, the desire to retain a pristine sense of the past is only possible through the technologies of mechanical reproduction such as cassette tapes, films, and so on.[6] Since historical reconstructions through these apparatuses introduce the heterotopic into the utopian or the linear, what we get here is precisely a heterogeneous, contradictory rendition of history by making memory and cultural fragments metonymic representations of the whole. While cassette culture reconstructs the past as a synchronic moment (old Indian films can be viewed endlessly), it also contaminates the diasporic idea of culture as belonging to the homeland alone. As Paul Gilroy has argued so persuasively in *The Black Atlantic: Modernity and Double Consciousness*, the newer technologies of cultural transmission accentuate the fact that cultural commodities travel swiftly, criss-crossing geographical boundaries, creating new and vibrant forms. The Bhojpuri-Hindi songs of the Indian singers Babla and Kanchan, for instance, combine Hindi film music with calypso/hip hop, while in Britain, Asian Bhangra and Indian groups such as Loop Guru (post-Ravi Shanker music crossed with cyber-religion) show obvious influences of reggae and soul music of black Africa.

In this respect, *The Satanic Verses* affirms the impossibility of millenarian diasporic narratives while at the same time stressing that these narratives invariably will be the starting point of any radical retheorizing of the diasporic imaginary, which, for Rushdie, is identical with modernism itself and may be read as a "metaphor for all humanity":

> If *The Satanic Verses* is anything, it is a migrant's-eye view of the world.
> It is written from the very experience of uprooting, disjuncture and
> metamorphosis [...] that is the migrant condition, and from which,
> I believe, can be derived a metaphor for all humanity. (*Imaginary*
> *Homelands* 394)

Rushdie goes on:

> *The Satanic Verses* celebrates hybridity, impurity, intermingling, the
> transformation that comes of new and unexpected combinations of

> human beings, cultures, ideas, politics, movies, songs. It rejoices
> in mongrelization and fears the absolutism of the Pure. *Mélange*,
> hotchpotch, a bit of this and a bit of that is *how newness enters the world*.
> It is the great possibility that mass migration gives the world, and I have
> tried to embrace it. *The Satanic Verses* is for change-by-fusion, change-
> by-conjoining. It is a love-song to our mongrel selves. (394)

The celebration of the hybrid – "the process of hybridization which is the novel's most crucial dynamic means that its ideas derive from many sources other than Islamic ones," writes Rushdie (403) – however, also leads to the endowing of the fiction itself with what Gilroy has called "an absolute and non-negotiable privilege" ("Cultural Studies" 190). The aesthetic order as somehow immune to a counter-attack through a non-aesthetic reading of the text has dominated much of the criticism that has been directed against Rushdie in the wake of Khomeini's *fatwa*. We shall return to the question of aesthetic privilege.

The Diasporic Avant-garde

The story of "migration, its stresses and transformations, from the point of view of migrants from the Indian subcontinent,"[7] nevertheless drops the old realist modes of writing and embraces the European avant-garde. Yet it also keeps its realist nose sharply in focus. This is partly because the book is as much about South Asians in a racialized Britain as it is an avant-gardist break in the history of "English" fiction.[8] Rushdie, in fact, is quite explicit about this dual agenda:

> [*The Satanic Verses*] begins in a pyrotechnic high-surrealist vein and
> moves towards a much more emotional, inner writing. That process of
> putting away the magic noses and cloven hoofs is one the novel itself
> goes through: *it tells itself*, and by the end it doesn't need the apparatus
> any more. (Interview with Blake Morrison 120)

It is, however, the use of non-European narrative forms, summed up in the Arabic narrator's correction of the reader's processes of naturalization through a phrase such as "it was so, it was not," that led Gayatri Spivak to remark that while *The Satanic Verses* was not part of the linear narrative of the European avant-garde, "the successes and failures of the European avant-garde is available to it" (41). Let us accept Spivak's proposition but give the text a further twist. Instead of using the phrase "European avant-garde," let us use the phrase "diasporic avant-garde" to mark out a generic space for a variety of literary texts that would use the European avant-garde to inter-rogate subject positions excluded or silenced by modernism by constructing allegorical or counter-hegemonic subaltern renditions of the geopolitical imaginary of South Asians in Britain.

At the risk of repetition, let me underline once again that *The Satanic Verses* is *the* text about migration, about the varieties of religious, sexual, and social filiations of the diaspora.[9] The work is the millenarian routed through the space of travel (the aeroplane replaces the ship) and then problematically rooted in the new space of the diaspora. In this respect the text's primary narrative is a tale of migrancy and the ambiguities of being an Indian (or Pakistani) in Britain. In the process, the work explores the disavowal of so many fundamental assumptions and values because of a massive epistemic violence to the intellect. The narrative, in fact, begins with people who have already lost their faith in religion and who now have a truly diasporic relationship with India. As Rushdie has explained, these people are the new travellers across the planet; having lost their faith, they have to rethink what death means to the living and how desire can find expression when people cannot love (Interview with Blake Morrison 120–21). One of the key phrases that recurs deals with being born again (to be born again, you have to die, says Gibreel to Saladin), and the diasporic world is very much the world in which one undergoes a rebirthing. In the case of Gibreel and Saladin, the context in which this occurs combines the fantastic free fall from an exploding plane (AI 420 from the height of Mt Everest, a full 29,002 feet[10]) with the realistic narrative of terrorism and hijacking. The combination of these two generic modes is striking, since it forecloses the possibility of naturalistic readings because the work reveals a kind of simultaneous *karma* and reincarnation: two people die and are immediately reborn as they were at the moment of their deaths. The rebirthing of Gibreel and Saladin, then, parallels, say, the rebirth of Amba as Shikhandin in the *Mahabharata*, the founding Indian text that is simultaneously diachronic and synchronic: it happened then, it happens now. One becomes someone else but keeps the earlier history/biography intact. The relationship between Rushdie's writings and the Indian epic tradition of generic mixing is a narrative we cannot go into here, but it is nevertheless important to refer to it, if only because it reminds us of the fictiveness of the text and its relationship to the traditional hybridity of Indian culture. Moreover, as Gibreel's song (from the film *Shree 420*) shows, the dominant cultural form of modern India, the Bombay film, the successor to the encyclopaedic pan-Indian epic tradition, constantly adapts itself to and indigenizes all global cultural forms, from Hollywood to Middle Eastern dance and music.

The "emigration" of Salahuddin Chamchawala from Bombay has close parallels with Salman Rushdie's own pattern of emigration. From the insertion of the well-known autobiographical "kipper story" (the young Rushdie was not allowed to get up from the dinner table until he had finished his kipper, which he didn't know how to eat!) to his own uneasy relationship with his father, there are striking parallels between Saladin and his creator. It is not Gibreel but Saladin who is reborn and who accepts the need for change: the nostalgia for the past (a house, one's ancestral religion, and so on) is not something one can live by but to which, in an act of both homage and acceptance of his father Changez Chamchawala, Saladin returns. The use of a fused sign – Salman and Saladin – allows Rushdie to enter into those areas, notably the body and the religious body-politic, that accentuate the diasporic condition. Relationships with women – Pamela Lovelace (wife), Mimi Mamoulian (professional partner), and Zeeny Vakil (mistress) – raise the interesting question of diasporic sexuality and gender relations. At the same time, the other autobiographical figure around "Salman" – Salman from Persia in the Mahound and Jahilia sections of the book – is also diasporic and connects with Islam as a political as well as religious revolution staged by "water-carriers, immigrants and slaves" (101). Even the radical Iranian cultural critic suppressed under the Shah's regime, and for many the harbinger of Khomeini's revolution, Jalal Al-e Ahmad (1923–1969), refers to one Salman-e Faresi (Salman the Persian) who "found refuge in Medina with the Muslims and played such an important role in the development of Islam" (16). This Salman-e Faresi may not have been the prophet's contemporary, but the connection between Iran (through the figure of Salman) and the advent of Islam underscores the strength of the Iranian furore against Rushdie. In Al-e Ahmad's reading of the Islamization of Iran, what is emphasized, perhaps too simplistically, is the idea of Islam being invited into Iran. Unlike earlier Western incursions, Islam, another Western ideology, is not an invasion but a response to Iran's own need to embrace the austere harmony of the "one."

It is through Saladin/Salman (Rushdie) that the new themes of diasporic interaction are explored. Saladin sees in the relics of Empire in the heart of London "attractively faded grandeur." Gibreel, on his part, sees only a "wreck, a Crusoe-city, marooned on the island of its past." When asked about his favourite films, Saladin offers a cosmopolitan list: "*Potemkin, Kane, Otto e Mezzo, The Seven Samurai, Alphaville, El Angel Exterminador*" (439), whereas Gibreel (the larger-than-life Bombay film actor modelled on Amitabh Bachchan and N. T. Rama Rao, the latter a hero-god in countless mythological films turned politician) offers a list of successful commercial Hindi films: "*Mother India, Mr India, Shree Charsawbees*: no Ray, no Mrinal Sen, no Aravindan, or Ghatak" (440). The lists, the choices made, the implied discriminations, the negotiations with the migrant's new land, all indicate the complex ways in which two diaspora discourses (the millenarian and the diasporic) work. Gibreel, for his part, does not undergo mutation but remains locked in the worlds of memory and fantasy. Saladin thus becomes the figure who is both here and elsewhere, and his return to the Motherland to be at his father's deathbed is perhaps the more cogent statement about the diasporic condition. Gibreel, on the other hand, acts out his actor's fantasies and becomes the conduit through whom (in his imagination) the Prophet receives the Quran. Blasphemy, therefore, falls not to the hybrid mutant but to the nostalgia-ridden Gibreel. Further, the mutant condition of Saladin (names in the diaspora are similarly mutated, a Hobson-Jobson discourse gets replayed) is both linguistic as well as physical: the he-goat with an erratic pair of horns and the owner of a name that moves between the Indian Chamchawala to the trans-Indian Spoono (English for *chamcha*, "spoon," though in Hindi/Urdu a *chamcha* is a sycophant gleefully doing his/her master's work). In all this, two ideas –newness and love – keep cropping up. For Dr. Uhuru Simba, "newness will enter this society by collective, not individual actions" (415). As for love, the combinations it takes – Gibreel/Rekha Merchant/Allie Cone; Saladin/Pamela Lovelace/Zeeny Vakil/Mimi Mamoulian – get complicated by other alignments: Jumpy Joshi/Pamela; Saladin/Allie Cone; Billy Battuta/Mimi; Hanif Johnson/Mishal Sufyan. All these relationships are part of the new diasporic combinations, a kind of necessary reprogramming of the mind in the wake of the diasporic newness. At the point of interaction where the old and the new come together – as is the case with the diaspora's encounter with the vibrant politics of the metropolitan centre – new social meanings get constructed, especially in the domain of psychosexual politics. Thus the capacious Hind and not the bookish Muhammad effectively runs the Shaandaar café: her great cooking is what improves the material condition of the family rather than Muhammad's Virgilian rhetoric, which has no value in Britain. Gender relations therefore get repositioned in the diaspora, and women begin to occupy a different, though not necessarily more equitable, kind of space. The manner in which a diasporic restaurant culture in Britain is actually based on wives as cooks is quite staggering. In another world, in the world of Jahilia, however, it is Hind, the powerful wife of the patriarch Abu Simbel who has to battle with another new idea: "What kind of an idea are you?" (335) is the question asked of the Prophet. Yet the idea of the "new" (the idea of the "post" in any modernity) also has a tendency to get fossilized, which is where another narrative of the diaspora, the millenarian, becomes the attractive, and easy, alternative. As a heterogeneous, "unread" text, *The Satanic Verses* has been appropriated, positively and negatively, toward both diasporic (hybrid) and essentialist ends. I will return to the latter in the context of Rushdie and the sacred. For the moment, I want to explore further the question of racial politics and diasporic identity.

Race, Identity, and Britishness

The late 1960s saw the emergence of a new racism in Britain for which Enoch Powell was the best-known, but not the only, spokesperson. In what seemed like a remarkable reversal of old Eurocentric and imperialist readings of the black colonized as racially inferior, the new racists began to recast races on the model of linguistic difference. This difference, however, had to be anchored somewhere, and the easiest means of doing this was by stipulating that nations were not imagined communities constructed historically but racial enclaves marked by high levels of homogeneity. Thus a race had a nation to which it belonged. The British had their nation and belonged to an island off the coast of Europe, and so on. In the name of racial respect and racial equality, this version in fact gave repatriation theorists such as Enoch Powell a high level of respectability in that, it was argued, what Powell stood for was not racism but a nationalism that the immigrants themselves upheld. What the argument simplified was the history of imperialism itself and the massive displacement of races that had taken place in the name of Empire. Nowhere was this more marked than in the Indian, African, and Chinese diasporas of the Empire. More importantly, however, the new racism was used to defend Britishness itself, to argue that in fact multiculturalism is a travesty of the British way of life, which now becomes extremely vulnerable. The only good immigrant is one who is totally assimilable, just as the only good gay or lesbian is someone who leads a closet life. Writes Anna Marie Smith:

> Only the thin veneer of deracializing euphemisms has shifted over this period, with blatantly racist discourse on immigration being recoded in discourse on criminality, inner-cities' decay and unrest, anti-Western terrorism, and multiculturalism. Indeed, the fundamentally *cultural* definition of race in the new racism allows for this mobile relocation of the racial-national borders to any number of sociopolitical sites. (62)

It is by way of the Sufyan family (Muhammad, the Bangladeshi schoolmaster with a weakness for European classics, his wife, Hind, and their daughters, Mishal and Anahita) that we enter into changing demographic patterns and race relations in Britain, as well as see how homeland family norms negotiate the new gender politics of diasporas. The Sufyan family lives on Brickhall Street, the old Jewish enclave of tailors and small-time shopkeepers. Now it is the street of Bangladeshi migrants or Packies/Pakis ("brown Jews" [300]) who are least equipped for metropolitan life. Thus, in Brickhall, synagogues and kosher food have given way to mosques and halal restaurants. Yet nothing is as simple as it seems in this world of the diaspora. The space of the Shaandaar Cafe B&B becomes the space of new labour relations between husband

and wife but also of new forms of sexuality. Mishal becomes pregnant by the second-generation diaspora Hanif Johnson, while Jumpy Joshi has sex with Pamela, even as her husband, Saladin, sleeps under the same roof. The diaspora here finally crumbles and falls apart because the pressures come not only from the newly acquired sociosexual field of the participants in the diasporic drama but also because that drama has to contend with racist hooliganism as the diaspora becomes progressively an object of derision to be represented through the discourse of monsterism. It is through this brand of fascism that death finally comes to the diaspora and to those associated with it. Both the café and the community centre are burned down. Hind, Muhammad, and Pamela die and suddenly there is no room for nostalgia, no room for the discourse of mysticism (469) that had sustained the discourses of the homeland. Instead, the imperative is to transform one's memory into modes of political action because the world is far too real (469). It is at this point in the narrative that diasporic identities get complicated by the presence in Britain of people who have already gone through the diasporic experience in other parts of the world. Having co-existed with Afro-West Indians, the Indian diaspora of the West Indies, for instance, is already a hybrid form. Thus Sewsunker Ram (Pinkwalla), the DJ, and John Maslama, the club proprietor, have political and cultural orientations that bring them close to the kinds of diasporic politics endorsed by a Dr. Uhuru Simba. The alignments at work here – Bengali, Afro-Caribbean, East Indian Caribbean, East African Indian, Sikh, Indian, Pakistani, Bangladeshi, and so on – gesture toward new forms of diasporic awareness and coalitional politics. From the Africanist ideal of Dr. Uhuru Simba to the multifaceted, decentred, simulative worlds of the Sufyan girls, Jumpy Joshi, and Hanif Johnson, one now begins to see not one legitimation narrative of the diaspora but many.

"The trouble with the Engenglish is that their hiss hiss history happened overseas, so they dodo don't know what it means," stutters S. S. Sisodia (343). When those who were instrumental in creating that history (as subject peoples on whose behest the Empire believed it was acting) are now within the metropolitan centres of the Empire itself, the idea of Britishness is threatened. Both the challenge and the threat are summarized elegantly by Iain Chambers, who writes:

> It is the dispersal attendant on migrancy that disrupts and interrogates
> the overarching themes of modernity: the nation and its literature,
> language and sense of identity; the metropolis; the sense of centre;
> the sense of psychic and cultural homogeneity. In the recognition of the
> other, of radical alterity, lies the acknowledgement that we are no longer
> at the centre of the world. (*Migrancy, Culture, Identity* 23–24)

Chambers's "we" here is the British, but the definition that he gives of the British is very much an intermediate one. It is a definition in which the subjects of the centre – the British as an ethnic entity – also begin to find that subjectivity is "interactively" constructed, on the move, so to speak. The cultural imperative that underlies Chambers's move is that the diaspora now invades the centre and makes prior, essentialist definitions of nation-states based on notions of racial purity (Enoch Powell), a historical relic of imperialism itself. It is the privileged site of that imperialist history and its constructions of Britishness that gets replayed in the doctrines of purity in postcolonial Britain. Yet, as I say this I think what is implicit in the Chambers thesis – the need for a radical pedagogy about ethnic identities – is precisely what needs underlining. How does one make decisive interventions in the curriculum so that Britishness itself is opened up for debate? It is the agenda of the agents who would transform the apparatuses of control through which the idea of the self is constructed that requires further examination.

A "post-diaspora community" in Britain, to use Rushdie's own phrase (*Imaginary Homelands* 40), now becomes a site from which a critique of Britishness itself (and the imperial relationship between the British and Indians that has a 300-year history) is now being mounted. The migrant living here and elsewhere would find it difficult to fit into, say, Margaret Thatcher's imperious definition of a Briton during the Falklands War. As Chambers again has stressed, any attempt to decipher this appeal to "British-ness" necessarily draws us into complex, contradictory, and even treacherous terrain, in which the most varied elements "entwine, coexist and contaminate one another" (*Border Dialogues* 15). For the Indian diaspora, this trope of "Britishness" has multiple identities and can be expressed in a variety of ways. To be British in a post-diaspora Britain is to be conscious of multiple heritages and people's conflicting participation in the long history of Britain. For many, an easy, unproblematic reinsertion into a utopic or linear narrative of the British nation is impossible. In *The Satanic Verses*, we get a strong affirmation of the undesirability of this version of linear history.

We are therefore faced with "the possibility of two perspectives and two versions of Britishness" (Chambers, *Border Dialogues* 27). One is Anglocentric, frequently conservative, backward-looking, and increasingly located in a frozen and largely stereotyped idea of the national – that is, English – culture. The other is ex-centric, open-ended, and multi-ethnic. The first is based on a homogeneous "unity" in which history, tradition, and individual biographies and roles, including ethnic and sexual ones, are fundamentally fixed and embalmed in the national epic, in the mere fact of being "English." The other perspective suggests an overlapping network of histories and traditions, a heterogeneous complexity in which positions and identities, including those relating to the idea of the "citizen," cannot be taken for granted and are not "interminably fixed but tend towards flux" (Chambers, *Border Dialogues* 27).

The peculiar irony of Rushdie's own anti-racist rhetoric is that he has been used to fuel racism: Muslim threat against Rushdie's life is used by the white majority to portray all Muslims as fundamentalists. As Rushdie himself has pointed out, "The idea that the National Front could use my name as a way of taunting Asians is so horrifying and obscene to my mind that I wanted to make it clear: that's not my team, they're not my supporters, they're simply exploiting the situation to their own ends" (Interview with Blake Morrison 115). The uses made of Rushdie in defence of "Britishness" imply a problematic incorporation of the name "Rushdie" into British citizenry. The appropriation of Rushdie by British writers in the name of the autonomy of the aesthetic order again has a similar agenda. Rushdie, the politically correct defender of the diaspora, is now the equally correct "British" citizen under the protection of Scotland Yard who is defended by Harold Pinter.

The Diaspora, the Sacred, and Salman Rushdie

The Satanic Verses is one radical instance of diasporic recollection or re-memoration. Any such rememoration asks questions of the diasporic subject: What is the status of its past, of its myths, of its own certainties? How has it constructed these certainties? Does anything or anybody have a hegemonic status within the diaspora itself? Or do we read diasporas, as I have suggested, through the Gramscian definition of the subaltern? Do the Imams of Islam (in Bradford or in Tehran or in Bombay) constitute a ruling group within the subaltern?

Can one reinvigorate one's myths? One kind of reinvigoration was endorsed by Indian diasporas created in the wake of the British indenture system. In these nineteenth-century diasporas, loss was rewritten as a totality through the principle of a reverse millenarianism. There was a golden age back there that we have forfeited through our banishment. Let us imaginatively re-create this golden age, which would leap over the great chasm created in our history through indenture. One of the grand templates of Indian diasporic millenarianism is the myth of Rama and his banishment. The alternative to this millenarian ethos is a version of rememoration in which the continuum of imperial history is blasted through a radical mediation on the conditions of migrancy and displacement. The recapitulation of one's history (and not just the reinvigoration of myth) leads to a confrontation with the narratives of imperialism itself. Where the old diaspora's myths, after all, were commensurate with the imperial narratives of totality (insofar as these myths were considered to be equally forceful from the subject's point of view), the

125

new diaspora attempts to penetrate the history of the centre through multiple secularisms. When, however, the interventions into secularity threaten an earlier memory, diasporas turn to versions of millenarian rememoration and retreat into an essentialist discourse, even though they know full well that the past can no longer redeem.

It is in this context that I would like to explore the intersection of the radical agenda of diasporas and the idea of the sacred. No reading of *The Satanic Verses* can be complete without considering the reception of the text in terms of the sacred. The sacred, in this instance, refuses to accept the aesthetic autonomy of the text and connects the narrator's voice unproblematically with that of the author. In his defence – and in the defence mounted on his behalf by the world literati – it is really the relative autonomy of art that has been emphasized. What this defence raises is a very serious question about whether a diasporic text that celebrates hybridity and rootlessness can be defended with reference purely to the privileged status of the aesthetic order. In the ensuing debates, the British South Asian diaspora has been read as a group that does not quite understand the values of a civic society and has the capacity to relapse into barbarism, precisely the condition that gave the Empire its humanist apology. If I return to the saturated discourses surrounding the Rushdie Affair, it is because the discourse reminds us of yet another kind of privilege, and one that questions the non-negotiable primacy of modernity itself.

Now here comes the difficult part of the presentation in the context of *The Satanic Verses* as a commodity with quite specific effects. The British Muslim response to *The Satanic Verses* has not been through the narratives of hybridity nor through an interventionist politics that would use *The Satanic Verses* to point out the massive contradictions between the diaspora and the ideology of "Britishness"; rather, it has been through a reappropriation of the myths of totality, of millenarianism, which were the survival mechanism of the old diaspora. In other words, the defence has been mounted not through a constantly revalidating and contingent subjectivity *in medias res* but through an unreal resistance based on the discourse of a prior diasporic mode of nar-rativization. *The Satanic Verses* as an intervention into the project of modernity now faces modernity itself as an unnecessary formation in diasporic culture. Clearly, the Bradford Imams cannot be both modern and anti-modern, but such indeed is the complex/contradictory narrative that is being articulated. Thus what we get is the second diaspora trying to cling to totalities, to the unreal completedness of the first, where, even for a Naipaul, there was never an unproblematic totality to aspire to in the first instance. The old diaspora, in spite of its ideologies of totality, could not have responded to *The Satanic*

Verses with the same sense of unqualified rejection. The *fatwa* against Rushdie originated in the diaspora – in Bradford – and not in Iran.

From the borders, from the interstices of existence, from the liminal, the diasporic subject uses, in Rukmini Nair and Rimli Bhattacharya's words,

> fragments of religious faith [...] [to] 'shore' up his existence, give him much needed stability in a hostile environment. When that stability is blown to bits by an author as well ensconced and integrated as Rushdie, panic results. The neurosis of *nemesis* replaces the certainties of *nostalgia*. (28–29)

One may disagree with Nair and Bhattacharya's use of "certainties," but the point is valid. What is missing from diasporic theory is a theory of the sacred based not on the idea of the sacred as a pathological instance of the secular in itself defined along purely modernist lines but as a point from which interventions can take place. In short, as Al-e Ahmad points out, the sacred is a source of metaphors of empowerment easily available for ethnic mobilization. In all our debates about the diaspora, the sacred is missing. I return to *The Satanic Verses*, which, by its very title, foregrounds something highly contentious in Islam and in Islamic definitions of the sacred. Racialized politics meets its sacralized other here. To emphasize this, to find how Rushdie reads the sacred and how the unified discourse of the sacred is used by the diaspora to defend a lost purity from within the hybrid, the hyphen, is not to say that *The Satanic Verses* is best read along these lines. What I am doing is using *The Satanic Verses* selectively to underline the dual narrative of the diaspora: the hyphen and the total, the fracture and the whole. Clearly, each has different historical antecedents for the diaspora: the hyphen is the presencing of the boundary where the politics of epistemic violence and a self-conscious redefinition of the project of modernity is located firmly within the global politics of migrancy (which also affects the construction of the non-diasporic subject); the sacred is a function of narratives that the almost self-contained diasporic communities constructed out of a finite set of memories. They gave permanence to mobility (the mothered space is always mobile – the child in the womb moves) by creating a fixed point of origin when none existed. The sacred refuses to be pushed to the liminal, to the boundary. It wants to totalize by centring all boundaries: the many and the one cease to be two dialectical poles. Since its narratives are transhistorical, the absurdity of the move for a disempowered diasporic community is overtaken completely by the illusory power of the act itself, from which the colonizer is excluded. This is true of all religious attitudes in the diaspora. As Ashis Nandy writes, "Hinduism in the diaspora, for example, is much more exclusive and homogenic. Out of feelings of inferiority, many Hindus have tried to redefine Hinduism according to the dominant concept of religion" (104).

In *The Satanic Verses*, Rushdie, in fact, connects the moment of newness itself with the diasporic performance in the sense that the Prophet's intervention into the staid politics and religion of Jahilia is made possible only through people who are always on the margins of society, "water-carrier immigrant slave" (104). The sacred is thus a means of radical self-empowerment, especially for those who work under the tyranny of the merchant classes of the Arab world. In that sacred discourse, the language, however, was not of the many, of the hybrid, but of the one. The radical, in other words, was not the idea of multiple narratives and contingency or coalitional politics, it was not the affirmation of the hyphen, but the starkness of the total, of the one:

> Why do I fear Mahound? [thinks the Grandee of Jahilia Abu Simbel]. For
> that: one one one, his terrifying singularity. Whereas I am always divided,
> always two or three or fifteen. [...] This is the world into which Mahound
> has brought his message: one one one. Amid such multiplicity, it sounds
> like a dangerous word. (102–03)

The radical "one," however, also carries a dangerous principle of female exclusion. Where the many have always found space for female goddesses, the Prophet, finally, excludes them from the position of divine intermediaries, though not before toying with the idea of their symbolic incorporation into the "new":

> Messenger, what are you saying? Lat, Manat, Uzza – they're all *females!*
>   For pity's sake! Are we to have goddesses now? Those old cranes,
> herons, hags? (107)

In the deserts of Arabia and at a particular historical moment, the radical, the new, could be conceived of only as an austere unity around the mathematical one. In the version of radical alterity that defines the modern diaspora, it is the many that must now splinter the impregnable fortresses of the one. This is the monumental irony of the debates around the book. The trouble is that the nation-state has never acknowledged the diasporic contribution to modernity, always reading them as the "one," always reading them as a dangerous presence in the West. At the height of the controversy surrounding the burning of the book, the British Home Minister responsible for Race Relations, John Patten, issued a news release entitled "On Being British" (18 July 1989), in which the ideology of the one is used to berate the excesses of another ideology of oneness. It can be seen that race relations in Britain itself produced a desire to return to the security of the past: both whites and Muslims in Britain return to their own essentialisms in moments of (perceived) crisis. Have the efforts of those who have struggled for a multiply centred nation-state therefore collapsed because the state itself created an environment in which a historical moment (that of the Prophet) would be dehistoricized, reshaped, and used as a defence of the diaspora itself? Homi Bhabha confronts these questions in *The Location of Culture*:

> The conflict of cultures and community around *The Satanic Verses* has been mainly represented in spatial terms and binary geopolitical polarities – Islamic fundamentalists vs. Western literary modernists, the quarrel of the ancient (ascriptive) migrants and modern (ironic) metropolitans. This obscures the anxiety of the irresolvable, borderline culture of hybridity that articulates its problems of identification and its diasporic aesthetic in an uncanny, disjunctive temporality that is, at once, the *time* of cultural displacement, and the *space* of the "untranslatable." (225)

Bhabha's examination of the politics of *The Satanic Verses* very quickly becomes a kind of aestheticization of the diaspora. The dominant semantics of this aesthetic may be stated through one of Bhabha's favourite metaphors, the metaphor of the "trans-." Applied to the diaspora, it means that for the diaspora a double time frame, a double space, is always, everywhere present. This is a good point, since the disjunctive temporality (both here and elsewhere; the space of present location and the rememoration of the past) is the diasporic condition. To ask the diaspora to function from one space, from one time, is to create what William Godwin in *Political Justice* (1793) called "impostures." Yet the decisive question remains: what political articulations indeed can be made from the position of a disjunctive temporality? And if this is also the condition of hybridity (the term goes back to the nineteenth-century botanists), then what hope is there for hybrids to become agents of change and not just positions that one may occupy for purposes of critique?

Clearly, Bhabha's reading of the diasporic subject within the European nation-state is more or less identical with the non-hegemonic or pre-hegemonic Gramscian subaltern whose histories are fragmented and episodic. In the context of the Rushdie Affair, we may ask, Does hegemony always suppress difference? Or does it entertain and even encourage difference provided that it is a difference that can be footnoted adequately in the grand history of Empire, which Sir Ernest Baker once referred to as a "mission of culture – and of something higher than culture" (qtd. in Asad 250)? When the hegemonic power loses its clarity of vision in terms of its own definition of unity, then a crisis erupts – and both Salman Rushdie and Homi Bhabha believe that post-imperial British society is in crisis. Terms such as cultural minorities, ethnics, blacks, New Commonwealth immigrants, multiculturalism, are all terms used by a hysterical centre that no longer knows how to normalize the Other in the nation within. It is then the celebration of difference by Rushdie that is endorsed by Bhabha:

> It has achieved this by suggesting that there is no such whole as the nation, the culture or even the self. Such holism is a version of reality that is most often used to assert cultural or political supremacy and seeks to obliterate the relations of difference that constitute the language of history and culture. [...] Salman Rushdie sees the emergence of doubt, questioning and even confusion as being part of that cultural "excess" that facilitates the formation of new social identities that do not appeal to a pure and settled past, or to a unicultural present, in order to authenticate themselves. The authority lies in the attempt to articulate emergent, hybrid forms of cultural identity. (qtd. in Asad 262–63)[11]

It goes without saying that social identities do need authenticating (Asad), but their authentication, according to both Rushdie and Bhabha, derives from our ability to continuously reinvent ourselves out of our hybrid cultural condition (Asad 263).[12] The sacred asks different questions: Hybridity for whom? Does the state apparatus always want homogeneity? Is it in its interest to pursue this? Or is difference (but difference within a panoptical power) the desired aim of the nation-state? At one level, how is postcolonial difference (as hybrid) to be rretheorized as postcolonial hybridity? Is hybridity the desirable aim or a fact of life? Does the sacred reject the aestheticization of culture? Is the sacred point of view homogeneous to begin with? The debates surrounding the aesthetic order, the diaspora, and the sacred reached a point of extreme dissonance once Khomeini invoked the *fatwa* against Rushdie. What the debates also underlined, in the general context of the relationship between diasporas and the nation-state, is that often the ground rules that govern the nation itself may not be applied uncritically to inhabitants who fashion themselves in ways that are not identical with those of the majority of the citizens of the state. By way of a lengthy conclusion, I want to examine the Rushdie Affair and its (mis)readings on the assumption that what we have in a diaspora's relationship to the nation is a case of what Lyotard referred to as the differend.

The Rushdie Affair and the Postcolonial Differend

The Rushdie Affair draws us toward what Jean-François Lyotard has referred to as the case of the differend, in which the aesthetic and the sacred are so opposed to one another that there is no equitable resolution of the differences. Indeed, I would be even more forthright. *The Satanic Verses* has generated a number of discourses that quite simply are incommensurable with each other on any count. Indeed, if one were to use Lyotard's legal terminology, we have a case of litigation in which there are no ground rules acceptable to all the parties concerned. At the extreme end is a position theorized by the Iranian intellectual Jalal Al-e Ahmad. In his intriguing book, *Plagued by the West*, Al-e Ahmad calls Westernization a pathology (*Gharbzadegi* or "western strickenness"), by which he means the manner in which Westernization functioning as a cosmetic ideal in the Orient effectively destroys the Iranian's understanding of his or her own culture. There is no room here for any kind of hybridity. Indeed, Al-e Ahmad writes,

> The west-stricken man has no personality. He is a creature lacking in originality. He, his house, and his speech are colorless, representative of everything and everybody. Not "cosmopolitan." Never! Rather he is a nowhere man, not at home anywhere. He is an amalgam of individuals without personality and personality without specificity. Since he has no self-reliance, he puts on an act. Although he is a master of politesse and charm, he never trusts those with whom he speaks. And, since mistrust is a watchword of our times, he never reveals his true feelings. The only thing which might give him away and is visible is his fear. Whereas in the West the individual's personality is sacrificed to the requirements of specialization, in Iran the west-stricken man has neither personality nor speciality. Only fear. Fear of tomorrow. Fear of dismissal. Fear of anonymity and oblivion. Fear that he will be discovered for what he is, a blockhead. (70)[13]

Clearly, Al-e Ahmad's pathologization of the hybrid would sit uncomfortably with hybridity as an essential component of the diasporic aesthetic – not simply uncomfortably, in fact, but in an incommensurable manner, because between Al-e Ahmad and Rushdie we see a clear instance of the differend at play. In the aesthetic domain, Rushdie's *The Satanic Verses*, then, bears witness to differends by finding idioms for them. Yet in the political domain the reaction to the text has been articulated through conflicting discourses that cannot lead to equitable resolution because the discourses presuppose rules of judgement that are totally at variance with each other. There is no effective law that could accommodate these two competing positions because there is nothing in law that relates, with equal detachment and validity, to both. It is here that the Rushdie Affair itself becomes modernity's test case for the differend, and one, I would argue, that is more interesting than other literary debates such as those over *Lady Chatterley's Lover* or *Lolita* or *The Power and the Glory*. To pursue the differend here, I will limit myself to a handful of statements made both for and against Rushdie.

The Satanic Verses had a dual audience: English readers in the West and people from the Indian subcontinent, whether in India, Pakistan, and Bangladesh, or the eight-million-strong Indian diaspora overseas. The fantasies recounted in the book are those of people who are Indian (especially Bombaywallahs), and much of the humour in the book is also very distinctly Indian, as are innumerable allusions that are readily accessible only to the ideal Indian reader. Rushdie's Islam, too, is Indian Islam with its mixture of strong Hindu elements. Not surprisingly, among non-white readers the book has been discussed most intensely by British Asians (largely British Muslims) and by Indians in India. In Pakistan and in Bangladesh, the critical reception has not been as great. For Indian Muslims its publication could not have come at a worse time. Already on the defensive in the wake of Hindu revivalism, the last thing the Muslims in India wanted to see was a book that exploded (or attempted to explode) Islam's non-negotiable position about Muhammad and the text of Gibreel's revelation. As the Persian saying goes, *Ba khuda diwana bashad/ Ba Muhammad hoshiyar* ("Take liberties with Allah, but be careful with Muhammad" [Naqvi 179]). Yet the Indian audience must have been of special significance to Rushdie because the first review of the book, by Madhu Jain (even before the book was launched in Britain), and interview with the author appeared in *India Today* on 15 September 1988. This was followed immediately by another interview with Shrabani Basu in *Sunday* (18–24 September 1988). The *India Today* issue also carried excerpts from the Mahound section of the book, clearly with the author's permission. The cynic could argue that this was a calculated risk by both Rushdie and Viking/Penguin, his publisher, and was aimed at creating vigorous but critical debates among the Indian intelligentsia.[14] However, politicians, too, read the review, and the Muslim Opposition MP Syed Shahabuddin, eager to fill the Muslim leadership vacuum in India, immediately asked the Government of India to ban the book.[15] Whether it was out of political expediency (the Muslim vote bank in India is huge) or out of a genuine worry that the book was indeed blasphemous, one does not know, but the book was banned within a month of the publication of Madhu Jain's review. Because the book was not officially launched until 26 September, it is unlikely that too many people had even seen the book before it was banned in India. In fact, the excerpts published in *India Today* were probably the only sections of the book that people had read. Before looking at Shahabuddin's own reading of the book, I want to go back very briefly to Jalal Al-e Ahmad's critique of Westernization in his remarkable *Plagued by the West*, because Al-e Ahmad positions the differend as the failure on the part of the Iranian Westernized bourgeoisie to understand and transform Iran's real, democratic concerns in the postwar period. Whether in regard to oil or to the dissemination of knowledge, Iran functioned under the Shah as an imperial outpost of the West. The Iranians themselves – at least those who belonged to the establishment – had acquired Western habits (through mimicry) but had lost their own much longer traditions of social concern and equity. Yet Al-e Ahmad also notes the crucial differend at the level of disputation when he writes, "whereas at one time a verse from the Koran or one of the traditions [hadiths] of the Prophet was enough to win an argument and put an opponent in his place, today quoting some foreigner on any subject silences all critics" (72). The other fear that Al-e Ahmad has is that Western liberalism contains within itself the seeds of fascism.[16] More precisely, and Al-e Ahmad returns to this point over and over again, he fears the manner in which an instrumental reason at the core of nineteenth-century Western liberalism transforms the self-reflexive and self-critical reason of the Enlightenment into an instrument of coercion that transforms the Orient into a collective body of superstitions from which Oriental subjects can be saved only if they can be made to think like Europeans. The massive investment in Oriental archives in the West, to which imperialists sent their Oriental students, is symbolic of a belief that only when the Orient can be archived in the West, and Orientals exposed to research principles based on Western bibliographic principles, will they ever be able to study their own cultures. Reformulated, the Western Orientalist argument goes something like this: Orientals cannot understand themselves because they have no theory of research. Nor do they have a systematic archive collected in one place that they can use as their data. They must either learn from the West or use the work of Western scholars who have had the benefit of years of training in analytical techniques. The Oriental replies: But you plundered our resources, and you never allowed us to develop research skills in languages that came naturally to us, because you connected research with the acquisition of a Western language.

If we return to Syed Shahabuddin's argument in the context of the foregoing, it soon becomes clear that he continues to read imperialism's instrumental reason as if this were the same interpretation of reason as that of the Enlightenment (and certainly Kant). It is also of some concern that in defending "Islam" from a perceived threat, he played into the hands of the Hindu fundamentalists for whom Shahabuddin's ire confirmed Islam's perceived (and erroneous) inflexibility and totally closed world view. In this version, Shahabuddin made a religiously correct statement but a politically naïve one. Let us explore the case a bit more. Shahabuddin's essay appeared in *The Times of India* on 13 October 1988. It is important to realize that by 1988 the right-wing Hindu fundamentalist Bharatiya Janata Party (BJP) had become an extremely powerful political party with strong grassroots support, especially in North India. The Ayodhya Affair had reached a point of no return, and, looking back, one can see that the destruction of the mosque was simply a matter of time. It is important for us to invoke Ayodhya here because what Shahabuddin is really speaking about is the feeling of the average Muslim in India who is now being told about this unpardonable affront to the Prophet on the part of a renegade Muslim. This information was not available to the average Indian Muslim before Shahabuddin politicized Rushdie. In the same essay, Shahabuddin then becomes a defender of the many avatars, *rishis* ("our religious personalities"), for which the Quran has no place at all. In making this naïve political remark, he in fact begins to speak precisely like the devil who can entertain a multiplicity of gods in the pantheon for the sake of civic harmony. In short, Shahabuddin speaks less like a Muslim and more like Rushdie at this point and fails to appease precisely the electorate he most needs to convince – the vast Hindu electorate. This kind of counter-reading is possible because even Shahabuddin's non-fictional prose has another agenda: to speak of national harmony, even as he invokes a fundamental fact of Indian life, which is that there is precious little intellectual dialogue between Hindus and Muslims in India precisely because Islam cannot countenance idolatry. The Hindu, on the other hand, cannot live without it. As an instance of the differend at play, Shahabuddin's rhetoric exposes the differend within India, and the need in that country too to discover other means by which dialogue can take place. The Hindu intellectual speaks with ease with the Marxist Aijaz Ahmad but has great difficulty following Shahabuddin. There are, then, three levels at which Shahabuddin operates. At the level of the Islamic defender of the faith, the claim is a simple one of Rushdie giving offence to Muslims who revere the Prophet as the perfect man and whose name the devout Muslim chants five times a day. The connection between Mahound and the Prophet is made explicitly in *The Satanic Verses*, which, of course, suggests that the book was written to offend.

The second text of Shahabuddin is different. It is based on Indian legal codes that explicitly state that offence to anyone's religion in India is punishable by fine and/or imprisonment (not by death, let us add) (Article 295A of the Indian Penal Code). Shahabuddin here invokes a variant of a law that exists, in different forms, in the West. In this instance, it is a case of litigation that can be mounted and/or defended successfully. However, it is the third text of Shahabuddin, the use of the Affair to underline Islam's own respect for other religions (even those that are not religions of the Book and condemned in the Quran), that is interesting. *The Satanic Verses* thus becomes a means by which Indian Islam distances itself from one of the fundamental characteristics of Islam (that the Hindu is essentially a *kafir*). In 1989 this was an important move on the part of thinking Muslims in India who saw Hindu fundamentalism as their greatest threat. How to appease the Hindu, how to emphasize that Islam never condoned the destruction of temples, how to use *The Satanic Verses* to become a defender not only of Islam but of the multitude of religions within India? Indeed, how to be another Rushdie and yet uncompromisingly anti-Rushdie? These are the texts that have emerged from the debates thus far, as they touch on Indian social and political life. And the strategy backfired. The vernacular press did not support Shahabuddin, and Rajiv Gandhi's banning of the novel was seen as another act of appeasement of the Muslims not long after the Shah Bano case, in which Muslim Sharia laws were allowed to override Indian secular law. In Britain, where the protest began with the Islamic Foundation in Leicester's director, Faiyazuddin Ahmad, and where Muslims did read the book closely, the protests were directed not so much against the author as against his publisher, Penguin Books, which was asked to withdraw the book and pay compensation to the Muslim community for sacrilege. It was also in Britain that pan-Islamic support was mustered and, finally, if we are to believe one version of the events, a request made to Khomeini to act on behalf of all aggrieved Muslims. The request, however, seems to have been anticipated in remarks made by a number of British Muslims, one of whom, M.H. Faruqi, in fact, wrote, "Perhaps it would be more salutary if the author is allowed to enter into Islamic jurisdiction and prosecuted under relevant law" (49). It hardly needs to be added that this "relevant law" condemns the offenders of Islam to death. Two points to Rushdie, two points to Islam, one to Hinduism (unwittingly).

It was against this furore that one would like to read Rushdie's most important defence, which was published on 22 January 1989. It is an interesting defence because it is straight out of the project of modernity that began – as many would argue persuasively, I believe – with the Enlightenment. The key to Rushdie's argument is to be found in his carefully written sentences against what he sees is the essentialist Islam of the "tribe of clerics," a "contemporary Thought Police" (Appignanesi and Maitland 74–75). The "Thought Police" have established the ground rules for the discussion of Islam, not Islam itself. Rushdie writes:

> They have turned Muhammad into a perfect being, his life into a perfect life, his revelation into the unambiguous, clear event it originally was not. Powerful taboos have been erected. One may not discuss Muhammad as if he were human, with human virtues and weaknesses. One may not discuss the growth of Islam as a historical phenomenon, as an ideology born out of its time. (Appignanesi and Maitland 74–75)

These are perfectly reasonable arguments, and not at all unusual among liberal intellectuals in the West, or, for that matter, in other parts of the world as well. However, in presenting the argument in these terms, Rushdie implicitly accepts that the book is a critique of Islam and, furthermore, assumes, against the evidence, that any religion can survive the kind of historicization that he has in mind. Since the spheres of religion and the state are not at all clearly demarcated in Islam, Rushdie's case makes sense only if the two spheres indeed were separate. The choice for civilization, as Rushdie argues, is simple: one has to choose between Enlightenment and barbarism. However, is the choice so straightforward that one can state quite simply, "It is time for us to choose"? Choose what? A secular sphere from which the Muslims are excluded and a religious sphere to which the laws of blasphemy do not apply? Diasporic ideology, as we have argued, resists the historical in favour of the mystical and universal. No matter how powerfully the argument is presented, it cuts no ice, even with British Muslims, as may be seen from Michael Foot's elegant defence of Rushdie. Foot's target text is Dr. Shabbir Akhtar's defence of the burning of the book in Bradford: "Any faith which compromises its internal temper of militant wrath is destined for the dustbin of history, for it can no longer preserve its faithful heritage in the face of corrosive influences," wrote Akhtar (*Agenda*, 27 February 1989; qtd. in Foot 243). The point that Akhtar misses is that if all religions were similarly militant against each other, especially in those nation-states in which one of the religious groups has been defined traditionally as the outsider, we would all be in a dreadful mess. What is there in Islam that needs the temper of militancy, and what is the political and social payoff of underlining this militancy? Foot's counter-argument is that the retreat from militancy has been Christianity's new-found strength, an argument with which Akhtar would not agree, or refuses to see. Clearly, the force of the argument (and Foot clearly scores strongly against Akhtar here) is not at issue. What is at issue is whether Foot (and Rushdie) can see Akhtar's argument. Millions of Muslims can, just as many Westerners cannot. Two points to Rushdie here, two to Islam.

We can, of course, go through any number of defences of Rushdie. One, however, that is of some importance is Carlos Fuentes's essay "Words Apart," which appeared in *The Guardian* on 24 February 1989, just over a week after the proclamation of the *fatwa*. Fuentes invokes Mikhail Bakhtin to make the case that the novel is *the* form of modernity, in which a multiplicity of languages and voices can expose the folly of a world view that locks itself into meaning. Such a world view – where "reality is dogmatically defined" – is that of the ayatollahs of this world. For them, the source of all meaning is a closed sacred text that allows for no disagreement. Fuentes then goes on to counterpoint absolute truth against the idea of constantly searching for the truth. He affirms Luis Buñuel's position: "I would give my life for a man who is looking for the truth. But I would gladly kill a man who thinks that he has found the truth" (246). The statement exaggerates, in a surrealist sort of way, but the point comes across clearly. It is this position that is reversed for those who have condemned Rushdie. They would gladly give their lives for those who claim to have found the truth and would murder the unbelievers or those incapable of living with absolutes.

We can cite many more instances of the debates surrounding the Rushdie affair, but the lines of the differend return to a simple opposition. Rushdie views the case as one in which justice can be meted out provided all parties concerned can talk about the issues, but within an Enlightenment framework in which the aesthetic object has a special place. As the Affair dragged on, Rushdie began to repeat the aesthetic argument. The book is fiction, a work of art, and therefore not subject to absolutely realist readings. In *Imaginary Homelands*, this position is extensively and monotonously argued. In an October 1994 interview, Rushdie stated that the work of art is essentially an aesthetic object and should be read through aesthetic categories (sensibility, organization, design, etc); its politics is only of secondary significance (Interview with Kerry O'Brien).

Conclusion: The Postcolonial Differend

Can one theorize the Rushdie Affair and make an intervention into diasporic aesthetic without repeating the rhetoric of intractability? I have suggested in the second half of this paper that the Rushdie Affair dramatically draws our attention to diasporic politics within a nation-state as an instance of the differend. Through the use of the phrase "the postcolonial differend," I now want to make some (in)conclusive remarks about the uses of the differend as a mode of analysis that goes beyond consensual politics. This is how Lyotard defines *differend* in the opening page of his book *The Differend*:

> As distinguished from litigation, a differend [*différend*] would be a case of conflict, between (at least) two parties, that cannot be equitably resolved for lack of a rule of judgment applicable to both arguments. One side's legitimacy does not imply the other's lack of legitimacy. However, applying a single rule of judgment to both in order to settle their differend as though it were merely a litigation would wrong (at least) one of them (and both of them if neither side admits this rule). (xi)

The most obvious modern instance of the differend is the claim on the part of certain revisionist historians such as Robert Faurisson and David Irving that the Holocaust needs to be rethought and the "facts" modified.[17] Faurisson, for example, disputes the very existence of gas chambers because he could not find a single individual who had actually seen a gas chamber with his own eyes. What is at issue here is the nature of the referent. Since reality is not "what is 'given' to this or that 'subject'" but a "state of the referent (that about which one speaks) which results from the effectuation of establishment procedures defined by a unanimously agreed-upon protocol" (Lyotard 4), it follows that any object of analysis or knowledge comes into being only insofar as it "require[s] that establishment procedures be effectuated in regard to it" (Lyotard 9). When the establishment procedures unproblematically link up diverging phrase regimens within discursive laws that are fixed, laws such as dialogue, consensus, and so on, the matter is resolved. However, when the linkages cannot be effectuated by virtue of a radical heterogeneity of the items – by virtue of their intrinsic incommensurability – then we begin "to bear witness to the different." Lyotard continues: "A case of differend between two parties takes place when the 'regulation' of the conflict that opposes them is done in the idiom of one of the parties while the wrong suffered by the other is not signified in that idiom" (9). To give the differend any real presence or effectiveness, to make it legitimate in spite of the absence of assimilative linkages between the phrase regimens of the competing ideas, one needs to recast the phrases themselves through new idioms in order that the elements that make up a phrase – its referent (what it is about, the case), its sense (what the case signifies), the person to whom it is addressed (the addressee), the person through whom the case is made (the addressor) – can be given new meaning. Lyotard speaks of silence, a negative phrase, as an example of something that has yet to be phrased: since it cannot be staged, it has no effectiveness.

The claim here is not that every dispute must be resolved but "how to argue for a nonresolvable heterogeneity (the basis for all true discussion) that is not a simple pluralism" (Carroll 80). What the Rushdie Affair dramatizes so forcefully is that "the diasporic imaginary" and "the postcolonial" are phrases in dispute because in moments of crisis the parties concerned present their case in a language and through sets of manoeuvres unacceptable to the other in a court of law. The conflict is not a simple opposition between us and them, the postcolonial and the nation-state, or the colonizer and the colonized; rather, it is a consequence of phrase regimens endemic to the worlds engendered by these terms.

It seems that Rushdie's works confirm the radical practice of heterogeneity where the differend is affirmed and not "suppressed or resolved" (Carroll 75). The subjects in his works do not exist outside or prior to the phrases through which they are constituted. There is, then, no supra real or a real outside the subject positions so constructed through which arbitration can take place. This does not mean that there is no room for correct or proper political action from a position of consensus or detachment (the image of the law); rather, the flight from spurious ground rules (the "authentic base," as some would say) draws attention to the problematic nature of the subjects in these works. A refusal to grant objective history (the real) priority and, furthermore, to see this reality as an instrument of totalitarianism and injustice because the victim's testimony is considered to be without authority leads Lyotard to claim that history (rationality) is really unjust in cases of the differend. One has to return to disarticulations, to silence, to feelings, to the corporeal, and not simply to the mental, for counter-hegemonic positions.

In this respect, the aesthetic order especially signals the possibility of alternative worlds that do not seek legitimation purely through facts. The aesthetic then contains unresolvable "heterogeneities" – Keats came close to it with his phrase "negative capability" – because unbridgeable gaps are left in "dispute." Lyotard sees this in Kant's own claim that the ethical, for instance, could not be deduced from the cognitive. The aesthetic, too, cannot be demonstrated through recourse to the cognitive and hence to reality. The Kantian sublime is thus a celebration of heterogeneity because, while it demands a certain universality, it does not assume that the universal is a given. The sublime celebrates antimony as the mind stretches it as far as it can. The mind embraces the sublime as if this were desirable and necessary and would continue to do so if reason were not to re-establish its law. Yet in that moment of celebration, in that dispute between faculties, in that incommensurable differend, no object can be represented that equals the idea of the totality.

In all this the urgent demand is that the differend should be listened to. The diasporic imaginary, as the littoral, is that which defies social assimilation with ease. If and when that assimilation occurs, diasporas disappear. Until then what we have to address – as a matter of justice – is the radical politics of heterogeneity. Since the differend ultimately is unresolvable, and phrases cannot be linked unproblematically, the differend, as David Carroll explains, "proposes strategies [...] of resisting [...] homogenization by all political, aesthetic, philosophical means possible" (87) – except, of course, for a genre of discourse such as the novel, which does link the various phrase regimens together. These phrase regimens, such as the cognitive, the prescriptive, the performative, the exclamative, the interrogative, in themselves represent mutually exclusive modes of representing the universe (Lyotard 128). The aesthetic then becomes a site for the differend to be presented even as the phrase regimens themselves remain incommensurable.

Ultimately, of course, Rushdie is speaking about justice for the diaspora. Is the concept of justice (not just the legal bourgeois term surrounding specific legal codes and acts) equally available to all citizens or is justice the prerogative of only those citizens who are part of a homogeneous British family that includes not only white Britons but also the assimilable black? What I have done is think through some of the radical incommensurabilities in the texts of Rushdie from the perspective of what Lyotard has called the differend, as both the staging of and engagement with difference as dispute. In the politics of the Rushdie Affair, we encounter phrase regimes that are in conflict. So firmly grounded are the opposing views in a particular ideological and epistemological formation that either, from the point of view of the given epistemology or truth conditions, is equally true and valid. Given such a persuasive rhetoric, even the question of a communicative community capable of arbitrating, consensually, is out of the question. In the case of the Rushdie Affair, compromise or justice is not possible because the grounds of the arguments are incommensurable. There are no winners and losers in the Rushdie Affair, only the presencing of the differend through agonistic discourses and politics. What must be recognized is that in this presencing there is no possibility of a recourse to the grand narratives of the centre or the nation-state (recall both Powell and Thatcher here). The grand narrative therefore is replaced by the local and by the differend, which, as I read it, is a phrase that designates precisely those conditions such as Rushdie's, where the rupture, the drift, the inconclusive begin to designate the diasporic condition itself. In diasporic theory we must bear witness to the differend.

Notes

1 My thanks to Jim Clifford, Iain Chambers, Christopher Connery, Stephen Slemon, Brett Nicholls, Maria Degabriele, Abdollah Zahiri, and Horst Ruthrof for their help in writing this paper.

2 I owe this phrase to Iain Chambers.

3 The poem reads:

> Let me tell you, boyo, bach: I love this place,
> where green hills shelter me from fear,
> jet fighters dance like dragonflies
> mating over unsteady, unafraid lambs,
> and in the pub a divorcée, made needy
> by the Spring, talks rugby and holidays
> with my protectors, drinks, and grows
> more lovely with each glass. So, too, do they.
> As for me, I must hide my face
> from farmers mending fences, runners, ponied girls;
> must frame it in these whitewashed, thickstoned walls
> while the great canvas of the universe
> shrinks to a thumbnail sketch. And yet
> I love the place. It remembers, so it says, a time
> older than chapel, druid, mistletoe and god,
> and journeys still, across enchanted pools,
> towards that once and future Avalon. (128)

4 See Rushdie, "Hobson-Jobson," in *Imaginary Homelands* (81–83).

5 Phoolan Devi was released on 19 February 1994 after spending eleven years in prison. She was imprisoned on charges of murdering eighteen upper-caste landowners. She turned a dacoit after she was gang-raped in her village of low-caste Hindus. Wanted in fifty-five criminal cases on charges including murder, kidnapping, and robbery, she gave herself up in February 1983, turned to politics, and was murdered in 2001. Her story has already been recorded in films and books. See Sen and Shekhar Kapu's film *The Bandit Queen*.

6 Millenarian narratives are an integral part of diasporic recollections and may be designated, for their respective diasporas, through terms such as the Indological, the Africological, and the Zionist.

7 *Observer,* 22 January 1989 (quoted in Apignanesi and Maitland, 75).

8 Two of the novels that Rushdie admires most are *Moby Dick* and *Ulysses*.

9 "[T]he book isn't actually about Islam, but about migration, metamorphosis, divided selves, love, death, London and Bombay," wrote Rushdie to the Indian Prime Minister Rajiv Gandhi (Apignanesi and Maitland 44).

10 Air India Flight 182 exploded in 1985, one of the more audacious acts of Sikh terrorism that actually originated, it seems, in the Canadian Indian diaspora. 29,002 feet was compulsory knowledge for geography students in the colonies.

11 Asad asks: "Does Bhabha mean (a) that it is not worth appealing to the past as a way of authenticating social identities because the act of articulating emergent identities authenticates itself or (b) that the past, albeit unsettled, is not worth contesting because it is merely an aesthetic resource for inventing new narratives of the self?" (263 n21).

12 Asad notes that to speak of cultural syncretism or cultural hybrids presupposes a conceptual distinction between pre-existing ("pure") cultures. Of course, all apparent cultural unities are the outcomes of diverse origins, and it is misleading to think of an identifiable cultural unity as having neutrally traceable boundaries (262).

13 Note that on his visit to an Islamic seminary in Qom, Naipaul chanced upon a book with a sepia-coloured cover that had been written by an Iranian who, the director of the seminary said, "had spent an apparently shattering year in England. This book was called *The West Is Sick*" (Naipaul 50).

14 See Naqvi 166–69.

15 Unless otherwise stated, my source for the debates surrounding *The Satanic Verses* and the fatwa against Rushdie's life is *The Rushdie File,* edited by Apignanesi and Maitland. See also Fischer and Abedi, chapter 7.

16 "One of the basic problems of Western civilization (in the Western countries themselves) is the constant threat of the seeds of fascism within the body of 19th century liberalism" (97).

17 See Lipstadt.

Works Cited

Al-e Ahmad, Jalal. *Plagued by the West (Gharbzadegi).* Trans. Paul Sprachman. New York: Caravan Books, 1982.

Anderson, Benedict. *Imagined Communities: Reflections on the Origin and Spread of Nationalism.* London: Verso, 1991.

Appignanesi, Lisa, and Sara Maitland, eds. *The Rushdie File.* London: Fourth Estate, 1989.

Asad, Talal. *Genealogies of Religion.* Baltimore: Johns Hopkins University Press, 1993.

The Bandit Queen. Dir. Shekhar Kapu. Perf. Seema Biswas. 1994.

Basu, Shrabani. Interview with Salman Rushdie. *Sunday*, India. 18-24 Sept. 1988. Appignanesi and Maitland. 32-33.

Bhabha, Homi. *The Location of Culture.* London: Routledge, 1994.

Carroll, David. "Rephrasing the Political with Kant and Lyotard: From Aesthetic to Political Judgements." *Diacritics* 14.3 (1984): 74–88.

Chambers, Iain. *Border Dialogues: Journeys in Postmodernity.* London: Routledge, 1990.

———. *Migrancy, Culture, Identity.* London: Routledge, 1994.

Clifford, James. "Diasporas." *Cultural Anthropology* 9.3 (1994): 302–38.

Faruqi, M.H. "Publishing Sacrilege Is Not Acceptable." Appignanesi and Maitland 48-49.

Fischer, Michael M. J., and Mehdi Abedi. *Debating Muslims: Cultural Dialogues in Postmodernity and Tradition.* Madison: University of Wisconsin Press, 1990.

Foot, Michael. "Historical Rushdie." Appignanesi and Maitland 242–44.

Fuentes, Carlos. "Words Apart." *The Guardian* 24 February 1989. Appignanesi and Maitland 245–49.

Gilroy, Paul. *The Black Atlantic: Modernity and Double Consciousness.* Cambridge, MA: Harvard University Press, 1993.

———. "Cultural Studies and Ethnic Absolutism." *Cultural Studies.* Ed. Lawrence Grossberg, Cary Nelson, and Paula A. Treichler. New York: Routledge, 1992. 187–98.

Jain, Madhu. Interview with Salman Rushdie. *India Today.* 15 Sept. 1988. Appignanesi and Maitland. 30-32.

Lipstadt, Deborah. *Denying the Holocaust.* New York: The Free Press, 1993.

Lyotard, Jean-François. *The Differend: Phrases in Dispute.* Trans. Georges Van Den Abbele. Manchester: Manchester University Press, 1988.

Naipaul, V.S. *Among the Believers: An Islamic Journey.* London: André Deutsch, 1981.

Nair, Rukmini Bhaya, and Rimli Bhattacharya. "Salman Rushdie: The Migrant in the Metropolis." *Third Text* 11 (Summer 1990): 17–30.

Nandy, Ashis. "Dialogue and the Diaspora: Conversation with Nikos Papastergiadis." *Third Text* 11 (Summer 1990): 99–108.

Naqvi, Saeed. *Reflections of an Indian Muslim.* Delhi: Har-Anand Publications, 1993.

Rushdie, Salman. "Crusoe." *Granta* 31 (Spring 1991): 128.

———. "Hobson-Jobson." *Imaginary Homelands: Essays and Criticism 1981–1991.* London: Granta/Viking, 1991. 81–83.

———. *Imaginary Homelands: Essays and Criticism 1981–1991.* London: Granta/Viking, 1991.

———. Interview with Blake Morrison. *Granta* 31 (Spring 1991): 113–25.

———. Interview with Kerry O'Brien. "Lateline." Australian Broadcasting Corporation Television. 4 October 1994.

———. *The Satanic Verses.* London: Viking, 1988.

Sen, Mala. *India's Bandit Queen: The True Story of Phoolan Devi.* Delhi: Indus/HarperCollins, 1993.

Shahabuddin, Syed. "You Did This with Satanic Forethought, Mr. Rushdie." *The Times of India* 13 October 1989. Appignanesi and Maitland 45–49.

Smith, Anna Marie. "The Imaginary Inclusion of the Assimilable 'Good Homosexual': The British New Right's Representations of Sexuality and Race." *Diacritics* 24.2–3 (1994): 58–70.

Spivak, Gayatri Chakravorty. "Reading *The Satanic Verses.*" *Third Text* 11 (Summer 1990): 41–60.

Tölölyan, Khachig. "The Nation State and Its Others: In Lieu of a Preface." *Diaspora* 1.1 (1991): 3–7.

Introduction: The Linked Histories of the Globalized World   The Fascist Longings in our Midst   Queer with Class: Absence of Third World Sweatshop in Lesbian/Gay Discourse and a Rearticulation of Materialist Queer Theory   Cross-Mirrorings of Alterity: The Colonial Scenario and Its Psychological Legacy   Mythologies of Migrancy: Postcolonialism, Postmodernism, and the Politics of (Dis)location   Postcolonial DefferendDifferend: Diasporic Narratives of Salman Rushdie

Keeping History at Wind River and Acoma   Modernity's First Born: Latin America and Postcolonial Transformation   Towards Articulation: Postcolonial Theory and Demotic Resistance   Postcolonial Theory and the "Decolonization" of Chinese Culture

*Postcoloniality is the condition of what we might
ungenerously call a comprador intelligentsia: of a
relatively small, Western-style, Western-trained, group
of writers and thinkers who mediate the trade in cultural
commodities of world capitalism at the periphery*

> —Anthony Appiah
> "The Postcolonial and the Postmodern" (149)

*As soon as any radically innovative thought becomes
an -ism, its specific groundbreaking force diminishes,
its historical notoriety increases, and its disciples
tend to become more simplistic, more dogmatic, and
ultimately more conservative, at which time its power
becomes institutional rather than analytical.*

> —Barbara Johnson
> "Nothing Fails Like Success" (11)

In the third world no one gets off on being third world.

> —Gayatri Chakravorty Spivak
> "What Is It For?" (77)

At the Margins
of Postcolonial Studies

KALPANA SHESHADRI-CROOKS

As the epigraphs above suggest, the "field" of (so-called) postcolonial studies, despite the ambiguity of its object of study, has reached that phase in its development in which, like every other revisionary discourse, it is melancholic about its new-found authority and incorporation into institutions of higher learning. This melancholic condition derives not only from postcolonial scholars' apprehension that institutionalizing the critique of imperialism may render it conciliatory but from other significant factors as well, such as their own (First World) place of speaking (which implicates them in the problematic of neo-colonialism), their criteria for political self-legitimation (that is, the impossibility of representing the Third World as anti-imperialist constituency, especially in the face of the retreat of socialism), and their peculiar immobility as a positive oppositional force for curricular change within the (American and British) academies. It is especially in the last sense that postcolonial studies differs from ethnic studies: for instance, it cannot, unlike African or Asian-American studies, commit itself to canon revision, which is essentially a minoritarian project. Although it is often associated with the impossible category of Third World literature, as a specific form of cultural studies it continually questions such totalizing concepts and thus maintains a critical if not hostile relationship to multiculturalism. The melancholia of postcolonialism also derives from the fact that today it faces, from within its own ranks, major criticisms and attacks against its very legitimacy and political viability.[1] The term itself has become suspect: a catch-all phrase for a post (read fashionable) Third Worldism.[2]

While postcolonial studies has yet to inform positively all scholarly inquiry today, it is not far-fetched to suggest that it has certainly acquired, if not power, a certain institutional cachet, or, to use Arif Dirlik's term, an "aura" of innovativeness. Evidence of this new-found cachet or mystique is lodged, for instance, in a footnote in Naomi Schor's fascinating defence mounted on behalf of French departments in the U.S. She writes:

> Commenting on the interest in postcolonialism, an eminent and respected colleague recently opined that Europe was dead. The statement seems astonishing in view of current (political) and future (economic) developments in that part of the world, which represents a population of 325 million and constitutes the second largest economic block in the world. (33)

What is interesting here is the assertion, by a scholar of such perspicuity as Schor, of the importance of Europe rather than the noting, for instance, of the imbrication of Europe and postcolonial states, or her colleague's peculiar disengagement of Europe from its others. In other words, she seems aware of the growing influence of a so-called postcolonial studies but seems unclear about its scholarly focus, be it the critique of the continuing power of Europe and North America over the Third World (as the work of Edward Said and Samir Amin would testify) or of its institutional place – that it is not a parallel discipline to English or French literary studies, but offers a critique of "national" literatures as such. It is inevitable that this sense of the postcolonial mystique renders the field, for most area- or period-based scholars, incoherent if not totally "bankrupt," to use Emily Apter's term.[3] While there is no doubt that the field has grown rapidly in the past few years, producing its own journals, conferences, book-publishing series, and jobs (the recent spate of readers and anthologies bears testimony to the phenomenon[4]), the field itself remains undefinable and amorphous in its outlines. While it is possible to valorize rather than lament specific aspects of this amorphousness (I will address this issue later in this essay), much of the melancholia from within and the mystification from without emerges, I would argue, from an inadequately enunciated notion of the margin. The largely mechanical connection, even conflation, of postcolonialism with American multiculturalism, despite its perceived difference, even distance, from the latter, has meant that the relation between postcolonial studies and other minority studies has remained under-theorized. What we compromise by neglecting to articulate the linkages between these two (largely academic) initiatives is not only a more textured or nuanced notion of the margin but the very possibility of a postcolonial critique. In the following, I consider briefly the ideological thrust of multiculturalism and postcolonialism through a reading of individual works by Charles Taylor and Iain Chambers, not so much to rehearse their differences as to show how both discourses share a notion of the margin (as a spatial category) and thus once more overlook the possibilities of a postcolonial critique.

According to Taylor in his "The Politics of Recognition," multiculturalism is based on the recognition of the dialogical nature of identity. The politics of recognition, as he defines it, is based not so much on the admission of historical injustice (as with affirmative action) but on contemporary coevality.[5] According to Taylor, insofar as identity is constituted in our relations with others, being ignored or being negatively represented could have a detrimental effect on one's sense of self. Thus the right of the powerless or of people in the minority to agitate for proper recognition (through inclusion of their cultural contributions into the curriculum) is deemed consistent with our notions of authenticity and dignity. As Taylor puts it,

> The reason for these proposed changes is not, or not mainly, that all students may be missing something important through the exclusion of a certain gender or certain races or cultures, but rather that women and students from the excluded groups are given, either directly or by omission, a demeaning picture of themselves, as though all creativity and worth inhered in males of European provenance. Enlarging and changing the curriculum is therefore essential not so much in the name of a broader culture for everyone as in order to give due recognition to the hitherto excluded. The background premise of these demands is that recognition forges identity. (65–66)

The key terms in Taylor's analysis of multiculturalism are recognition and respect, or the equal right to dignity. Taylor locates the concept of multiculturalism squarely in Western liberalism, and much of his characterization of multiculturalism as the quest for recognition is undergirded by a subjectivist notion of authenticity:

> Being true to myself means being true to my own originality, which is
> something only I can articulate and discover. In articulating it, I am also
> defining myself. I am realizing a potentiality that is properly my own. This
> is the background understanding to the modern ideal of authenticity, and
> to the goals of self-fulfillment and self-realization in which the ideal is
> usually couched. (31)

This sense of authenticity, Taylor (quoting Herder) suggests, can be extended
to "the people" as well, an idea that then inaugurates the modern form of
nationalism. Decolonization, according to Taylor, is "to give the peoples
of what we now call the Third World their chance to be themselves unimpeded" (31); in other words, it is a way of returning them to their authentic
selves. It is obvious from this emphasis on authenticity that Taylor will
privilege traditional and integrated societies, but the key issue in his argument apropos multiculturalism is judgement. No society, he argues, can
be judged (as worthy or worthless) before it has been studied with respect.
Taylor deplores as hypocritical at worst and condescending at best the form
of multiculturalism that demands not just respect and recognition but equal
worth before study. As a presumption, he will allow

> that it is reasonable to suppose that cultures that have provided the
> horizon of meaning for large numbers of human beings, of diverse
> characters and temperaments, over a long period of time – that have, in
> other words, articulated their sense of the good, the holy, the admirable
> – are almost certain to have something that deserves our admiration and
> respect, even if it is accompanied by much that we have to abhor and
> reject. (72–73)

Yet *real* judgements of worth, he suggests, must be reserved until after study,
a study that will transform our standards of judgement, that will achieve "a
fusion of horizons," in Gadamer's sense of the phrase, which will then enable
us to form judgements of worth on a comparative basis. Judgements of value
and worth "cannot be dictated by a principle of ethics," writes Taylor; they
"are ultimately a question of the human will" (69). Of course, the fact that a
transformation of one's standards of judgement in studying a given culture
may make comparative study impossible does not seem to trouble Taylor too
much, invested as he is in the core authentic self that apparently can alter its
perceptions of a culture without changing its fundamental vision of global
cultural differences. To sum up, in Taylor's notion of multiculturalism,
hierarchy between groups can be redressed through recognition and respect
for the other's authenticity. Marginalized people must be dealt with fairly
(63), and all cultures must be given the right to survive in their authenticity.

Such a formulation necessarily assumes the following: integrated cultures; traditional long-surviving cultures; stable national, ethnic, and cultural identities; the possibility of studying and completely understanding the other; comparative studies; and finally, "authentic" judgements of others based not on ethics but on human will. Taylor's multiculturalism is thus an epistemology of the other that can only make sense within the Christian liberal tradition that he invokes as its proper context. For our purposes, his analysis is useful as a reminder of two aspects of multiculturalism as practiced in the U.S.: a) it is essentially supplicatory; for all its talk of revisionism, it asks to partake in the privileges of the centre; and b) it is essentially a reinforcement of Western liberalism. On a more mundane level, we see these claims borne out in Peter Brooks's letter to the editor of the *New York Times* on 19 December 1994. Addressing Yale's latest albatross, the $20-million gift from Lee Bass (which has since been returned) to establish a Western civilization program, Brooks says most trenchantly: "Western civilization versus multiculturalism is a false opposition." As Roger Rouse argues in his recent analysis of the bourgeois management of the crisis of the nation-state in the age of transnationalism, the greatest significance of conservative monoculturalism, which argues for "a single culture and identity" for the U.S. (381), and of corporate liberal-multiculturalism, which appropriates the radicalism of left/liberal arguments, lies in their

> relationship of complementary opposition. Always offering at least the illusion of significant choice, they have seemed to fully exhaust the field of imaginable alternatives and, in doing so, they have endowed their commonalities [their emphases on bourgeois class positions, nationalism, and educational and political reform] with a powerfully constraining force. (385)

We would do well to remember this point in our discussions of the alliance between postcolonialism and multiculturalism: far from undermining the hegemony of Western civilization, multiculturalism merely expands its frontiers both geographically – world culture itself is appended to the United States – and pedagogically – as the universal system of knowledge both in terms of method and ideology.

The discipline of a so-called postcolonial studies, however, is a much more ambiguous one pedagogically, given that it is not really a minority studies. Rather than enhancing the girth of Western liberalism, postcolonial studies, if it is possible to speak of it as a unity or to generalize its political impulse, would work to examine the conditions by which a group arrogates to itself the function of granting or denying recognition and respect. Furthermore, it would seriously call into question Taylor's advocacy of studying the other for comparative purposes as another form of imperialism or orientalism: one that reinscribes the Western cultural relativist as universal subject with the other serving as informant.[6] However, I would argue that it is the critique of positive knowing, of rationalism, even of humanism and values of radical transformation when undertaken under the sign of postcoloniality, which awkwardly positions postcolonialism as neither liberalism nor (an orthodox) Marxism, that has generated the crisis within this subdiscipline. In other words, it is at this point of differentiation from liberal multiculturalism (which characterizes itself as marginality studies) that postcolonial discourse becomes politically vulnerable. Before I take up this theme with reference to Aijaz Ahmad's influential Marxist denunciation of the field on the grounds of its postmodern biases, however, it is imperative to see how the agenda of postmodern criticism again embarrasses "postcoloniality" by once more characterizing it as the discourse of the margin (as the space of otherness), by placing it at the vanguard of cultural and political critique.

Affirmative action and multiculturalism, in their liberal modes, conceptualize the margin spatially, as the excluded and unintegrated other. In some ways, these initiatives posit a utopian moment in which the marginal as such will cease to exist, with power circulating freely and fluidly connecting and equalizing all points of habitation. In this conception, the marginal is the space of agitation, of subversion, and thus of theoretical innovation. Yet, if, with George Yudice, we re-examine the notion of marginality as an "essentially" innovative space, we realize the futility of such a claim, which can only be made through an evasion of material history:

> There was a time when to be "marginal" meant to be excluded, forgotten, overlooked. Gradually, throughout this century, first in the discourses of anthropology, sociology, and psychoanalysis, "marginality" became a focus of interest through which "we" (Western culture) discovered otherness and our own ethnocentric perspectives. Today, it is declared, the "marginal" is no longer peripheral but central to all thought. (214)

What is worth noting here is the way in which the spatial margin – that is, margin as subject position – becomes also the source of rejuvenation of the centre, where knowledge as positive knowing is made possible. The academic industry of postcolonial studies has gained the status of a phenomenon within this paradigm of positivity. Thus, despite its contrary political impulses (as I will show in my reading of Iain Chambers), it is aligned uncritically (by liberalism and postmodernism) in an analogical relationship with multiculturalism and thus faces the consequence of melancholia or debilitation. To elaborate: what this subdiscipline is perceived to offer today that, ostensibly, no other minority or ethnic studies does is not so much a revolutionary method, inventive theories, or even new fields of inquiry, but quite literally (and perhaps crudely) an exotic new frontier, a hitherto unaccounted-for margin that must be tamed or theorized: it is here we tell ourselves that a theory will be made that will express in dazzling synchronicity and relationality the disparate and incorrigible issues of race, ethnicity, gender, nation, class, and Eurocentrism, as well as the conditions of marginality, migration, and minoritization. For many scholars situated outside of the field, postcolonial cultural studies seems to or is exhorted to offer the possibility of a radically revised history: a relentlessly dissident method of reading that will alter the way business is done in and out of academia. An excellent and particularly compelling example of this kind of exhortation is Iain Chambers's *Migrancy, Culture, Identity*, in many ways an exemplary book.

In the chapter entitled "The Broken World," Chambers argues that the presence of increasingly vocal postcolonials in the metropolis not only challenges the univocity of European thought construed as reason, logic, universal, and objective but further confounds the comfortable binarisms of self and other, margin and periphery, English and native. The significant consequence of this disruption of categories, according to Chambers, however, is the exposure of the notion of authenticity: its fascist potential when deployed as Europeanness or Englishness, and its derivativeness when deployed simplistically as Negritude (*pace* Senghor) or nativism. For Chambers, unlike Taylor, authenticity is not a subjective category but a structural one that positions actors outside modernity. "To relinquish such a perspective" of authenticity or of returning to the roots, writes Chambers (quoting Johannes Fabian), "leads us to recognise a post-colonial and post-European context in which historical and cultural differences, while moving to different rhythms, are coeval, are bound to a common time. 'Communication is, ultimately, about creating shared Time'" (74). In other words, insofar as (that suspect category of) authenticity, either of the self or the objectifiable other, is enabled by the imperialist logic of modernity that positions others as occupying another temporality, the recognition of coevality in the postcolonial world means that claiming authenticity is no longer "feasible." "Post-colonialism is perhaps the sign of an increasing awareness that it is not feasible to subtract a culture, a history, a language, an identity, from the wider, transforming currents of the increasingly metropolitan world. It is impossible to 'go home' again" (74). For Chambers, the poetics of postmodernism best expresses this condition of homelessness and inevitable hybridity. Naming the cultural fusions in world music and other art forms as the "metropolitan vernacular," he interestingly circumvents the Marxist problematic of postmodern aesthetics as a symptom of late capitalism by resorting to the notion of local market demands versus the totalizing agency of capitalism (76–77).[7] Further, he asks: Are phenomena such as world music not engaging in

> a movement of historical decentering in which the very axis of center and periphery, together with its economic, political and cultural traffic, has, as a minimum, begun to be interrogated from elsewhere, from other places and positions? For is it not possible to glimpse in recent musical contaminations, hybrid languages and cultural mixtures an opening on to other worlds, experiences, histories, in which not only does the "Empire write back to the center," as Salman Rushdie puts it, but also "sounds off" against it? [...] The master's language is transformed into creole [...] and all varieties of local cultural refashioning, as it moves to a different tempo in a "reversal of colonial history." (84–85)

What is most commendable about Chambers's analysis is his insistence that the margin/centre dichotomy be thoroughly dispersed. >From within this productive confusion, he suggests, may arise two consequences: the exposure of the state apparatus in all its repressive and ideological operations and a recognition of the implication of the citizenry in all forms of repression:

> Previous margins – ethnic, gendered, sexual – now reappear at the center. No longer restricted to the category of a "special issue" (*e.g.* "race relations"), or "problem" (*e.g.* "ethnic minorities," "sexual deviancy"), such differences become central to our very sense of time, place and identity. (86)

Despite (or perhaps because of) his utopian futurism, however, there are several logical problems in Chambers's argument. First is his inadvertent totalization of the postcolonial subject. In his single-minded determination to blow up the centre, the postcolonial construed as the logical agent of sedition is made to carry the bomb. Less metaphorically, it is Chambers's assumption that all migrant subjects inevitably constitute a subculture that is untenable. It is this unstated assumption that enables him to construct pantheons of black artists (68–69) and postcolonial discourse theorists (70)[8] as being collectively (even consensually) engaged in the critique of the Occident in a manner that elides serious differences between these writers and ignores these writers as occupying (academically and performatively) an internally conflictual space. As Stuart Hall puts it with reference to black British cinema,

> Films are not necessarily good because black people make them. They are not necessarily "right-on" by virtue of the fact that they deal with the black experience. Once you enter the politics of the end of the black

subject you are plunged headlong into the maelstrom of a continuously contingent, unguaranteed, political argument and debate: a critical politics, a politics of criticism. You can no longer conduct black politics through the strategy of a simple set of reversals, putting in the place of the bad old essential white subject, the new essentially good black subject. Now, that formulation may seem to threaten the collapse of an entire political world. (28)

In other words, Chambers's vision of resistance does not enter into that phase of political engagement that Hall rightly has characterized as the shift from a "relations of representation," which involves counter-racist narratives and a struggle over the access to representation, to a "politics of representation," which involves theorizing not only the differences of race, ethnicity, and culture but also the "struggle around positionalities" (28):

There is another position, one which locates itself *inside* a continuous struggle and politics around black representation, but which then is able to open up a continuous critical discourse about themes, about the forms of representation, the subjects of representations, above all, the regimes of representation. Once you abandon essential categories, there is no place to go apart from the politics of criticism and to enter the politics of criticism in black culture is to grow up, to leave the age of critical innocence. (30)

Secondly, in his critique of authenticity secured by the argument about temporal non-coevality, Chambers elides Fabian's recommendation to "create" coevality for proper communication with a "recognition" of coevality given the condition of postcolonialism. Thus coevality, or the lack of it, becomes merely false consciousness; what is important, Chambers seems to suggest, is that we recognize that we are "really," that is to say, "authentically," coeval. The problem with this logic is twofold. First, the situating of authenticity as a spatial category, and that of hybridity as a temporal one, effectively locates authenticity (insofar as space is conceived non-historically) on another temporal register outside the transforming currents of time. Second, authenticity is somehow made to depend on disjunct temporalities and vice versa, and thus the absolute pronouncement – one can never go home again. Thus the postcolonial is not only always-already hybrid, but she is so always with reference to the West. What Chambers is unable to visualize in his delineation of postcolonial ontology, which is really an idealization of the migrant as postcolonial paradigm, are forms of cultural practice – musical or otherwise – that adapt to and march in step with Western hegemony but define themselves as "authentic" insofar as they continue to be indifferent to the West for purposes of validation, perpetuation, and aesthetic evaluation. This form of authenticity, however, must be distinguished from Taylor's more subjectivist and essentialist notion. In other words, authenticity can be better understood in performative rather than ontological terms. The vigorous state of traditional music in the North and South of India is an example of this form of authenticity, and its practitioners not only presuppose the possibility of going home but would probably argue (despite their itinerant lifestyles) that they have never left in the first place.[9] In other words, I am suggesting that Chambers's implication of authenticity in non-coevality is a *non sequitur* and has the curious effect of recasting the erstwhile "dead native" as hybrid. The overall effect, as I implied earlier, is the construction of the postcolonial as an authentically dissident or marginal subject. It is in response to this interpellation that postcolonial studies falls into melancholia and sometimes political disarray.

While it may appear that Taylor's liberal multiculturalism and Chambers's dissonant politics of "no respect" are aversive, what is interesting in both their analyses is the way in which the terms "authenticity," "hierarchy," and "margin" carry enormous burdens of significance. Briefly: while for Taylor (the recognition of) authenticity as "a vital human need" (26) is an individualist category that directly impinges on one's self-esteem and sense of well-being, for Chambers, authenticity is a structural notion, a subject position – an impossibility in the modern world because it implies hierarchy: "Subordinate subjects have invariably been ordained to the stereotyped immobilism of an essential 'authenticity,' in which they are expected to play out roles, designated for them by others [...] for ever" (38). Hierarchy, for Taylor, means non-reciprocal "other dependence" (44–51); for Chambers, it means temporal non-coevality. For Taylor, hierarchy can be undone with respect and recognition (temporality and modernity being non-factors in his analysis); for Chambers, on the other hand, hierarchy can be undone only through hybridity and confusion of categories. Modernity, as Chambers construes it, is univocal and imperialist and cannot accommodate authentic differences.[10] Both Taylor and Chambers agree, then, that equality and difference are contradictory and inevitably based on a notion of sameness. Yet Taylor is willing to let the contradiction lie, while Chambers wants to create equality in order that difference becomes a basis for identity rather than alienation. For Taylor, the margin is "them," the others who must be dealt with and managed: "The challenge is to deal with their sense of marginalization without compromising our basic political principles" (63). The West, he implies, is guilty and can redress the problem. For Chambers, the margin is the site of subversion – it must be made to arrive at the centre and disrupt it. For both Taylor and Chambers, however, as I mentioned earlier, the margin is a source of rejuvenation. A future moment must be posited when it will be either incorporated or dissolved and hierarchy will be undone.

Gayatri Spivak has addressed most notably the profound contradictions of this liberal/postmodern demand in her essay "Who Claims Alterity?" Regarding the position of marginality (construed as a potentially subversive space) sometimes claimed by but often imposed upon postcolonial subjects, Spivak writes of this ideological entrapment:

> [T]he stories of the postcolonial world are not necessarily the same as the stories coming from "internal colonization," the way the metropolitan countries discriminate against disenfranchised groups in their midst. The diasporic postcolonial can take advantage (most often unknowingly, I hasten to add) of the tendency to conflate the two in the metropolis. Thus this frequently innocent informant, identified and welcomed as the agent of an alternative history, may indeed be the site of a chiasmus, the crossing of a double contradiction: the system of production of the national bourgeoisie at home, and abroad, the tendency to represent neocolonialism by the semiotic of "internal colonization." (274–75)

The consequence of this poorly analyzed double contradiction is that by homogenizing and masking the contingent otherness of postcoloniality into an undifferentiated margin, the political efficacy of a "postcolonial" critique is weakened considerably. However, it is actually in its points of differentiation from such homogenizing notions of the margin, more precisely in its critique of positive knowledge alluded to earlier, that postcolonial studies faces its greatest challenges. It is not simply that being marginal is no longer a possibility, but that some of the ways in which the margin as sign and standard (as a measure of value and as political cause) get deployed produce some of the impasses in our field.

We can conceive of margin/marginality in two ways: a) as subject position – the excluded other that must be coaxed into the centre through incorporation, inversion, hybridization, revolution; or b) as irreducible other – the condition for the production of our discourse (and all positive knowledge) that must be acknowledged as asymmetrical and irrecuperable. The former speaks the positive discourse of rights; the latter the negative discourse of limits.[11] In *The Order of Things*, Michel Foucault characterizes the modern episteme as marked by the emergence of Man in his finite spatiality as the object of positive knowledge:

> At the foundation of all the empirical positivities, and of everything that can indicate itself as a concrete limitation of man's existence, we discover a finitude – which is in a sense the same: it is marked by the spatiality

of the body, the yawning of desire, and the time of language; and yet
it is radically other: in this sense, the limitation is expressed not as a
determination imposed upon man from outside (because he has a nature
or a history), but as a fundamental finitude which rests on nothing but
its own existence as fact, and opens upon the positivity of all concrete
limitation. (315)

In other words, it is no longer a question of knowing the limits of knowledge,
as with classical philosophy, but of discerning the constitutive negativity, the
otherness, the irrecuperable, the "unthought" that makes positive knowing
possible.[12] It is this latter notion of the margin, of course, that has enabled
the most powerful critiques of anthropology, orientalism, and comparative
philology.[13] Said's *Orientalism*, which was the first significant attempt to
disclose the constitutive function of this margin for Western knowledge,
attests to the fact that such critiques are often implicit in the deconstruction
of the "metaphysics of presence"; more explicitly, they may be channelled
through Foucault's notions of the limit and of power/knowledge. That so
many analyses of colonialism, following in the wake of Said's work, have
reiterated the shadow of this margin is the precise bone of contention between
postcolonialists and a so-called orthodox Marxism, represented most vocally
by Aijaz Ahmad, who attacked Said's *Orientalism* in his *In Theory: Classes,
Nations, Literatures*. But let us attend in greater detail, if briefly, to Ahmad's
problems with a so-called postcolonial discourse.

In his essay "The Politics of Literary Postcoloniality," Ahmad characterizes
postcolonial literature and cultural criticism as offsprings of a postmodernism that they disseminate zealously (10).[14] Ahmad does not explain what he
specifically means by the term *postmodernism* (other than by positing the
untenable proposition that it is an anti-Marxism), nor does he explain why
the term should be self-evidently disparaging. Rather, he illustrates his thesis
that postcolonialism is the progeny of postmodernism by fastening on short
passages from Gayatri Spivak and Homi Bhabha and then performing close
readings of them after the manner of deconstructive literary critics. While
there is much in Ahmad's essay that merits close attention, I shall focus on his
interpretation of Spivak and those themes that he designates as characteristic
of postcolonial postmodernity – hybridity and contingency (ambivalence is
mentioned but not analyzed) – to show that despite his call for a return to a
fundamental Marxism, his own critique is caught up in the contradictions
that attend totalizations of any kind, be they Marxist or postcolonialist.

For instance, in his reading of Spivak's often-quoted passage in which she
asserts that the concept metaphors of "nationhood, constitutionality, citizenship, democracy, socialism" are "effectively reclaimed" in postcoloniality as

"regulative political concepts" for which "no historically adequate referent may be advanced from postcolonial space" ("Scattered Speculations" 281), Ahmad mounts his polemic on what turns out to be a contradictory ground. In his quotation, he elides the following: Spivak says, "Within the historical frame of exploration, colonization, and decolonization, what is *effectively* reclaimed is a series of regulative political concepts, the supposedly authoritative narrative of whose production was written elsewhere, in the social formations of Western Europe" (281). By choosing to elide the question of ideological regulation, which invokes Althusser's notion of ideology (in general) as having no history,[15] Ahmad can read the phrase "no historically adequate referent" literally as about "political history" (4). There is socialism and nationalism in India, he reminds us; we only have to remember the masses who vote for the communist ticket and the fact that it was the nationalist struggle and not colonialism that invested India with nationhood. The literalism here is a consequence of what Ahmad marginalizes: Spivak's insistence that socialism, nationalism, etc., insofar as they function as regulative political concepts, effectively resituate struggle within the frame of imperialism. This is not a denial of history but a comment on the limits of historiography itself. Yet the literalism permits Ahmad to read ideological critique here as free-floating dehistoricizing postmodernism, thus re-enacting, in the name of Marx, what Spivak problematizes: ideological regulation. Yet Ahmad is not consistently an orthodox Marxist, for in his consideration that perhaps Spivak is speaking of these concepts in terms of "the European origin of these words" (5), he expresses his consternation thus:

> Even with regard to concepts, I did not know that mere origins – ("myth of origins?") – mattered all that much in postmodern discourse, nor does it seem appropriate that everything that originates in Europe should be consigned so unilaterally to the "heritage of imperialism," unless we subscribe to an essentialist notion of an undifferentiated Europe where everything and everyone is imperialist. (5)

Here the problem with Spivak is that she is not being constructionist enough for Ahmad, and is slipping into a premodern "dangerous" notion of origins and essences. From what was first a charge of too much postmodernism, Ahmad now castigates Spivak for not being postmodern enough for his purposes.

Nevertheless, postmodernism continues to function as a peculiar catch-all phrase of derision for Ahmad, usefully encapsulating poststructuralism, deconstruction, and, of course, colonial discourses. The most egregious example of this totalizing impulse is evident in his critique of Bhabha's notion of hybridity. What is peculiar in Ahmad's reading of Bhabha is that he attributes a "celebratory" tone to the latter, believing that the notion "partakes of a carnivalesque collapse and play of identities, and comes under a great many names" (13). While it may be beside the point to engage in an argument on the "correct" interpretation of hybridity, which I understand to mean not an arbitrary mixture of cultures and a surplus of pleasure but the uncanny and undermining effect produced by the incompatibility of discourses in unequal power relations,[16] it must be acknowledged that the notion of carnivalesque subversion is more evocative of Bakhtin than of Bhabha. Ahmad's real quarrel with Bhabha's notion of hybridity, however, is twofold: a) it dispenses with "a sense of place, of belonging, of some stable commitment to one's class or gender or nation [which] may be useful for defining one's politics"; and b) it is "posited as the negation of the 'organic intellectual' as Gramsci conceived of it" (14). The point about stable identities is an old one; we have already encountered it in relation to Charles Taylor. The fact that such stability may not be easily available in this age of total capitalist penetration and that, in fact, such (commodified) commitment to "one's class," at this historical moment, may produce fascisms of the sort Ahmad himself laments in India and elsewhere is not considered at all. This is because Ahmad is not so much interested in the question of the nature or grounds of political commitment but rather in the deployment of Marx and Gramsci as prophylactics of postmodernism. Thus Bhabha's bracketing of the organic intellectual is again read as travesty rather than on its own terms. While I do not want to open a discussion of Gramsci's concepts or Bhabha's reading of them at this point, it would be salutary to recall Gramsci's declared view of intellectual orthodoxy in his "The Study of Philosophy":

> Who is to fix the "rights of knowledge" and the limits of the pursuit of knowledge? And can these rights and limits indeed be fixed? It seems necessary to leave the task of researching after new truths and better, more coherent, clearer formulations of the truths themselves to the free initiative of individual specialists, even though they may continually question the very principles that seem most essential. (*Selections* 341)

"Organic intellectual" is not a term that transparently signifies social good. Like everything else, the possibilities of such leadership need to be "elaborated," in the Gramscian sense of the term, in its contingent and specific historicity.

This leads us to the next point that Ahmad invokes as characteristic of postcolonial postmodernity – the theme of contingency as mediated once again through Bhabha's quotation of Veena Das (Ahmad, "Politics" 14–15). For Ahmad, the emphasis on the contingent nature of a given (caste or class) conflict is an act of de-historicization and political passivity. It is de-historicizing because it recommends that "when it comes to caste conflicts, each historical moment must be treated as *sui generis* and as carrying within itself its own explanation [...] [and] that the understanding of each conflict be confined to the characteristics of that conflict. [...] What is denied [...] is that caste is a structural and not merely contingent feature in the distribution of powers and privileges" (15). Furthermore, "when the theorist [...] denies the structural endurance of histories and calls upon us to think only of the contingent moment[,] we are in effect being called upon to overlook the position of class and caste privileges from which such theories emanate and such invocations issue" (15). The consequence of such anti-structuralist analysis for Ahmad is political passivity:

> Such premises preclude [...] the very bases of political action. For the idea of collective human agent (*e.g.*, organised groups of the exploited castes fighting for their rights against upper-caste privilege) presumes both what Habermas calls communicative rationality as well as the possibility of rational action as such; it presumes, in other words, that agencies are constituted not in flux and displacement but in given historical locations. (15–16)

There are at least two unexamined contradictions in Ahmad's argument: a) the opposition between the historicity of conflict and contingency, and b) the alliance between a structural reading of history and rational action. Much of the problem has to do with Ahmad's untheorized notion of conflict and its relation to history in the first place. For Bhabha, as I understand him, the analysis of conflict as contingency is reliant on the notion of conflict as constitutive of history or historical change rather than on a view of conflict as a factor in an idealist progression of an objective and real history. In Ernesto Laclau's terms, in so far as "identities and their conditions of existence form an inseparable whole" (21), "the conditions of existence of any objectivity that might exist must be sought at the level of a factual history" (22). For instance, to such a question as "Is the English revolution of the seventeenth century the bourgeois-democratic revolution?" Laclau responds:

> The "bourgeois-democratic revolution," far from being an object to be identified in different latitudes (France, England, Italy) – an object that would therefore establish relations of exteriority with its specific conditions of existence in different contexts – would instead be an object that is deformed and redefined by each of its contingent contexts. There would merely be "family resemblances" between the different "bourgeois-democratic revolutions." This allows the formulation of questions such as: how bourgeois was the democratic revolution in the country X?; or rather, how democratic was the bourgeoisie in context Y? (22)

Thus, for Laclau, and for "postcolonials" such as Bhabha and Das, the analysis of conflict requires that "the very categories of social analysis [...] be historicized" (Laclau 22) in a movement that "radically contextualizes" rather than de-historicizes conflict.

Furthermore, Ahmad concludes that radical historicization or contingency, because it involves no structural understanding of history, is incompatible with "communicative action" (in Habermas's sense of the term). In doing so, he generates a further confusion by collapsing structuralist theories of history with the more consciousness-based theories of Habermas and even Lukács. The relationship between Habermas's notion of communicative action (which is based on Enlightenment notions of progress) and the more structural notions of history (which one associates with Althusser and Balibar) does not seem self-evident or in any way a logical connection. Again, the problem here is Ahmad's refusal to engage with the fundamental question of identity as such; thus his analysis falls into a kind of idealism that Gramsci would characterize as "common sense." My point is that Ahmad's denunciation of postcolonialism as anti-Marxist (due to its association with postmodernism) seems highly dubious given that Marxism is not some sort of ready-made grid that can be imposed upon social realities; rather, Marxism is itself a highly conflictual discourse whose terms and concepts must be constantly negotiated if they are to be made useful. The fact remains that issues of ideology, structure, and conflict or historical change, insofar as they must be negotiated and redefined in their contingency, do radically call into question our totalization of knowledge. To dismiss such inquiry as ludic postmodernism because of its compatibility with Derrida's critiques of philosophy or with Foucault's rewriting of historiography seems hasty at best and authoritarian at worst. The problem with Ahmad's criticisms of postcolonial discourse is that he refuses to acknowledge, at the fundamental level of political orientation (*i.e.*, the investment in class and race politics), the continuity between his own position and that which he repudiates as the brood of postmodernism.

But to return to the question of postcolonial studies as marginality studies: one consequence of deploying an undifferentiated notion of the margin is that postcolonial studies has been stereotyped as an acceptable form of academic radicalism.[17] This has meant that scholars, once intimately – even emblematically – associated with the postcolonial, resort to distancing themselves from this "PC" term by denouncing it from within. What it comes down to is an anxiety over the loss of the margin, which results in the redrawing of lines and a struggle over the margin itself. As R. Radhakrishnan puts it in "Postcoloniality and the Boundaries of Identity,"

the critic intellectual is divorced from the politics of solidarity and
constituency. The critic is forever looking for that radical "elsewhere" that
will validate "perennial readings against the grain," and the intellectual
is busy planning multiple transgressions to avoid being located
ideologically and/or macropolitically. (761)

The notion of the margin as the site of struggle for the outermost limit, then,
takes on a new meaning as it is fetishized and reified as the "dislocated" and
authoritative *critical position*, which then reveals the "real" stake in these
battles: the margin as turf.[18]

My task here is not to ride out in defence of postcolonial studies, even if
such an object existed for the purpose. Rather, what I am interested in are
the consequences that attend the deployment of an undifferentiated notion
of the margin. I suggest that the exploration of postcoloniality from the point
of view of the margin (as the excluded and the limit) can be thought of as
the realm of postcolonial scholarship. While we cannot cease to uncover the
politics of marginalization that provides the impetus to criticism, we also need
to conceive of the "politics of criticism" as elaborated by Stuart Hall as an
ironic project. By this I mean that postcolonialism must rehearse continually
the conditions for the production of its own discourse or be doomed to fall
into a form of anthropology.[19] As Barbara Johnson suggests in the context of
deconstructio, "any discourse that is based on the questioning of boundary
lines must never stop questioning its own" (14). If postcolonial studies can be
said to possess any pedagogical efficacy at all, then that energy arises from its
indeterminate location and failure to recoup the margin. The conflationary
(counter) critiques mentioned above, then, cannot be located "outside" of
the field and thereby be made to engender what Said, in his "Intellectuals in
the Post-Colonial World," terms a "politics of blame." It is undeniable that
the debates generated by these critiques are not only salient to the project
of postcolonial studies but are themselves indicative of the thankful lack
of triumphalism of the field – or so it seems, as long as they do not divert
discussion from the issues about larger material determinants to a skirmish
over or at the margin. To quote R. Radhakrishnan again,

> Postcoloniality at best is a problematic field where heated debates and
> contestations are bound to take place for quite a while to come. My
> point here is that whoever joins the polemical dialogue should do so
> with a critical-sensitive awareness of the legitimacies of several other
> perspectives on the issue. In other words, it would be quite futile and
> divisive in the long run for any one perspective such as the diasporic, the
> indigenous, the orthodox Marxist, etc., to begin with the

> brazen assumption that it alone has the ethico-political right to speak
> representatively on behalf of "postcoloniality." Such an assumption can
> only take the form of a pedagogical arrogance that is interested more
> in correcting other points of view rather than engaging with them in a
> spirit of reciprocity. No one historical angle can have a monopolistic hold
> over the possible elaborations of the "post-colony," especially during
> times when master discourses in general, *e.g.* modernity, nationalism,
> international Communism/Marxism, are deservedly in disarray. (762)

Another reason for the lack of triumphalism of postcolonial studies pertains to its institutional and theoretical amorphousness: it has no theory to speak of, concerned as it is with micro-cultural and micro-political practices and issues. Unlike other area studies, postcolonial studies has no identifiable object: it would be impossible to suggest that it pertains to one or the other area of the world or that it is confined to a period, genre, or theme; nor can it name a stable First or Third World subject as its legitimate speaker (as can, for instance, women's studies, Afro-American studies, or gay and lesbian studies). >From this perspective, it may be acceptable to claim that postcolonial studies is concerned more with the analysis of the lived *condition* of unequal power-sharing globally and the self-authorization of cultural, economic, and militaristic hegemony than with a particular historical phenomenon such as colonialism, which may be plotted as a stage of capitalist imperialism. It is interested, above all, in the materialist critique of power and how that power or ideology seeks to interpellate subjects within a discourse as subordinate and without agency. In some ways, it is this amorphousness that permits it to be simultaneously self-critical and oppositional. As well, it is this free-form aspect of postcolonial studies that makes it the target of both the Right and the so-called Left. Yet perhaps it is this shapelessness, this refusal to stay still, to define itself or defend itself, that makes postcolonial studies a particularly hospitable interstice from which to work out the paradoxes of history (the temporality of modernity) and colony (imperialism and nationalism).

Notes

1 As R. Radhakrishnan points out, "The important thing to notice here is the overall culturalist mode of operation: in other words, we are not talking about postcolonial economies, histories, or politics. The obsessive focus is on postcoloniality as a cultural conjuncture" (751).

2 See Ella Shohat's essay "Notes on the 'Post-Colonial'" for an elaboration of this theme.

3 Apter writes: "It seems that the theoretical and political categories of postcolonialism, even as they burgeon and become increasingly sophisticated, are also becoming more rapidly used up and, in many instances, altogether bankrupt. Preludes and prefaces that take great pains

to situate the writer/viewer in a redemptive practice that is ultimately a reenactment of just what she or he is trying to avoid (the voyeurism of 'other-gazing'), all these verbal markers and narrative devices repeat the colonial gesture of self-authorization" (299).

4   In an essay written in 1991, Vijay Mishra and Bob Hodge argue that Bill Ashcroft, Gareth Griffiths, and Helen Tiffin's *The Empire Writes Back* (1989) was the first attempt to substitute the erstwhile category of Commonwealth literature with that of postcolonial writing. Although this book came out eleven years after Said's *Orientalism,* which most scholars consider as the inaugural text of the field, I agree with Hodge and Mishra that for all of its problems, *The Empire Writes Back* did perform an important pedagogical function:it put a teachable text on the market that summarized the limits and possibilities of this new field of inquiry. Hodge and Mishra's essay has been reprinted recently in a reader entitled *Colonial Discourse and Post-Colonial Theory,* edited by Patrick Williams and Laura Chrisman. This reader reprints the seminal essays marking the debates and concerns of the field. For other notable anthologies of postcolonial "theory," see Adam and H. Tiffin; Slemon and H. Tiffin; Whitlock and H. Tiffin; Ashcroft, Griffiths, and H. Tiffin (The Post-Colonial Studies Reader); C. Tiffin and Lawson; and White.

5   For a characterization of affirmative action as a recognition of past historical injustice see Shelby Steele's problematic but nevertheless important argument in *The Content of Our Character: A New Vision of Race in America* (1990), chapter 7.

6   See also S.P. Mohanty's "Us and Them" and Anthony Appiah's "The Postcolonial and the Postmodern."

7   For an explanation of the "Marxist problematic," see Harvey, *The Condition of Modernity,* and Jameson, *Postmodernism or, the Cultural Logic of Late Capitalism.*

8   For instance: here, in the crisis of enunciation, we can also recognize a potential convergence of radical feminist theory – Luce Irigaray, Carla Lonzi, Hélène Cixous, Alice Jardine, Rosi Braidotti, Jane Flax, Susan Hekman, Judith Butler – with its sustained critique of the presumptions of occidental discourse: a convergence that is directly inscribed in the work of Gayatri Spivak, Trinh. T. Minh-ha, bell hooks, Paul Gilroy, and Homi Bhabha, for example, and that is destined for greater dialogue (70).

9   See James Clifford's "Travelling Theories" for a discussion of this notion of authenticity.

10   For excellent reconsideration of the monological views of modernity, see Fuchs.

11   I am indebted to Drucilla Cornell's monumental book *The Philosophy of the Limit* for an understanding of this concept as a primarily ethical demarcation. See especially chapter 3.

12   For a neo-Marxist formulation of negativity (as the critique of reason and totalizing politics) as the foundation of radical politics and history, see Laclau.

13   See Bernal; Clifford and Marcus; and Said, "Representing the Colonized: Anthropology's Interlocutors."

14   He writes: "[T]he term 'postcolonial' also comes to us as the name of a discourse about the condition of 'postcoloniality,' so that certain kinds of critics are 'postcolonial' and others not. [...] Following on which is the attendant assertion that only those critics, who believe not only that colonialism has more or less ended but who also subscribe to the idea of the end of Marxism, nationalism, collective historical subjects and revolutionary possibility as such, are the true postcolonials, while the rest of us, who do not quite accept this apocalyptic anti-Marxism, are not postcolonial at all [...] so that only those intellectuals can be truly postcolonial who are also postmodern" (10).

15   See the section on ideology in Althusser's "Ideology and Ideological State Apparatuses" (159– 61).

16   See Bhabha's essays "Signs Taken for Wonders" and "Articulating the Archaic" in *The Location of Culture.*

17   For an understanding of the concept of stereotyping, see Bhabha, "The Other Question."

18   It can be argued that the skirmish over the margin is not peculiar to postcolonial studies, and that feminism, in fact, seems to be at the centre of such battles. The siege of a perceived orthodox feminism by an ostensibly radical feminist wing is a sign of such battles. However,

what is distinctive about postcolonial battles over the margin is the way in which the very terms and field of study are themselves contested, with the metaphor of the subaltern acting as the category of de-legitimation.

19 For a sweeping though provocative critique of so-called postcolonial cultural studies' failure to conceive of colonialism in plural and local terms, see Thomas.

Works Cited

Adam, Ian, and Helen Tiffin, eds. *Past the Last Post: Theorizing Post-Colonialism and Post-Modernism*. 1990. Hartfordshire, UK: Harvester Wheatsheaf, 1991.

Ahmad, Aijaz. *In Theory: Classes, Nations, Literatures*. New York: Verso, 1992.

——. "The Politics of Literary Postcoloniality." *Race and Class* 36 (1995): 1–20.

Althusser, Louis. "Ideology and Ideological State Apparatuses (Notes Towards an Investigation)." *Lenin and Philosophy and Other Essays*. Trans. Ben Brewster. New York: Monthly Review, 1971. 127–86.

Appiah, Anthony. "The Postcolonial and the Postmodern." *In My Father's House: Africa in the Philosophy of Culture*. New York: Oxford University Press, 1992. 137–57.

Apter, Emily. "Ethnographic Travesties: Colonial Realism, French Feminism, and the Case of Elissa Rhais." *After Colonialism: Imperial Histories and Postcolonial Displacements*. Ed. Gyan Prakash. New Jersey: Princeton University Press, 1995. 299–325.

Ashcroft, Bill, Gareth Griffiths, and Helen Tiffin. *The Empire Writes Back: Theory and Practice in Post-Colonial Literatures*. London: Routledge, 1989.

——. eds. *The Post-Colonial Studies Reader*, New York: Routledge, 1995.

Bakhtin, Mikhail. *Rabelais and His World*. Trans. Helene Iswolsky. Bloomington: Indiana University Press, 1984.

Balibar, Etienne, and Immanuel Wallerstein. *Race, Nation, Class: Ambiguous Identities*. New York: Verso, 1991.

Bernal, Martin. *Black Athena: The Afroasiatic Roots of Classical Civilization*. Vol. 1. New Brunswick: Rutgers University Press, 1987.

Bhabha, Homi. *The Location of Culture*. New York: Routledge, 1994.

——. "The Other Question: Stereotype, Discrimination and the Discourse of Colonialism." *The Location of Culture*. New York: Routledge, 1994.

Brooks, Peter. "Colleges Need to Question, Not Just Celebrate, Western Values." *New York Times* 19 December 1994: A18.

Chambers, Iain. *Migrancy, Culture, Identity*. London: Routledge, 1994.

Clifford, James. "Travelling Theories." *Cultural Studies*. Ed. Lawrence Grossberg, Cary Nelson, and Paula Treichler. New York: Routledge, 1992. 96–116.

Clifford, James, and George Marcus. *Writing Culture: The Poetics and Politics of Ethnography*. Berkeley: University of California Press, 1986.

Cornell, Drucilla. *The Philosophy of the Limit*. New York: Routledge, 1992.

Dirlik, Arif. "The Postcolonial Aura: Third World Criticism in the Age of Global Capitalism." *Critical Inquiry* 20 (1994): 328–56.

Fabian, Johannes. *Time and the Other*. New York: Columbia University Press, 1983.

Foucault, Michel. *The Order of Things: An Archaeology of the Human Sciences*. New York: Vintage, 1973.

Fuchs, Martin. Introduction. "India and Modernity: Decentering Western Perspectives." Special issue of *Thesis Eleven* 39 (1994): v–xiii.

Gramsci, Antonio. *Selections from the Prison Notebooks*. Trans. Quintin Hoare and Geoffrey Nowell Smith. New York: International Publishers, 1971.

Habermas, Jürgen. *The Philosophical Discourse of Modernity: Twelve Lectures*. Trans. Frederick G. Lawrence. Cambridge: MIT Press, 1987.

Hall, Stuart. "New Ethnicities." *Black Film British Cinema*. Ed. Kobena Mercer. London: ICA Documents 7, 1988. 27–31.

Harvey, David. *The Condition of Postmodernity*. Oxford: Blackwell, 1990.

Jameson, Fredric. *Postmodernism or, the Cultural Logic of Late Capitalism*. Durham: Duke University Press, 1991.

Johnson, Barbara. "Nothing Fails Like Success." *A World of Difference*. Baltimore: Johns Hopkins University Press, 1987. 11–16.

Laclau, Ernesto. "New Reflections on the Revolution of Our Time." Trans. Jon Barnes. *New Reflections on the Revolution of Our Time*. London: Verso, 1990. 3–85.

Mishra, Vijay, and Bob Hodge. "What is Post(-)Colonialism?" 1991. Williams and Chrisman 276–90.

Mohanty, S.P. "Us and Them: On the Philosophical Bases of Political Criticism." *The Yale Journal of Criticism* 2 (1989): 1–32.

Pratt, Mary Louise. *Imperial Eyes: Travel Writing and Transculturation*. New York: Routledge, 1992.

Radhakrishnan, R. "Postcolonialism and the Boundaries of Identity." *Callaloo* 16 (1993): 750–71.

Rouse, Roger. "Thinking through Transnationalism: Notes on the Cultural Politics of Class Relations in the Contemporary United States." *Public Culture* 7 (1995): 353–402.

Said, Edward. "Intellectuals in the Post-Colonial World." *Salmagundi* 70–71 (1986): 44–81.

——. *Orientalism*. New York: Vintage, 1978.

——. "Representing the Colonized: Anthropology's Interlocutors." *Critical Inquiry* 15 (1989): 205–25.

Schor, Naomi. "The Righting of French Studies: Homosociality and the Killing of 'La pensée 68.'" *Profession* 92. New York: MLA, 1992. 28–34.

Shohat, Ella. "Notes on the 'Post-Colonial.'" *Social Text* 31/32 (1992): 99–113.

Slemon, Stephen, and Helen Tiffin, eds. *After Europe: Critical Theory and Postcolonial Writing*. Mundelstrup: Dangaroo, 1989.

——. "Scattered Speculations on the Question of Cultural Studies." *Outside in the Teaching Machine*. New York: Routledge, 1993. 255–84.

——. "'What Is It For?' Gayatri Chakravorty Spivak on the Functions of the Postcolonial Critic." Interview with Gloria-Jean Masciarotte. *Nineteenth-Century Contexts: An Interdisciplinary Journal* 18 (1994): 71–81.

——. "Who Claims Alterity?" *Remaking History*. Ed. Barbara Kruger and Phil Mariani. Seattle: Bay Press, 1989. 269–92.

Steele, Shelby. *The Content of Our Character: A New Vision of Race in America*. New York: St Martin's, 1990.

Taylor, Charles. "The Politics of Recognition." *Multiculturalism: Examining the Politics of Recognition*. Ed. Amy Gutmann. New York: Routledge, 1994. 25–73.

Thomas, Nicholas. *Colonialism's Culture: Anthropology, Travel, Government*. New Jersey: Princeton University Press, 1994.

Tiffin, Chris, and Alan Lawson, eds. *De-Scribing Empire: Post-Coloniality and Textuality*. New York: Routledge, 1994.

White, Jonathan, ed. *Recasting the World: Writing after Colonialism*. Baltimore: Johns Hopkins University Press, 1993.

Whitlock, Gillian, and Helen Tiffin, eds. *Re-Siting Queen's English: Text and Tradition in Post-Colonial Literatures*. Atlanta: Rodopi, 1992.

Williams, Patrick, and Laura Chrisman, eds. *Colonial Discourse and Postcolonial Theory*. New York: Columbia University Press, 1993.

Yudice, George. "Marginality and the Ethics of Survival." *Universal Abandon? The Politics of Postmodernism*. Minneapolis: University of Minnesota Press, 1988. 214–36.

Introduction: The Linked Histories of the Globalized World   The Fascist Longings in our Midst   Queer with Class: Absence of Third World Sweatshop in Lesbian/Gay Discourse and a Rearticulation of Materialist Queer Theory   Cross-Mirrorings of Alterity: The Colonial Scenario and Its Psychological Legacy   Mythologies of Migrancy: Post-colonialism, Postmodernism, and the Politics of (Dis)location   Postcolonial DefferendDifferend: Diasporic Narratives of Salman Rushdie   At the Margins of Postcolonial Studies

Modernity's First Born: Latin America and Postcolonial Transformation   Towards Articulation: Postcolonial Theory and Demotic Resistance   Postcolonial Theory and the "Decolonization" of Chinese Culture

Keeping History
at Wind River and Acoma

MARY LAWLOR

Among the small frame houses and government buildings clustered together at Fort Washakie, Wyoming, a village of 1,700 people on the Wind River Indian Reservation, stands a white Victorian structure that houses the Shoshone Tribal Cultural Center. The building stands out from the prefabricated homes and corrugated sheds that surround it. More stately and aged, it seems a misplaced image of domestic elegance whose height and architecture speak to its importance as a vault of tribal history and a museum of contemporary culture. Yet there is a certain shabbiness about the house – the porch sags, the screen door needs replacing – that suggests that the history and culture preserved there are not, after all, such vital components of life at Fort Washakie.

The idea of a "cultural center," located in a particular place and display-ing objects to satisfy a spectator's curiosity, is in most ways antithetical to traditional Shoshone methods for maintaining history and culture. Oral narratives, ceremonies, and dances performed those functions in the past, and they still have that authority in contemporary life. Yet this museum-archive makes available to non-Indians as well as Indians the elements of Shoshone culture and history that the tribe itself is willing to contribute to the multi-textured fabric of "American" public culture. In this sense, the Cultural Center presents not a gateway nor even a vestibule to the inner sanctums of a more private and sovereign tradition but a sampler of historical material that mutually situates Shoshone and Euro-American cultures in the history of the United States – surely a significant factor in the construction of Shoshone-American identity in the late twentieth century. In this essay I want to offer some observations about the ways that materials of displayed culture and narratives of history offered to the public at Wind River and at a second Indian community, the Acoma Pueblo in New Mexico, both assert a place for Native Americans in the larger picture of U.S. cultural development and, in varying degrees, contest the dominant narratives of European America.

One of the most extensive collections in the Shoshone Cultural Center's archive consists of a series of articles and essays devoted to Sacajawea, the young Shoshone woman who participated in the Lewis and Clark expedition from 1805 to 1806.[1] Originally from the Lemhi Shoshone group of what is now southern Idaho, Sacajawea was abducted in her early teens by a group of Hidatsa hunters and taken to their villages along the northern bend of the Missouri River. Subsequently, Sacajawea came to be in a liaison with the French trapper Toussaint Charbonneau, who very likely bought or won her from the Hidatsa captors.[2] During the autumn of 1804, Charbonneau enlisted with the Lewis and Clark expedition, then quartered near the Mandan villages just south of Hidatsa country. Sacajawea gave birth to her son with Charbonneau, Baptiste, the following winter, and in the spring of 1805, when the expedition set out again for the sources of the Missouri, she and the child accompanied Charbonneau. Her familiarity with the area of the Missouri headwaters was useful to the expedition, and her ability to speak Shoshone was important in negotiations with the people there, whose help was necessary for the expedition's successful portage to the Rocky Mountains.

The written materials at the Shoshone centre offer various details of Sacajawea's contribution to the expedition, but many of them focus particular attention on the narrative of her life afterwards. The course of that life is much debated. One argument has it that she lived for only a few years after the expedition, died in 1812 at approximately the age of twenty-four, and was buried near Fort Manuel, a short-lived trading post on the border of North and South Dakota. This account is for the most part subscribed to by Euro-American historians, whose evidence comes from contemporary diaries and letters of men who encountered Charbonneau and his wife in St. Louis and at Fort Manuel in 1811 and 1812.[3] The other argument constructs a very different story of Sacajawea's life by claiming that she died in 1884 at Wind River, after having lived there for many years as a highly respected member of the community and thus as an important figure in local history.

The Shoshone Cultural Center as an institution supports the latter account, as do most of the Shoshone people living on the reservation today. Several Euro-American writers whose commentaries make up part of the Cultural Center's collections also subscribe to this story, but the 1812 argument is represented as well in the archival materials. Asked if the argument that runs contrary to the Center's own position ever tempted local readers to think differently on this question, a Shoshone researcher told me that no one at Fort Washakie was ever bothered by it because they knew Sacajawea was there, buried outside of their hamlet.

Indeed, a short drive outside of Fort Washakie leads to Sacajawea Cemetery, in the midst of which stands a large gravestone, marked with the epigraph "Sacagawea, A Guide With the Lewis and Clark Expedition, Identified By Reverend J. Roberts Who Officiated at Her Burial." Those who think Sacajawea died at Wind River in 1884 believe she is in fact buried here, and they have named the cemetery after her. Oral histories related by tribal elders in the early twentieth century to the Euro-American researcher Grace Hebard serve now as textual evidence for this identification.[4]

Their story is supported in a statement written in 1935 by John Roberts, an Episcopal minister at Wind River from 1883 until 1945.[5] Roberts explains that the woman he knew as Sacajawea had through the years related to her family incidents of her experience with the Lewis and Clark expedition, and that this information came to him via the Indian agent at the time who had Sacajawea's history from her adopted son, Bazil. As the epigraph indicates, Roberts officiated at her burial in 1884.[6]

In both of these accounts, Sacajawea is considered a brave, generous, and intelligent person whose contributions to the expedition were estimable and whose place in the historical record is highly valued. In this respect, the Shoshone tribal characterization agrees with that of the Cultural Center and, indeed, with that of the culture at large. As an actor in the chronicle of the American nation, Sacajawea has achieved a good deal of popular recognition in the culture at large; and through her the Shoshone people have been acknowledged in mainstream history more than they might have been otherwise. Since her first appearance as a central figure of the Lewis and Clark expedition in Eva Emery Dye's 1902 novel *The Conquest*, she has become the subject of much popular fiction, a virtual icon of U.S. romantic nationalism.

In such a role, Sacajawea might seem to present a figure of ambiguous cultural value among Indian people, since the expedition spearheaded a Euro-American settlement history that overtook the space and resources of all Native American peoples in the trans-Mississippi West. Sacajawea's sisters in expeditionary fame, Pocahontas of the Virginia Powhatans, who assisted John Smith at Jamestown, and the Aztec-born La Malinche, translator and mistress to Cortés in Mexico, have both acquired complex reputations as sensitive diplomats and exceptionally canny women who at some level betrayed their people. Certainly this is more apparent in the case of La Malinche, but the complications of both women's roles as negotiators and interpreters between indigenous leaders and white political-entrepreneurial missions are evident in the extensive scholarship and popular writing on both.[7]

No such ambiguity envelops the figure of Sacajawea. It is evident that the Wind River Shoshone want to claim her as their own. Indeed, the iconic image of Sacajawea, with wind-blown hair and babe on her back, a "Noble Savage" pointing the way west, is affirmed not only in white statues and storybooks but also in the writing of one of the most influential Native American cultural analysts and poets of the present day.[8] Paula Gunn Allen, a radical feminist, celebrates Sacajawea's strengths in the following terms:

> When Eva Emery Dye discovered Sacagawea and honored her as the guiding spirit of American womanhood, she may have been wrong in bare historical fact, but she was quite accurate in terms of deeper truth. The statues that have been erected depicting Sacagawea as a Matron in her prime signify an understanding in the American mind, however unconscious, that the source of just government, of right ordering of social relationships, the dream of "liberty and justice for all" can be gained only by following the Indian Matrons' guidance. (27)

To support her position, Allen then quotes from a 1905 speech by the suffragette Anna Howard Shaw, which begins with the words, "Forerunner of civilization, great leader of men, patient and motherly woman, we bow our hearts to do you honor" (27).

Allen's praise assumes much about Sacajawea's abilities to make choices and decisions in her role as Charbonneau's bought wife and as figurehead of the Corps of Discovery.[9] In *The Sacred Hoop*, Allen's zeal to represent Native American feminine authority as a general, viable phenomenon results in what appears to be a somewhat wishful interpretation of Sacajawea's character.

All of this suggests that the Wind River reputation, as well as the hagiography of Sacajawea in other quarters, begs some critical inspection. In that portrait, half of the historical scholarship on the topic of her death is ignored, and the politics of her co-operation with Lewis and Clark are left unaddressed. In their representation of Sacajawea, the Cultural Center's staff and most of the Shoshone people living at Wind River would seem to subscribe to the dominant culture's valuation of her and, in the process, identify the Shoshone people with those values by according her such a representative and central position in their own history. Perhaps one of the more patent notices of this fact is that the grave marker at Wind River dedicated to her includes, near the bottom and in small print, the notice "Erected by the Wyoming State Organization of the National Society of the Daughters of the American Revolution, 1963."

In certain schools of contemporary postcolonial cultural studies, the position on Sacajawea expressed at the Shoshone Cultural Center would likely be met with some degree of opprobrium, since it indicates assimilation rather than anything particularly Shoshone. There are other ways of looking at this picture, however. The first thing to reconsider is the neglect of the evidence for Sacajawea's death in 1812. In my own experience of studying the characters of United States expeditionary narratives, the 1812 date of death has always seemed the more compelling: passages from journals are cited, with dates, names (though not Sacajawea's), and places indicating where Charbonneau was seen with his "Snake" (an Anglo term for the Shoshone commonly used in the early nineteenth century) Indian wife, who had participated in the Lewis and Clark expedition. These journals were kept by travellers whom contemporary historians can identify by occupation and origin; indeed, their names ring with familiarity: Brackenridge, Bradbury, Luttig.

But why take this, finally, as the truth rather than the 1884 story? As I spoke with people at Fort Washakie and reviewed their archival material, I found myself "coming around," as it were, to a more agnostic position. Swayed in part by their obvious desire to claim Sacajawea, by the accounts of the people who remembered knowing her at Wind River, and by the power of the Sacajawea Cemetery with its solemn, indeed sacramental, argument for ownership, I began to feel that my attraction to the 1812 argument had been based too exclusively on the textual biases of Western historiography. One thought in particular disrupted the clarity of my earlier position – the fact that everyone involved in this debate admits to Charbonneau's having been a profligate lover, marrying what Harold Howard calls "Indian girls" all over the Western country until he was an old man (185). Any wives he had before 1811 might have accompanied him from St. Louis to Fort Manuel. The researchers at the Shoshone Tribal Cultural Center explain that they are approached constantly, through the mail and over the phone, by people who claim to be Charbonneaus and who wonder if their ancestor might have been Sacajawea. This fact is not necessarily testimony to the multiplicity of Charbonneau's amorous connections, but it does point to the difficulty of establishing secure identities in such a case. Moreover, as Howard has indicated, there is a good deal of contemporary oral evidence of Sacajawea's presence in what are now Wyoming and Montana, in which she is identified in the same terms as those used to describe her in the journals of Brackenridge, Bradbury, and Luttig. She is the former wife of a "Frenchman" or of someone whose name is spelled something like "Charbonneau," and she once accompanied Lewis and Clark to the Pacific.

The significance of this debate in a sense calls for reconsideration of the second objection to the Wind River reputation noted above – namely, the lack of commentary on the politics of Sacajawea's co-operation with Lewis and Clark. We have no evidence to indicate that Sacajawea was in any position to make choices or decisions in joining the expedition or in determining any of its activities, other than to advise certain geographical directions. The problem arises when one considers the fact that the Shoshone people have embraced her for having had this experience. How else, after all, would she even be known in the historical record; what, one might ask, is there about Sacajawea to appreciate besides this role? I think an appropriate response is simply that she is recognized. Several posters and pamphlets at the Cultural Center label her "Sacajawea, Recognized Shoshone Woman." As caretakers of her legacy, the women who manage the museum and the people represented by it are directly associated with her. Sacajawea's recognition is not theirs, but it is as close as they are likely to come to substantial acknowledgement within the American public sphere, and that is no small effect of Sacajawea's influence. While it is true that the Center indirectly connects its values with those of the dominant culture's historiography by affirming Sacajawea's heroic status for having assisted Lewis and Clark, the fact that the expedition served to raise her to national fame seems far more significant at Wind River than the broader ideas or aims that the expedition was intended to actualize.

Yet another perspective on Sacajawea's character and destiny in local oral commentary further attests to the way in which the Wind River community asserts its possession of her memory, outside of the roles she occupies in the more hegemonic narrative. As one of the women who work at the Cultural Center told me, many people at the reservation now feel that Sacajawea should have left Charbonneau rather than accompany him on the expedition. His womanizing and ill treatment of his wives seem deplorable by their contemporary standards, and the retrospective advice, or admonition, to Sacajawea effectively separates her from him by prescribing her proper action, even if that action never occurred.

On the other hand, the comment made to me by the woman at the Center would also seem to imply that Sacajawea's participation in the expedition was not a matter of her choice but part of the generally "bad deal" that she had with Charbonneau. This seems quite plausible. We know, after all, that much of Sacajawea's young life was spent in captivity after her childhood, during which she had apparently been promised by her father to another man. Taken together with the fact that she was probably bought or won by Charbonneau, this information can lead one to construct an image of her that is not so much that of a strong-willed and determined individual as that of a woman whose own desires are quite unreadable, since her actions are so evidently determined by the series of men we know were in her life, including Lewis and Clark.

The expedition was designed and controlled at a distance by the "Great Father" in Washington, as Lewis and Clark referred to President Thomas Jefferson in their pre-composed orations about the new nation and the Indians' part in it, which they periodically delivered along their way. The bad deal they offered, which the Indians could not refuse, is writ small in the deal offered to Sacajawea herself and to her descendants who must rely on her for any recognition within the larger culture. In her capacity as guide and interpreter, Sacajawea acts and speaks for the interests of Lewis, Clark, Jefferson, and the mix of European Enlightenment and Romantic national ideas for which they stood. As we know her from the expedition texts, she never speaks for herself.

By claiming Sacajawea as one of their ancestors and at the same time imagining her separated from the man who connected her with the activities through which her recognition and, very likely, their knowledge of her comes, the people at Wind River mark their own minor recognition in the narrative of U.S. history while also posing a counter-voice to that history. The critique is aimed at the set of patriarchal relations that kept Sacajawea in a compromised situation, and an indirect connection exists between that patriarchal structure and the national project to which she and Charbonneau contributed. The irony, of course, is that if Sacajawea had cut her connection to Charbonneau, she presumably would never have participated in the expedition and thus would never have been an instrument of mainstream history.

However, in the account of Sacajawea's longer life, ending in 1884, she does in fact leave Charbonneau several years after the expedition when he has taken yet another, younger wife, whom he demonstratively favours to the disadvantage of the increasingly mistreated Sacajawea. From this point on, she figures as a much more self-directed character. Taking her daughter and adopted son with her, she travels to Montana and lives with a group of Comanche, marrying a man named Jerk Meat, who is kind and generous to her. Sometime after his death, she joins the Fremont expedition of 1843 for a short time and finally settles during her last years at Wind River.[10]

This account thus constructs Sacajawea as one who is in a position to make some choices and who, in doing so, parts from the man who once treated her badly and determined the course of her life. Accordingly, within this narrative the Fremont expedition is simply a temporary vehicle for passage to Wind River rather than another opportunity for contributing to U.S. official exploration of the West. By the time she arrives at Wind River, the historical character shaped in this narrative is appropriately renamed Wadze-Wipe, "Lost Woman." Disconnected from any sort of tribal or marital relations, she is on her own, a figure of feminine independence who still does not speak and thus still is not known, but who opts for life with her people, finally, rather than for association with the white culture of whose history she is now a part.

In this position, Sacajawea's character as expedition participant, and the potential charge of collaboration that it bears, is revised, as she is written out of the earlier histories and resituated with the Indians. In subscribing to this narrative of Sacajawea's life, the Shoshone people at Wind River claim her participation in that project as well as her distance from it. To understand her in this way is to accord her neither the role of grand matriarch of Native American female strength nor that of heroine of U.S. colonialism but rather to portray her as one who turned away from white history in a complex refusal of recognition by the mainstream audience. In doing so, Sacajawea enacts for the Indian audience a version of what William Bevis refers to as "homing in" in much contemporary Native American literature – that is, returning to a locus of Native American community and identity after a time of wandering without cultural structure, precisely as a lost woman.[11] The exclusivity of Shoshone culture is maintained in this narrative, even as it constitutes part of the history that belongs generally to "American" public culture.

2

The museum and information centre at Acoma Pueblo, like the Shoshone Tribal Cultural Center at Fort Washakie, has a special place in relation to the village in which it is located and whose culture it offers to public view. Unlike the Shoshone Center's idiosyncratic appearance, however, the adobe Acoma museum looks like most buildings in the area. This fact, however, cannot be read as an indication of harmonious blending with the local culture, for the structure sits alone below the imposing mesa of Sky City, where visitors are permitted only in the company of Native guides.

Like other museums, that of Acoma has the effect of reducing the complexities and incompleteness of history and culture to a decontextualized, exoticized collection for tourists' consumption. Artifacts of Acoma history and culture, particularly pottery, are on display; the cases are filled with pieces dating back as far as the tenth century, many of which are placed beside recently made clay pots that resemble them precisely in shape and design. This display of continued competence in the ancient craft certifies the traditionalism of present-day potters; it also defines these works as copies and as products of an effort to duplicate earlier technologies and aesthetics as if no time or sensibility interceded between then and now. Other display cases offer the paraphernalia of nineteenth-century battles – bows and arrows, guns, war bonnets, U.S. Army uniforms, and charts, maps, texts that trace the course of Acoma's history with the Europeans since the seventeenth century. Just like any display case in any museum around the world, these offer the objects as synecdoches of the history of which they are parts. The Shoshone museum does the same, and one cannot help but notice how little the reduction does for the representation of cultural integrity. Rather, these institutions seem at first glance to cater to the curiosity and interests of visitors.

Yet in Acoma, unlike Wind River, the home of the objects in the museum and the subject of its history, Acoma itself, is visible from the doorway, approachable via a short, winding drive up the steep mesa wall. After registering and paying an admission fee to visit Sky City, tourists are shuttled in small buses to the venerable Pueblo. Once atop the mesa, a guide leads each group through a range of narrow streets and narrates Acoma's history. Pottery is for sale from vendors who appear as if on cue, and visitors are notified in advance of the two-minute time limit allowed for making purchases at any particular stand along the route. Picture-taking is permitted with the purchase of a ticket at the information centre, but the church interior and graveyard cannot be photographed, and permission must be requested from Acoma's residents before anyone can take their portraits.

When our bus arrived at the Pueblo, a young man in dark glasses rose and introduced himself as our guide. After restating the rules, he led us off the bus into a small square, where he began narrating Acoma's history from the thirteenth-century settlement to the present. At one time inhabited by more than one thousand people, the Pueblo now has about thirty year-round occupants who take up some thirteen of the approximately four hundred houses; the rest are used only in summer and during holidays. These population figures seemed to imply at the outset of the tour that life in Acoma is simultaneously an actual and a performed phenomenon, for much is made of the fact that it is the oldest continuously occupied village in the continental United States. With only thirty people to sustain this identity year-round, several of whom are involved in the tourist trade, Acoma may be construed as a kind of quaint memorial to its former living self. A woman in our group asked the guide if he lived there. No, he said; like most of his generation, he had chosen to live where schools and jobs were within easier reach. By his account, most Acoma people live within the region and return to the mesa often, even if they cannot call themselves residents. During our visit, approximately twenty-five or thirty people turned out to sell goods, and a few others emerged here and there, going about their business without referring to us. Aside from these, we saw only other tourists, who, like mirrors of ourselves, would appear now and then in groups at the end of a street or across a plaza.

Thus the Pueblo appeared remarkably empty. It seemed to exist, by and large, as a perfect but modest display: like the contemporary imitations of ancient pottery, present-day life in Acoma seems committed to the forms and styles of an uncontaminated, classical past. Isolated and remote, the Pueblo indeed looks disconnected from the culture and history that surround it and have framed it as a reservation.

Indeed, the framing of Acoma as a perfect remnant is so intense that it seems to work against authenticity and the preservation of "real" culture. The museum displays and the controls over tourists at the Pueblo contribute to a sense that this is all a sort of para- or pseudo-experience. Yet there are clearly other dimensions to this story, too, and what appears at first to be a concession to tourism that sustains the status-quo perception of Native American culture as exotic and intellectually collectible is only the beginning. The tone of imitation and display in the tour soon starts rebounding onto the tourist, for as much as it makes Acoma look like a fossil trying to perform the part of a living community, the tour continually calls attention to itself as a tour and thus positions the visitor as a self-conscious stranger whose presence in the village is in some sense already scripted. Our comments and questions echoed off the close walls as if they had been asked many times before; the confined spaces through which we walked seemed themselves to prescribe body movement and posture. With no other sounds or activities in which to contextualize our own, we seemed the only players on an otherwise quiet and empty stage. We had paid to look at the Pueblo itself and were given an opportunity to see ourselves in Acoma as part of the bargain.

The invitation to view the village as an object of the spectator's interest was patently and visibly limited. The narrow channels of the tourist's Acoma, sealed off from the domestic interiors of sparsely occupied homes; the few residents, whose exchanges with the visitors have only to do with selling goods; and the rules of the game, which control the visitor's visual experience as well as her movements – all of these conditions of the tour work to wall off the unvisited quarters of the Pueblo. Its unseen residents, engaged in whatever banal or dramatic activities, are free from the curious eye of the stranger. Beyond the walls, daily life went on among however few people actually live there, and whatever their regard for the visitors, it was not for us to see.

Our guide's narrative worked in concert and counterpoint with this chiselled experience. His distantly ironic tone and the memorized sound of his material kept the fact of our being "on tour" continuously in focus. He did not dwell at length on the horrors of Spanish occupation or the manipulations of the Anglo-American government. Rather, his basic rhetorical method was to string together different kinds of information – for example, the measurements of a wall, followed by a particular practice of contemporary life, then an anecdote of local folklore – and, in conclusion, to narrate one of the many horrors committed by the Spaniards at Acoma during the sixteenth and seventeenth centuries. Finally, without a pause or change in pitch, he would ask in an uninviting and monotone voice, "Are there any questions?"

His discourse, however, did have the potent effect of bringing his listeners into the history he narrated by making their (our) European predecessors as much a part of the story as his own. Perhaps more than the particular data, however, the tone of irony in his oration had this strangely effective way of implicating the listeners' culture in the account of his own. On the surface, this strategy would seem to have had no effect on the majority of tourists in our group. Some of them seemed uninterested in questions of history or culture and chose to ask instead about the physical construction of the village. A gregarious older man, rotund and flushed from the walk and the heat, was particularly curious about the composition of the adobe, and his probings led to questions by others on the same topic, as well as to the matter of the shift in building trends from adobe to brick. Similar discussion arose concerning pottery: when did people begin using ceramic instead of simple clay, and what were the differences in firing? A khaki-clad, tense-looking young man with the demeanour of an anxious graduate student asked a few tentatively formulated questions about the density of walls, strength of beams, and so on. Others, like this fellow's female companion, covered in white cotton and veiled in gauze, never touched or questioned anything. The guide was probably accustomed to this range of interest, for he seemed to have ready at hand all sorts of information about heights, depths, and lengths of nearly every structure we encountered. Such dialogues recurred several times during our visit, particularly after the guide had been describing some of the atrocities committed by the Spaniards. His phrase, "Are there any questions?," which typically followed these descriptions, often had the odd effect of eliciting queries about building materials. Its way of deflecting attention to the simple materiality of Acoma's construction left the unaddressed questions of history dangling in hollow air.

Dialogues of this sort tended to focus on spatial measurements and the construction of boundaries, the sort of data regularly offered at such tourist sites. Yet, whether or not our guide was merely anticipating the typical interests of tourists when he responded to these questions as thoroughly as he did, it was impossible to resist thinking that there was something allegorically appropriate in the discourse about the composition of walls and ceilings. These are data that appeal strongly to rationalist imaginations and can give one the sense of possessing real knowledge about space and objects in a strange location. Boundaries are also very important in most Native American societies, where spiritual as well as geographical and political limits are crucial to the articulation of community and identity. Rather than elicit transgressive desire, as boundaries commonly do in Euro-American culture, however, they are respected and preserved as the marks that indicate home. All the talk about walls and what material is used to construct them seemed to me like a walking trope for the barriers existing between our guide and his culture, on the one hand, and, on the other, the traditions of the Anglo tourists, which include the desire to know about the Indians and Acoma.

To my mind, the guide's presentation seemed rich enough to satisfy familiar touristic desires at the same time that it could be said to position the tourist as one who is also returning to Acoma, to a scene preserved from history where the determinations of European culture in the lives of indigenous people are massively evident. His genre permitted him to lecture very subtly to his audience and to present for its consumption the details of a limited number of horrors in a history that belongs to them as much as it does to the Indians. The stories of Spaniards enslaving Indians and throwing reluctant or recalcitrant workers over the mesa's rim, of beatings, mutilations, and forced conversions, made the tourist recognize the European past in the conditions and situations that the guide narrated concerning the history of his own people.

Looked at in this way rather than as an inauthentic reproduction of Native American life, the tourist's Acoma would seem to be the product of a concerted and well-organized effort on the part of the people who claim the Pueblo as their home to preserve a traditional lifestyle from the curiosity of strangers. Rather than speculate on the traditional content of what we do not see, however, it seems more plausible to consider what we do see and what we are not told unless we ask. The relation of self-representation for the tourist trade to actual tradition is difficult to trace because it is a continuously renegotiated part of that tradition.[12] A few more details of our conversations with the guide may serve to indicate how the issue of traditionalism was evinced by this particular tour through Acoma.

My companion asked the guide at one point how extensively traditional religious practices were followed in present-day Acoma. He replied that they are still followed by many, but added that this does not mean people have relinquished Catholicism. Neither does it suggest some sort of hybrid faith. Given the intensity of their ancestors' sacrifices in the long and bloody process of the establishment of the Spaniards' religion, he remarked, the contemporaries of Acoma feel that if they do not maintain their Catholicism, the ancestors will have suffered and died in vain. Yet the two sets of religious practices are kept largely separate. Only on two occasions during the year are they joined: on September 2, the feast day of St. Stephen, patron saint of the Pueblo, and for four days during the Christmas season. The guide was very clear on this point, as if he wanted particularly to disabuse people of the notion that Native American Catholicism, like the Native American Church, always mixes indigenous with Christian forms.[13] Yet he gave little information about Native religion, other than to explain what the *kiva* was and to point out a few other places in the village where festival events take place. His narrative included more information on the history of Christianity in the pueblo. Again, in this sense the tour and accompanying narrative concentrated attention on the European presence in Acoma's history and kept the data of the guide's own culture and ritualistic traditions to a minimum.

The two centres of religious practice at Acoma, the church and the *kiva*, seem to illustrate this point in their very different architectural forms. The disparity suggests the respectively announced and unannounced relations to spirituality that they represent. Between them, one sees a contrast something like that between the Vietnam and Lincoln Memorials in Washington, D.C.[14] These secular temples, located in close range of each other, differ markedly in their conceptualizations of the histories they recall. The Lincoln Memorial, projecting the transcendent authority of U.S. democracy in the figure of the hallowed president, rises nearly thirty meters above the park in which it is located, visible from kilometers away, while the Vietnam Wall is almost hidden, designed to work with the landscape to evoke a different but equally "deep" range of emotions. St. Stephen's at Acoma, like many European Catholic churches, rises well above the heights of all other structures in the village, and its two bell towers reach upward for another 2.5 meters or so. The crosses planted above them fade at a distance, but there is no mistaking the Christian design of the highly visible building itself. The victory of the mission over indigenous secular as well as spiritual powers is advertised across the land. The *kiva*, on the other hand, sits in a row of houses made from the same adobe stucco and brick, largely unnoticeable from the outside. Beyond

179

our guide's identification of it, there was no evidence that this particular structure was other than one of the houses. We were not taken inside and we were told only a few details about how one enters the *kiva*, how long one stays, who goes in and who does not.

I will not attempt to analyze the differences in conceptualization and practice of spirituality that the church and *kiva* suggest, since they have been addressed extensively by scholars of comparative religion. It is worth remarking, however, that the contrasting notions of power implied by the two buildings seem to have had curious effects upon the guide's own sense of religious identity. Whatever powerful spiritualities are sponsored by the *kiva*, they do not fuel evangelical practices nor demand overt expressions of belief from those who are not already inclined. The Church, on the other hand, has been notorious for these things, and its political power through history has left its mark on contemporary life. The *kiva*'s silent reverence for the spiritualities it hosts and the lack of attention it calls to itself seemed to be respected in our guide's spare references to the religion practiced there and in his insistence on its discreteness from Catholicism. Yet it was not at all clear that he was especially devoted to Native religion or that he was purposely preserving from public knowledge its values and practices. My companion, whose own religious imagination is rather eclectic, asked the guide where he stood on these matters. He replied that he was "sort of stuck in between" things, but offered nothing more to explain what this meant. He admitted with great candour that he did not know the old stories very well, since they had been passed along to him, as he claimed they often are, by grandparents who had not really listened very carefully. Nor does he speak Keresan, the language of Acoma Pueblo.

In this peculiar position of representing the village to outsiders while remaining something of an outsider to its traditions himself, our guide resembled other famous go-betweens, Sacajawea among them, whose lives are situated in at least two cultures but who are "proper" to neither of them. Yet in most ways, it seems that he was quite representative in precisely this in-between status. His comment about the stories being passed down incorrectly implied a dilution of older forms and practices generally, in an era in which for several generations indigenous customs have been in competition with those of Europe and the United States and in which the inheritance of culture has become a somewhat kaleidoscopic process, with once-opposing terms shuffled into different and still-changing relations.

On such an eroded and heterogeneous cultural terrain, differing religious forms may be compartmentalized clearly, but the standards for determining what gets considered imported and what has the status of Native are not always easy to predict. My friend asked if "the Protestants," meaning evangelicals, had become much of a presence in the Pueblo. The guide answered that "some people are jumping the fence. You can see the missions along route 40." Route 40, formerly route 66, is the major interstate highway between Gallup and Tucumcari, but at points it digresses into a desolate-looking road that might be described as a belt of former strip culture. Abandoned gas stations, bars, and restaurants from the 1950s and 1960s languish along its length; the ghost cabins of defunct motels line up in shabby disrepair. Here and there a Baptist, Seventh-Day Adventist, or Mormon mission punctuate the desolation.

The fence-jumping phenomenon that, according to our guide, represents only about ten percent of the population, occurs off the mesa, in an environment whose aesthetic appeal is probably evident only to students of American landscape history. Protestantism is not gaining much of a foothold in Acoma itself, which accordingly represents it as a marginal movement. Catholicism, by contrast, stands on this side of the fence; indeed, our guide's explanation that the people of Acoma would not give up their Catholicism because their ancestors had sacrificed and suffered so much for it affirms what might be called the "negative inclusion" that the Church enjoys within the Pueblo culture. In this sense, compared to Protestantism, the Catholic Church acquires a virtually indigenous status, a "rootedness" that persists even if practiced in complete separation from Native religion. If our guide's condition of being "stuck in-between" is a matter of moving back and forth between two compartmentalized religious bases of cultural identity, then he is not culturally mixed but doubled.

Such a characterization and the complex dynamics that produce it speak to the difficult subject (in every sense) of postcolonial identity. Nonetheless, I will risk saying that this model of cultural doubling seems like something of an ideal, and that the maintenance of subjectivity that it presupposes is more schematic and linear than one would think possible. If, on the other hand, the guide's condition is a matter of really, literally, being "stuck in-between," such that he inhabits neither a Native nor a European cultural imaginary but some as yet unarticulated zone that runs parallel to both, then a whole range of questions arises about what constitutes the "traditional," "indigenous," and "Native." Whether tradition is something experienced as such in certain practices or recognized intellectually, as it were, from an abstracted point of view becomes a significant issue, since it bears heavily, although not exclusively, on the question of who determines what tradition is.

These are not new questions but in the context of late twentieth-century American cultural formations, they have to address as well the puzzling area of Native-hosted tourism and Indian self-representation in the market of public culture. In the wake of the Columbian quincentenary and the many revisionary critical interpretations of conquest history sponsored by that anniversary, respect for Nativeness in the United States is probably higher than it has ever been, even as the status-quo response to Indians retains the familiar tones of exoticization, "Noble Savagism," and race prejudice. For Native Americans, and for non-Natives who seek to learn from them about systems and ideas that the West badly needs to inculcate, the returning or "homing in," in William Bevis's terms, to indigenous community and identity is no direct route, as most people who are interested know by now.

It is easier these days to speak of reconstruction and reinvention than of return. Accordingly, much attention has been devoted to the notion of hybridization among indigenous peoples of the Western hemisphere, as if this were in some way a desirable and particularly rich way of being. Yet for our tour guide at Acoma, I would venture to say hybridization was at best a source of wry, ironic humour, at worst a source of confusion and alienation. He works, like many people in this country today, in a service industry, but in addition to entertaining and educating, his service is to challenge the status-quo knowledge of the typical tourist. The familiar southwestern vacation experience of visiting an Indian reservation is framed by thick walls of resistance. The much-discussed brick and adobe walls of the houses perform this role literally by limiting visitors' access to the "inner life" of Acoma. Rhetorically, the guide did the same with his narrative skills and with his authentic lack of knowledge.

3

Sacajawea's historical afterlife is as vexed in some ways as her life itself: it is another story of captivity, servitude, and partial escape. The mainstream record eventually positions her as a quintessential element of U.S. national culture, while alternative accounts work to distance her from that position and to recuperate her for Native American representation. Her recognition among Indian as well as Euro-American audiences results from her place as a Native American woman participating in the expedition. Thus the oppositional value she acquires in Native America exists within the fabric of contemporary U.S. public culture generally. Yet the story of her long life among the Comanche and Shoshone gives us a solitary Sacajawea who guides no one but wanders somewhat haphazardly in the direction of Wind River. The Shoshone here are not quite her own people, and the place is not her home, any more than the expedition was something in which she chose to participate. Rather than returning to her country of origin and to her aboriginal self, she becomes Lost Woman, a somewhat worldly veteran of losses, gains, and strange experiences in a frontier of many cultures. Similarly, the possession of Sacajawea at present-day Wind River does not foster a classic Shoshone identity but instead affirms the interconnection of the tribe's history with that of the United States. The recognition that identification with Sacajawea allows is simultaneously oppositional to and embedded in the terms of the larger public culture.

The tour leader I encountered at Acoma revised the relationship between Native guide and European travellers evident in older expedition narratives so that the Native, rather than showing the Europeans something they do not really know, offers them some of their own history. His mild manners and Elvis Presley haircut, his dress and dark glasses are familiar details of a particular kind of "cool" persona that one sees almost anywhere in the United States these days. Characteristically "American," our guide conducted a tour through Acoma that implicitly critiqued the roles of the visitors as unimplicated strangers. Some of the tourists were more interested in the history of adobe walls than in the history of the European presence, and for all I know they had their reasons. My companion and I went with the expectation of learning about the old culture, but our guide and the women who run the Shoshone Cultural Center demonstrated in very interesting ways that Native Americans have found their own way of teaching history at Wind River and Acoma.

Michel de Certeau, who studied extensively the history and politics of indigenous and European relations in the Western hemisphere, wrote in *The Practice of Everyday Life* that

> the ambiguity that subverted from within the Spanish colonizers'
> "success" in imposing their own culture on the indigenous Indians is
> well known. Submissive, and even consenting to their subjection, the
> Indians nevertheless often made of the rituals, representations, and laws
> imposed on them something quite different from what their conquerors
> had in mind; they subverted them not by rejecting or altering them, but by
> using them with respect to ends and references foreign to the system they
> had no choice but to accept. They were other within the very colonization
> that outwardly assimilated them; their use of the dominant social order
> deflected its power, which they lacked the means to challenge; they
> escaped it without leaving it. The strength of their difference lay in
> procedures of "consumption." (xiii)

Our Acoma tour guide affirms de Certeau's account, while updating it in somewhat different terms, for in his representation, rather than glossing their own cultural practices with those of the dominant culture, the Indians of contemporary Acoma, like those of Wind River, have appropriated familiar methods of mainstream tourism and historiography, and in the process offer Euro-Americans information about their own culture and history. In this sense, the Indians have "consumed" some of the narrative mechanisms of late twentieth-century U.S. culture and have, in de Certeau's terms, made for themselves a place as "other within the very colonization that outwardly assimilated them." Thus, it seems, they have "escaped it without leaving it."

Notes

1 Several different spellings of her name are used, even among contemporary writers. "Sacajawea" generally is considered the Shoshone spelling and translates as "Boat Launcher." "Bird Woman" is the equivalent of the Hidatsa "Sacagawea." "Sakakawea" is a variant spelling of the Hidatsa name and is common in North Dakota, particularly in the area of the Mandan, Hidatsa, and Arikara Reservation at Fort Berthold. Lewis and Clark multiply these spellings many times over, each of them using at least five or six variations of the name in their journal entries.

2 Harold P. Howard writes in his book *Sacagawea* that at this point in her life, she "was now one of Charbonneau's chattels" (17). Howard's account of this exchange is that Charbonneau "had probably acquired her in a gambling game or by barter" (17). Howard's is considered by several contemporary academic historians to be one of the more respected narratives of Sacajawea's life and role in the Lewis and Clark expedition. While his book presents the evidence for both sides of the debate described below concerning the date of Sacajawea's death, he subscribes to the conclusion of most Euro-American historians – namely, that she died in 1812, shortly after the expedition ended.

3 See Ronda; Lewis and Clark, *History*; Wissler; Larson: Schroer; and Howard (191).

4 Hebard's *Sacagawea: Guide of the Lewis and Clark Expedition,* published in 1932, was to a great extent based on interviews with Shoshone people living at Wind River who told Hebard that they had known Sacagawea, also known by them as Porivo and Wadze-wipe, or Lost Woman, during her later years. Hebard's argument has not been given much credit by other historians, who claim that she ignored the evidence of contemporary witnesses Henry Brackenridge, John Luttig, and John Bradbury that Sacagawea died much earlier. Hebard has also been criticized for wrongly assuming that Sacagawea was mistaken for one of Charbonneau's other wives by Brackenridge, Bradbury, and Luttig. See Howard, 157–58. For a summary of Hebard's oral sources, see Howard, 178–84.

5 1945 is the date given for Roberts's death, which occurred while he was still working at Wind River, in *Wind River: The People and Place,* published by the North American Indian Heritage Center. Howard writes in his *Sacajawea* that Roberts remained at the reservation for forty-nine years after his arrival in 1883, which would mean that his time there concluded in 1934 rather than 1945. No sources for these dates are given in either text.

6 Roberts narrates his experience in "The Death of Sacajawea." An enlarged print of his article is on display at the Shoshone Tribal Cultural Center.

7 On La Malinche's reputation, see, for example, Todorov; and Paz. Discussions of Pocahontas's reputation appear, for instance, in Dearborn and in Sundquist.

8 Since 1904, six statues have been erected to Sacajawea in different parts of the United States. In addition, four mountain peaks, two lakes, a state park, a spring, at least five historical markers, an airplane, and a Girl Scout camp have been named after her. She also has been the subject of three musical compositions, several paintings, a museum, the design of a silver service, and much other memorabilia. All of these memorials have been sponsored or produced by European-Americans. For a list, see Howard, Appendix A.

9 Concerning Sacajawea's place in the expedition, William Clark wrote in his journal for the expedition that "her presence reconsiles [*sic*] all the Indians as to our friendly intensions [*sic*], a woman with a party of men is a token of piece [*sic*]" (quoted in Moulton 2: 266). Later, as they entered the Columbia River, Clark noted that "the Umatilla people apparently were pacified at the sight of Sacajawea: as soon as they saw the Squar wife of the interperters [*sic*] they pointed to her and informed [the others who had not seen her]. [T]hey imediately [*sic*] all came out and appeared to assume new life, this sight of This Indian woman, wife to one of our interprs. confirmed those people of our friendly intentions, as no woman ever accompanies a war party of Indians in this quarter" (qtd. in Lewis and Clark, *Journals* 5: 306).

10 See Hebard; Cody; Eastman; and Howard 175–82.

11 See Bevis.

12 In 1979 when Peter Matthiessen tried to visit Acoma, it was still not open to tourism, and, with his Mohawk travelling companion Craig Carpenter, he was effectively shunned from the mesa. They were pleased with this experience, and in spite of the denied access, Matthiessen did gather a very distinct impression of the Pueblo and its peoples' attitudes toward strangers. In *Indian Country*, he recorded this peculiar tourist experience in the following way:

> Although it could trade on what must be the most striking location of all the pueblo villages of the Southwest, Acoma has so far resisted the temptation of both electricity and running water, and its people are silent and reserved. Resistance to the intrusion of our truck was so manifest in the dead silence of the stone dwellings in the rock that we turned around and left immediately, on a shared impulse, feeling exhilarated rather than rejected, as if we had glimpsed a rare vanishing creature without scaring it away. (301)

13 The Native American Church developed early in the twentieth century and combines elements of Sun dance religion, peyotism, and Christianity. It is still practiced by many peoples at the present time, but legal issues concerning preservation of and access to sacred places as well as the consumption of peyote have in many instances complicated the performance of rituals. See Deloria; Slotkin; and Aberle.

14 The contrasts between these monuments have been analyzed, for example, by Sturken.

Works Cited

Aberle, David F. *The Peyote Religion among the Navaho*. Chicago: Aldine, 1966.

Allen, Paula. *The Sacred Hoop: Recovering the Feminine in American Indian Traditions*. Boston: Beacon Press, 1986.

Bevis, William. "Homing In." *Recovering the Word: Essays on Native American Literature*. Ed. Arnold Krupat and Brian Swann. Berkeley: University of California Press, 1987. 580–620.

Cody, Mae. "Sacajawea." Wyoming Sacajawea Collection. Shoshone Tribal Cultural Center, Fort Washaki, Wyoming.

Dearborn, Mary. *Pocahontas's Daughters: Gender and Ethnicity in American Culture*. New York: Oxford University Press, 1986.

de Certeau, Michel. *The Practice of Everyday Life*. Trans. Steven Randall. Berkeley: University of California Press, 1984.

Deloria, Vine, Jr. "Trouble in High Places." *The State of Native America*. Ed. M. Annette Jaimes. Boston: South End Press, 1992. 267–290.

Eastman, Charles. Original Letters, 1925. Hebard Collection. University of Wyoming Library.

Emery Dye, Eva. *The Conquest: The True Story of Lewis and Clark*. Chicago: A.C. McClurg, 1902.

Hebard, Grace Raymon. *Sacagawea: Guide of the Lewis and Clark Expedition*. 1932. Los Angeles: Arthur Clark, 1957.

Howard, Harold P. *Sacagawea*. Norman, OK: University of Oklahoma Press, 1971.

Larson, T. A. "Where is Sacajawea Buried?" Unpublished essay. Wyoming Sacajawea Collection. Shoshone Tribal Cutural Center, Fort Washaki, Wyoming.

Lewis, Meriwether, and William Clark. *History of the Expeditions under the Command of Lewis and Clark*. Ed. Elliott Coues. 4 vols. New York: Harper Bros., 1893. New York: Dover, 1965. 3 vols.

———. *The Journals of the Lewis and Clark Expedition*. Ed. Gary E. Moulton. 8 vols. Lincoln: University of Nebraska Press, 1983–1987.

Matthiessen, Peter. *Indian Country*. New York: Penguin, 1984.

Paz, Octavio. *The Labyrinth of Solitude*. New York: Grove Weidenfeld, 1985.

Roberts, John. "The Death of Sacawajea." *Indians at Work: A News Sheet for Indians and the Indian Service*. Washington, DC: Bureau of Indian Affairs, 2.16. 1 April 1935.

Ronda, James P. *Lewis and Clark among the Indians*. Lincoln: University of Nebraska Press, 1984.

Schroer, Blanche. "Sacajawea: The Legend and the Truth." *In Wyoming* (Winter 1978): 20–28; 37–43.

Slotkin, James S. *The Peyote Religion*. Glencoe, IL: Free Press, 1956.

Sturken, Marita. "The Wall, the Screen, and the Image: The Vietnam Veterans Memorial." *Journal of American Culture* 13 (1990): 37–40.

Sundquist, Asebrit. *Pocahontas & Co.: The Fictional American Indian Woman in the Nineteenth Century*. Atlantic Highlands, NJ: Humanities Press, 1987.

Todorov, Tzvetan. *The Conquest of America*. 1982. Trans. Richard Howard. New York: Harper and Row, 1987.

Wind River: The People and Place. St. Stephens, WY: North American Indian Heritage Center, 1989.

Wissler, Clark. *Indians of the United States*. Garden City, NY: Anchor Books, 1966.

Introduction: The Linked Histories of the Globalized World   The Fascist Longings in our Midst   Queer with Class: Absence of Third World Sweatshop in Lesbian/Gay Discourse and a Rearticulation of Materialist Queer Theory   Cross-Mirrorings of Alterity: The Colonial Scenario and Its Psychological Legacy   Mythologies of Migrancy: Post-colonialism, Postmodernism, and the Politics of (Dis)location   Postcolonial DefferendDifferend: Diasporic Narratives of Salman Rushdie   At the Margins of Postcolonial Studies   Keeping History at Wind River and Acoma

Towards Articulation: Postcolonial Theory and Demotic Resistance   Postcolonial Theory and the "Decolonization" of Chinese Culture

Modernity's First Born:

Latin America and
Postcolonial Transformation

BILL ASHCROFT

There is considerable resistance to the idea of Latin American postcoloniality.
How and on what basis can we establish links between Latin America and
other colonized regions? Can a word such as *colonialism* really refer to the
historical experience of Latin America? We are told that Latin America is
different, and particularly that the features of its colonization from 1492 are
different from British imperialism from 1757. They occurred, says Santiago
Colas, "at different historical moments, the colonizers belonged to different
nations and to different classes within those nations, and the nations in turn
occupied different international positions. Moreover, the 'distant territories'
were geographically distinct, the 'implantations' were accomplished through
different financial and technical means, and the inhabitants had developed
distinct social and cultural habits" (383). To this I would add the radically

different institutional location of literary study in English and Spanish cultures (see Baldick; Viswanathan).

So Latin America is under threat from a new colonizing movement called "colonial and postcolonial discourse," yet another subjection, it would seem, to foreign formations and epistemologies from the English-speaking centres of global power. I want to suggest, however, that an obsessive fear of the word *postcolonial* is misplaced. There may be good reason for fearing the hegemonic effects of new global discourses, but if we forget for a minute that the term appears to be one more in a long line of "posts" and attempt to understand the significance of colonization and its postcolonial engagements, we may discover that Latin America gave ample evidence of its postcoloniality long before the emergence of "colonial and postcolonial discourse" from the metropolitan academy.

The problem with the debate on postcolonialism in Latin America is that it has been skewed from the beginning by a rather eccentric view of postcolonialism, largely resting on the assumption of its emergence from poststructuralism, which has led to an understandable resistance to its neo-hegemonic discursive character. A debate in the *Latin American Research Review* in 1993 illustrates both how a limited definition of postcolonial theory has been readily accepted and how questions about its validity have arisen. The use of the phrase "colonial and postcolonial discourse" itself indicates the extent to which the historical event of colonialism, its discursive machinery, and postcolonial engagements with it have been blurred.

The "field" or "movement," it is assumed, emerged in the 1980s from a dissatisfaction with previous approaches to colonial analysis. Patricia Seed's *Latin American Research Review* article in 1991, which stimulated this debate, sees postcolonial discourse as synonymous with the colonial discourse theory initiated by Edward Said's *Orientalism*. In addition, she claims that the interest in the textual and discursive aspects of colonialism is a direct inheritance of poststructuralism. But not only should Said's own work be distinguished from poststructuralism (see Said, *World*; Ashcroft, "Conversation"); this privileging of colonial discourse theory developed in *Orientalism* misrepresents the very complex emergence of postcolonial studies over several decades. Postcolonial analysis, even in its most overtly theoretical form, has been a function of the activity of writers and critics since the nineteenth century, burgeoning in the work of Frantz Fanon and other intellectuals writing in the wake of independence.

Hernán Vidal's stubbornly ethnocentric contention that the proliferation of literary criticism in Latin America "saw the importation of North American New Criticism, Russian Formalism, German Phenomenology and French Structuralism" (115) demonstrates very clearly the perceived threat to

Latin American intellectual integrity posed by outside critical movements. Such a fear appears, itself, to emerge from a tendency to homogenize the complex range of social experiences co-existing on the continent. Outlining two strands of literary criticism, which he calls "technocratic criticism" and "culturally oriented criticism" (116), Vidal sees the emergence of "colonial and postcolonial discourse" as the creation of a category of research that attempts to endow these two approaches "with a degree of affinity that they have not previously had" (116).

However, this can be understood in another way. The employment of "technocratic" criticism is a clear example of the tendency of colonized peoples to appropriate the formations, discourses, and theoretical strategies of a dominant discourse in making their voice heard. Such a process of appropriation has a long history in Latin American cultural production. Contemporary postcolonial criticism is not a product of the eighties, the decade in which it began to become more fully described, but a consequence of many decades of postcolonial writing in the former British and French colonies resulting in an uneasy and sometimes fractious alliance among such fields as Commonwealth literary studies, Black studies, and the emergent colonial discourse theory.

If we take the position that rather than a product of the experience of colonized peoples in the French- and English-speaking world, postcolonialism is the discourse of the colonized, that it does not mean "after colonialism" since it is colonialism's interlocutor and antagonist from the moment of colonization, then "postcolonial discourse" can be seen to emerge from the creative and theoretical production of colonized societies themselves. This averts the problems raised by the movement toward a new critical orthodoxy resulting from the expropriation of the field by contemporary centres of academic power. If, rather than a new hegemonic field, we see the postcolonial as a way of talking about the political and discursive strategies of colonized societies, then we may more carefully view the various forms of anti-systemic operations within the global world system.

Postcolonialism is generated by a simple realization: that the effect of the colonizing process over individuals, over culture and society throughout Europe's domain was vast and produced consequences as complex as they are profound. Not all postcolonial discourse is anti-colonial, nor can it ever, in any of its various forms, dispense with that comparatively simple moment of history that began to churn its social consequences around the world. These consequences have long been the subject of attention by Latin American historians and critics. Walter Mignolo, ostensibly rejecting postcolonialism, cites the postcolonial critique of Edmundo O'Gorman in *The Invention of America*, which demonstrated that "language is not the neutral tool of an honest desire to tell the truth [...] but an instrumental tool for constructing history and inventing realities" (122). Similarly Mignolo cites Angel Rama's *La ciudad letrada,* which offers a theory about the control, domination, and power of alphabetic writing (122): "O'Gorman and Rama exemplify the perspective of social scientists and humanists located in and speaking from the Third World. They are in some sense contemporary examples of the 'intellectual other'" (123). Mignolo's complaint is that O'Gorman did first what Said and Todorov did two decades later. O'Gorman and Rama were already, several decades ago, critiquing a key feature of colonial discourse: the power of language to construct and dominate the world of the colonized.

Mignolo is correct in suggesting that postcolonialism is not a child of poststructuralism conceived in the metropolitan academy for the benefit of an annoyingly ungrateful postcolonial world. It is born in the struggle of colonized intellectuals to appropriate the discursive tools of imperial discourse and to interpolate their own realities and cultural activities into the global arena. The examples of O'Gorman and Rama could be multiplied many times over. Postcolonial discourse is significant because it reveals the extent to which the historical condition of colonization has led to a certain political, intellectual, and creative dynamic in the postcolonial societies with which it engages.

So, we see that objections to postcolonial analysis have been based on a limited and academically defensive view of the discourse and that postcolonial analyses have been a feature of Latin American intellectual life at least since the fifties. But there remains a strong belief in the essential difference of Latin American postcoloniality even in those who favour its approach. Santiago Colas has adapted the theory of ideology developed by Slovenian theorist Slavoj Žižek to define the ideology of Latin American postcolonial culture ("Creole"). But how identifying, how distinct is this ideology? Is the difference of Latin America more a function of desire than reality?

Although Žižek's notion of ideology is not as different from Althusser's as he would like to believe, the explanation of the function of ideology as "not to offer us a point of escape from our reality but to offer us the social reality itself as an escape from some traumatic real kernel" (Colas, "Creole" 384) does provide a useful entry to Latin American postcolonial culture. This functions, according to Colas, "as an ideology that converts the persistence of colonial relations and its effects [...] into the precondition for the articulation of a nonmetropolitan identity. The culture then represses this conversion, leaving that identity seemingly self-constituted and self-sufficient – in a word, independent" (384). According to Colas the production of ideology in Latin America is driven by "the unconscious desire for the persistence of colonial relations in terms both of dependence on the former colonial or imperial power and of social inequality within the new nation" (385). In effect, Colas has provided a theory of ideology that is not limited to Latin America as he claims, but in fact astutely assesses the complex structure of colonial relations in all settler colonies. If we see that the postcolonial begins from the moment of colonization, then we understand that "the unconscious desire for the persistence of colonial relations" and the conscious desire for separation and independence are two positions which can exist side by side in any colonized space, but in the settler colony may so overlap that they can become subject positions adopted by the same subject. Perhaps inadvertently, Colas has demonstrated one way in which the inclusion of Latin America can begin to transform the field of postcolonial studies. The complexity of Latin American postcolonial society, far from lending itself to the concept of some Latin American essence, provides the ground for an increasingly sophisticated understanding of postcolonial relations throughout the world.

Latin America, Colonialism, and Modernity

The most energetic debate on the subject of Latin America and postcolonialism concerns the character and antiquity of the historical condition of colonization. This is where the inclusion of Latin America not only widens the scope of postcolonial theory but demonstrates how deeply colonial discourse is rooted in global culture. I consider this issue in response to a complaint made by Santiago Colas about *The Empire Writes Back*, which suggests that a discussion of the literatures of former British colonies may be "of interest and relevance" to the literatures of former Spanish colonies. Colas rightly points out that the developments in former Spanish colonies may be "of interest and relevance" to the study of English postcolonial culture and indeed, as he says, "may fundamentally change understandings of that culture" ("Creole" 383). Indeed, Latin America fundamentally changes our view of the postcolonial. The antiquity and character of its colonization, the longstanding reality of its hybridized cultures, the "continental" sense of difference that stems from a shared colonial language, the intermittent emergence of contestatory movements in cultural production – all radically widen the scope of postcolonial theory.

Jorge Klor de Alva asserts in "Colonialism and Postcolonialism as (Latin) American Mirages" that "the very notions of colonialism and imperialism came from the modern experiences of non-Hispanic colonial powers and only subsequently and improperly were imposed on the Spanish American experience from the sixteenth to the eighteenth centuries" (5). But what is an "improper" use? Does the cultural provenance of theory invalidate such categories as epistemological tools? Indeed, is there any system of analysis that does not have a valid retrospective function? I would go further than this

193

and say that such retrospective analysis has deeply transformed discussion of the British Empire as well. After all, imperialism is a very recent concept, formulated in the 1880s scramble for Africa and consolidated in the late nineteenth-century expatriation of British capital. But there is no good reason why we cannot use the term to retrospectively describe five centuries of European expansion.

Indeed the colonization of Latin America obliges us to address the question of postcolonialism at its roots, at the very emergence of modernity. Nineteenth- and twentieth-century British imperialism demonstrates the centrifugal movement by which the precepts of European modernity and the assumptions of the Enlightenment have been distributed hegemonically throughout the world. By including Latin America, as Peter Hulme advocates, we find that imperial expansion is more than the dispersal of European cultural values and assumptions into a Eurocentrically mapped world; it reveals itself as the enabling condition of that very process by which a modern Europe is conceived. Europe's world empire *is* modernity!

Latin America then, the "first-born child" of modernity, is simultaneously "worlded" by Europe, as Spivak puts it, and relegated to the periphery of that world. Spivak uses this term to describe the way in which the colonized space is brought into the "world" – that is, made to exist as part of a world essentially constructed by Eurocentrism:

> If [...] we concentrated on documenting and theorizing the itinerary of
> the consolidation of Europe as sovereign subject, indeed sovereign and
> subject, then we would produce an alternative historical narrative of the
> "worlding" of what is today called "the Third World." (128)

However, the process of European expansion, which began in its modern form with the invasion of America, was an enabling condition of the "worlding" of Europe itself. Imperial expansion, the engine of modernity, gave European societies a sense of their distinction from the traditional premodern societies they invaded, a difference that was taken to be superiority, a status that propelled the continuing discourse of empire itself. The transcultural realities of postcolonial experience are present from this moment as the embedding of global difference begins the process by which the colonized world becomes a crucial factor in the imagining of Europe.

Modernity, which usually refers to those modes of social organization that emerged in Europe from about the sixteenth century, broadly represented by the discovery of the "New World," the Renaissance and the Reformation, does not actually emerge as a concept until the eighteenth century. The invasion of Latin America began a process that, two centuries later, had come to constitute, as Habermas says, "the epochal threshold between modern times and the middle ages" (*Philosophical Discourse* 5). Clearly, this is quite a different concept of modernity from the one Colas has asserted "is consolidated and reaches its highest expression in the 1960's" (*Postmodernity* 24). The threshold of "The Modern World" is the confluence of the three great world systems – imperialism, capitalism, and the Enlightenment. Modernity is fundamentally about conquest, "the imperial regulation of land, the discipline of the soul, and the creation of truth" (Turner 4), a discourse that enabled the large-scale regulation of human identity within both Europe and its colonies.

Thus the emergence of modernity is coterminous with the emergence of Eurocentrism and the European dominance of the world effected through imperial expansion. Europe constructed itself as "modern" and constructed the non-European as "traditional," "static," "prehistorical." History itself became the tool by which these societies were denied any internal dynamic of capacity for development. Latin America, the first-born child of modernity, remained relegated to the status, if not the fact, of the premodern because this continent represents the first instance of the "worlding" of modern Europe. It was in the relationship with Latin America that the energetic Manichaean rhetoric of European cultural expansion was first conceived, from Montaignes's essay "On Cannibals" to Shakespeare's *The Tempest* to Darwin's debasement of the Tierra del Fuegans in *The Voyage of the Beagle*. This binarism remains firmly in place today in various guises, most notably as the distinction between the "international" and the "parochial."

The imperial origins of modernity give us a different perspective on the contemporary eagerness to define Latin American cultural productions as postmodern. Rather than the period of the disappearance of imperialism, the "postmodern" remains the site of its ultimate diffusion into global systems of economy and culture. There are several ways of conceiving postmodernity. We can see it as superseding modernity, in which case it appears to give credence to history, the discourse it claims to have overcome. We can see it as a cultural phenomenon focussed in postmodernism, the "aesthetic reflection on the nature of modernity" (Giddens 45). Or we can see it as modernity's discovery of the provisionality and circularity of its basic premise, the "providential" power of reason. This discovery can be exemplified in Nietzsche's realization that the Enlightenment replaced divine providence with the equally transcendental providence of reason (Habermas, *Philosophical Discourse*). Divine will was replaced by human autonomy, but it was a socially and culturally situated autonomy. In effect, providence was replaced by the temporally and spatially empty dominance of the European Subject. The "providential" rise of reason coincided with the rise of European dominance over the rest of the world and subject-centred reason the philosophical centre of European dominance through the Enlightenment.

The postmodern hinges, then, on the provisionality at the centre of modernity. According to this view, postmodernity is coterminous with modernity and represents a radical phase of its development. But in the same way postcolonialism is coterminous with colonization, and the dynamic of its disruptive engagement is firmly situated in modernity. The postcolonial begins from the moment of colonization, but it is from that moment a recognition of, and a contestation of, the hegemonic and regulatory dominance of the "truth" of modern Europe.

My contention is that postcolonialism and postmodernism are both discursive elaborations of postmodernity, which is itself not the overcoming of modernity, but modernity coming to understand its own contradictions and uncertainties. They are, however, two very different ways in which modernity comes to understand itself. Postcolonial theory reveals the socially transformative dimension of postmodernity, which actually becomes occluded by aesthetic postmodernism. This is because postcolonialism, with its locally situated meanings, refills a time and space that are "emptied" by modernity and constructs a discourse of the real that is based on the material effects of colonial dominance.

Indeed, we can only understand modernity, and hence postmodernity and globalism, if we understand the trajectory of imperial expansion. Anthony Giddens, in talking about modernity and globalism, provides a classic example of the blind spot that occurs when we fail to take imperialism into account. Asking if modernity is a Western project, he replies that in terms of the two great modern systems, the nation-state and capitalism, the answer must be yes. But, he asks, is modernity peculiarly Western in terms of its globalizing tendencies? "No," he says. "It cannot be, since we are speaking here of emergent forms of world interdependence and planetary consciousness" (175). So, by this account, globalism is an emergent process that just happens to come from everywhere! But clearly there would be no global modernity without the history of European expansion. The transcultural complexity of globalism certainly depends upon the transformations enacted by local uses and appropriations in various regions, but these do not take place outside a dialectical process of enculturation and contestation set up by the colonizing process. It is precisely the continuing reality of the imperial dynamic that a postcolonial reading exposes. For Latin America the hegemonic spread of global economy and culture is a significant threat to its modes of cultural location. But just as significantly, globalism can be seen as a direct legacy of the process of Eurocentrism begun several centuries ago.

We can view globalization as either the dynamic operation of nation states or the operation of a single world system. Clearly, while nations are still the principal actors within the global political order, corporations are recognized as the dominant agents in the world economy. The question remains, what is the function of the local in this structure? A *testimonio* such as *Let Me Speak!* by Domatila Barrios de Chungara provides a rich site for a postcolonial analysis because it demonstrates the way in which individual lives are affected by a global system of capital initiated as the economy of the empire of modernity. This novel is amenable to Marxist and Feminist readings, but an understanding of the colonial roots of the system that now appears worldwide helps to explain the racially based cycle of oppression and poverty that presents itself as the Bolivian economy. Common opinion is, she says, that

> "Bolivia is immensely rich, but its inhabitants are just beggars." And
> that's the truth because Bolivia is dominated by the multinational
> corporations that control my country's economy. (20)

Barrios de Chungara's complaint is familiar, but she is the victim of a system begun four centuries ago. Immanuel Wallerstein's world systems theory compellingly asserts that the capitalist system has been *the* world economic system since the sixteenth century and that one cannot talk about economies in terms of the nation state, nor of "society" in the abstract, nor of "stages" of development, because each society is affected by, indeed, is a part of, the capitalist world economy (Wallerstein, *Modern World System* 391). The proposition of one world capitalist system in operation since the sixteenth century radically affects how we view not only world economics but also national politics, class, ethnicity, and international relations in general. The theory has no place for local transformations or political change, but it is a useful critique of the historicist idea of a nation's economic growth, particularly in its approach to the economies of Latin America.

One traditional Marxist view of economic development sees all economies as passing through a series of stages, so it would see these economies as existing at a pre-bourgeoisie, pre-industrialized stage of development. But world systems theory holds that these economies are already a part of the capitalist world system; they are not an earlier stage of a transition to industrialization but are undeveloped because they are "peripheral, raw-material producing" areas, on the margins of, and exploited by, the industrialized world. So economies such as Bolivia's are undeveloped not because they are at any early stage of industrialization but because they are marginalized by the world system. Similarly, we can say that Latin America is not at a stage of development that has left the need for postcolonial analysis behind, but that its cultural productions are a lingering consequence of its imperial history; it still lies at the edges of the world system.

The imperialism of the capitalist system maintains its energy through the same kinds of rhetoric of exclusion that drives the imperial project. The miners, the peasants, all those struggling against capitalist exploitation are invariably Indians. The Bolivian situation is a classic example of the centripetal and global system of capital that continues to marginalize and exploit those on the periphery. But *Let Me Speak!* reveals the limitations of Wallerstein's theory. The lives of individuals, and particularly their taking control of the discursive tools of the dominant powers, can effect a transformation in the local effects of the world system and ultimately in the world system itself. Capitalism is a radical example of the globalizing impetus in modernity – what happens in a local neighbourhood is likely to be influenced by factors operating at an indefinite distance away. But equally, the local community can take hold of the global influence and transform it to local uses.

Strategies of Transformation in Latin American Cultures

The key dynamic of postcolonial discourse, one that affects the survival of local communities within global culture, is that of transformation. In particular the historical experience of colonization has resulted in the mechanics of a transformative appropriation of modernity by colonized societies. Such transformation is *transcultural* – that is, not only are local events affected by the operation of global factors, such as world money and commodity markets, but the global economy of representation is affected itself also by processes of local transformation. Furthermore, this dialectic does not generally occur at the level of the nation-state, an entity that is itself firmly incorporated in global systems of power.

There are many strategies of transformation in Latin America cultures. These strategies come under the rubric of a process I call interpolation (Ashcroft, "Interpolation"), in which the colonized culture interpolates the dominant discourse in order to transform it in ways that release the representation of local realities. The appropriation of language, the utilization of discursive systems of representation such as literature or history, the entering and taking over of systems such as economics or politics are all examples of the colonized culture taking the dominant forms and making them "bear the burden" of a different experience, as Chinua Achebe says of the English language. Postcolonial strategies focus on the political and historical reality of colonialism and are directed at transforming its discourses and institutions. Individual modes of resistance and transformation may have particular local exigencies, such as the oppression of Bolivian miners. But there is an epistemological substrate to the discursive dominance of colonialism that affects all colonized societies within the world system.

To represent modernity as a major revolution in the social life of European, and hence, world society at a particular time in history, a view that only came about in the Enlightenment, is to employ the historical consciousness that is a characteristic of modernity itself. Modernity may be better represented by those discontinuities that signify the most radical divisions between the modern and the premodern and that had the profoundest effect on "premodern" societies – namely, the separation of time and space, the loosening of social relations from the prominence of locality, and the "reflexive ordering and re-ordering of those social relations in terms of continual inputs of knowledge" (Giddens 17). Postcolonial transformation, which is directed at the engagement with and reorientation of colonizing discourses, is at base an engagement with the deepest reorientations of modernity, whether the colonized societies are premodern or not. It is not only "traditional" societies that employ these strategies; rather it is modernity that has constructed them as sites of contention within the postcolonial world.

The sites of postcolonial engagement that appear the most contentious are those that stem from the most radical shift in modern consciousness, the shift in the consciousness of time, because this reorientation generated the most disorienting features of colonial regulatory power. These were the emptying of time and space by separating them from location and the "disembedding" of social relations from locality, which resulted in the "lifting out of social relations from local contexts of interaction and their restructuring across indefinite spans of time and space" (Giddens 21). Indeed, the global change in the concept of a world itself is related in some way to this revolution in modern thought. The most profound disruption, therefore, of premodern social life was not the military destruction wreaked by colonial invasion, nor the importation of disease, nor the imposition of colonial language, nor the depredations of colonial administrations, for all their devastating effects ... but the invention of the mechanical clock.

This one invention and the associated Gregorian calendar metonymize the universal power of European expansion, the hegemony of the capitalist world system, and the most powerful and regulatory discourses of imperialism. The dislocating power of colonial language; the mapping of the world; the naming and regulation of distant lands; the emptying of space and the suppression of place; the surveillance of the colonized; the discourse of history; systematic education; the erection of imperialism's entire spatial and temporal binarism with its invention of race, of cannibalism and primitivism, and its distinction between the spirituality and transcendence of Europe and the materiality and primitivism of the periphery – all these represent modes of imperial control that in turn generate strategies of resistance and transformation in Latin American cultural production.

Three sites of cultural change – language, place, and history – situate perhaps the most profoundly complex interchanges of cultural formation and transformation. In many respects the key to these strategies lies in the use of language. A persistent argument of ethnocentric resistance is that to speak in the colonizer's language is to remain colonized. But an equally persistent argument of postcolonial writers is that the language may be appropriated for the writer's own purposes, its rhythms and syntax changed to correspond to a local idiom. This is the position taken by Angel Rama in *Transculturacion narrativa en America Latin*. In this book he adapts Cuban anthropologist Fernando Ortiz's conceptualization of local Latin American culture as a "transculturation" or *neoculturacion* of metropolitan models to the task of generalizing the literary phenomenon of neoregionalism, represented by authors such as Rulfo, Arguedes, Guimaraes Rosa, and Marquez. *Neoculturacion* is a more global term for the operation of the postcolonial strategies of appropriation and interpolation. This happens at various levels and in virtually every form of cultural discourse, particularly literature, but nowhere more powerfully than in the medium of *testimonio*.

Testimonio

Latin America is not only the beginning of modern Europe's self representation but also the site of the most powerful postcolonial textual production of modern times: a *testimonio* is a novel or novella-length narrative told in the first person by a narrator who is also the actual protagonist or witness of the events she or he recounts. Associated almost exclusively with Latin America, *testimonio* offers an unparalleled example of interpolation: the insertion of an oppressed postcolonial reality into the master discourses of literature and history. It does this by coming into being at the margins of both, entering a "zone of indeterminacy" from which genraic expectations are disrupted. The writings of indigenous subjects of settled colonies provide the greatest range of autobiographical and *testimonio*-like texts. But in no place outside Latin America has the form achieved the kind of genraic focus, readership, consistency of subject matter, and rich development as it has in this region since 1970.

The political urgency, the determination of the narrator to speak for the community, to adopt a subject position that conflates the personal and the political in what may be dangerous – even genocidal – conditions makes the form recognizable across various ethnic, national, and political boundaries within the region. A *testimonio* such as *I, Rigoberta Menchú* is an example of a genre at the margins of literature, occupying a zone of indeterminacy

The conqueror's culture is used specifically to protect the people from the conqueror. Similar issues arise in the production of the testimonial text itself in which the interlocutor might be accused of manipulating or exploiting the material the informant provides to suit her own cosmopolitan political, intellectual, and aesthetic predilections (Beverley 20). But this overlooks the power of the interpolation of the story of the Guatemalan Indians to reach an influential international audience.

Clearly one of the central themes of testimonial literature is the violation of human rights of members of the community by agents of the state. If established literature can be seen as a "cultural form" complicit in this domination, a form of epistemic violence that either implicitly or explicitly sustains these material brutalities, then their appropriation by oppressed peoples seems problematic. But postcolonial analysis has shown the extent to which the appropriation of dominant discursive forms throughout the world has been effective in the counter-discursive project of postcolonial societies. Testimonial literature, by interpolating itself at the juncture of literature and history, puts into question both the standard forms and the very ideas of literature and of history

Colonialism and History

If historicism is the naturalization of empty time, then these texts denaturalize time by inscribing the practices of denaturalization that are constantly present in communal life. Menchú shows how the Quiché ceremonies conflate history in such a way that the Spanish invasion is made to seem an aspect of present experience. All the ceremonies are conducted in terms of an explicit binarism that contrasts a putatively unchanging tradition with the contamination of the white man. It is not unlikely that this motif in the ceremonies is a rather contemporary one, developed for purposes of resistance, but it has an extremely important ideological effect upon the daily lives of the Indians.

Historicism fixes the indigenous subject at a static moment in the past, a prehistory located under the sign of the primitive, of a primal innocence or barbarity. This is the static historical moment from which history, the record of civilization, begins. In response to this, the Quiché Indians continually reinscribe the arrival of the white man in their rituals and ceremonies, thus exposing the originary colonial moment as a prominent feature of the present. Time is dismantled so that the location of the indigenous subject by history in a fixed time of primitive innocence is disrupted. By showing the distant historical event of invasion as an aspect of the present of Indian consciousness, the time of the colonized Indian is constituted as the present time, and thus a time amenable to change and alteration in a political sense, while also being the time of a changeless tradition. The fascinating aspect of this disruption of time is that the present oppressors are not "white" in the sense of being Spanish, but are *mestizos* produced by centuries of intermarriage. By continually reinscribing the colonizing event as a permanent feature of the continuing present, the "history" of Latin American independence and hybridization has, according to many Latin American critics, made the region inaccessible to postcolonial theory and is itself disrupted and denaturalized by at least one colonized group.

However, the tactic is problematic because on the one hand it perpetuates the myth of an unchanging Quiché ethnicity and culture, a myth that is contested at every level of contemporary Quiché life, and on the other it binaristically reinstates the predominance of the colonizing power of the "white man." The preservation of cultural purity is also undermined by the way it puts the people at the mercy of the government. Not only are the Indian groups at the mercy of the dominant landowning class because they cannot speak Spanish, but they cannot communicate with one another and thus organize a united front. Such an organized resistance can only come about once the relevant aspects of the dominant culture are appropriated.

The most extreme and horrific struggle represented in the book is the struggle of the gaze of history described by Menchú in a scene in which the army gathers the villagers from miles around to watch the torture, degradation, and burning alive of their relatives and friends. Nothing could more powerfully demonstrate the way in which colonial power inscribes itself on the bodies of its subjects. The torture and disfigurement seems more than a brutal inflicting of pain; its depravity rests on an organizing principle – that of the "ordered" power of the state (the body politic) against which the bodies of its subjects are rendered subhuman.

Yet the most profoundly brutal aspect of this act is its excessive and violent attempt to control the gaze of the community. The act of forcing the people to watch this appalling spectacle is to interpellate them as the objects of genocidal authority, as powerless voyeurs of their own abjection. Apart from its obvious function of terrorizing the people, it operates discursively as a metonymy of the historical gaze – they are forced to watch their own violation. The gaze in which they are interpellated is the gaze of history. It is this terrorism of the gaze that Menchú's interpolation into history is specifically designed to reverse. By revealing the appalling horror of these actions in this book, by constructing an audience of Spanish and hence English speakers, she appropriates the power of the historical gaze and turns the gaze of the reader and hence of history onto these criminals. By this means of interpolation, the gaze of history itself is reversed.

Conclusion

The *testimonio* of indigenous groups is a relatively uncontentious subject for a postcolonial analysis. But I want to suggest that the real relevance of such analysis to Latin America emerges in that engagement with modern time consciousness and its effects, which occurs in a great range of social groups – *mestizo* or *ladino*, urban or peasant, bourgeois or working class. One example is Juan Rulfo, who is a much more contentious case for a postcolonial analysis. A canonical figure, he is legendary in Latin American literary studies, a formative figure whose brief career is credited with penetrating "by sheer force of poiesis into the epical and even mythical unconscious of peasant Mexico" (Larsen 51). Rulfo is often credited with modernist innovation, his *Pedro Paramo* "a bold excursion into modern techniques of writing" (*Burning Plain* ix). But his postcoloniality becomes apparent through the medium of Angel Rama's use of the concept of transculturation. Reading Rulfo's use of language in *Pedro Paramo* and *The Burning Plain*, Rama shows how language becomes the site of a conflict between the colonizing modernity of the language and the inflection of a localized place:

> The author has become reintegrated with the linguistic community and speaks from within it, with unimpeded use of its idiomatic resources. [...] Here we have the phenomenon of "neoculturation," to use Ortiz's term. If the principles of textual unification and the construction of a literary language of exclusively aesthetic invention can be seen as corresponding to the rationalizing spirit of modernity, by compensation the linguistic perspective that takes up this principle restores a regional world view and prolongs its validity in a form yet richer and more interiorized than before. It thus expands the original world view in a way that is better adapted, authentic, artistically solvent, and, in fact, modernized – but without destruction of identity. (Larsen 56–57)

The percepfion of Rulfo's "reintegration with the linguistic community," speaking "from within it," is a metaphoric and essentialist description of language that would be better expressed metonymically. Rulfo does not so much speak from within local idioms as metonymically signify the local in his language variation. The fact that Rulfo's language does not actually correspond to the speech patterns and narrative forms of Jaliscan countryfolk (54) is immaterial to the metonymic operation of the language variation, which inscribes not authentic identity but metonymic difference. Rama's analysis is nevertheless very much in the nature of a postcolonial reading because the use of language by a Spanish speaker is seen to be adaptable to modes of reinscription of the local, creating a metonymic gap in which the difference of the local can be imagined (see Ashcroft, "Constitutive Graphonomy" and "Is That the Congo?").

Transculturation in Rama's formulation represents the appropriation of the dominant language for the purpose of reinscribing place, which Rama refers to as the "regional world view." The primacy of place in premodern settings has been largely destroyed by the separation of time and space and the "disembedding" of social groups from the significance of locality. The process of "re-embedding" is very clear in Native American *testimonio*. But place remains as a significant site of contention in modern colonial cultures as well. Rulfo's writing demonstrates how a settler culture invents a language that reinvents place. An "appropriation" of language such as Rulfo's metonymically links the language to place in a way that reinvents it in the process of reinscribing it. The separation of time and space that is central to modernity is redressed metonymically by the use of language in this way, which reinscribes the concept of local difference. Crucially, this is not a feature of a clash between a premodern culture and a modern discourse. Colonialism embeds the cultural anxiety attending its emptying out of local space and this becomes a site of contention in a range of colonized societies.

The consideration of Rulfo and Menchú brings together two very different writers, periods, sub-cultures, and classes in Latin American literary history. Yet they reveal to us that the operation of the transformative strategies of postcolonial discourse, strategies that engage the deepest disruptions of modernity, are not limited to the recently colonized, nor to the premodern societies who are still the most marginalized victims of modernization. Postcolonial strategies are those set in motion by the huge effects, both material and discursive, of colonization, no matter how distant the event. This is because colonialism is the militant material working of European modernity, the repercussions and contradictions of which are still in evidence in the global structure of neo-colonial domination.

Works Cited

Ashcroft, Bill. "Constitutive Graphonomy: Towards a Postcolonial Theory of Literary Writing." *Kunapipi* 11.1 (1989): 58–73.

———. "Is That the Congo? Language as Metonymy in the Postcolonial Text." *World Literatures Written in English* 29.2 (1989): 3–10.

———. "Interpolation and Postcolonial Agency." *Factions and Frictions*. Special Issue *New Literatures Review*. Ed. Paul Sharrad, et al. 28/29 (1995): 176–89.

———. "A Conversation with Edward Said." *New Literatures Review* 32 (1997): 3–22.

Baldick, Chris. *The Social Mission of English Criticism 1848–1932*. Oxford: Clarendon, 1987.

Barrios de Chungara, Domatila. *Let Me Speak!* Trans. Victoria Ortiz. Mexico City: Siglo 21, 1978.

Beverley, John. "The Margin at the Center: On *Testimonio* (Testimonial Narrative)." *Modern Fiction Studies* 35.1 (1989): 11–27.

Colas, Santiago. "Of Creole Symptoms, Cuban Fantasies, and Other Latin American Postcolonial Ideologies." *PMLA* 110.3 (1995): 382–96.

———. *Postmodernity in Latin America: The Argentine Paradigm*. Durham: Duke, 1994.

Giddens, Anthony. *The Consequences of Modernity*. Cambridge: Polity, 1990.

Habermas, Jurgen. "Modernity versus Postmodernity." *New German Critique* 22 (1981): 3–14.

———. *The Philosophical Discourse of Modernity*. Trans. Frederick Lawrence. Cambridge: Polity, 1987.

Klor de Alva, Jorge. "Colonialism and Postcolonialism as (Latin) American Mirages." *Colonial Latin American Review* 1.1–2 (1992): 3–23.

Larsen, Neil. *Modernism and Hegemony: A Materialist Critique of Aesthetic Agencies*. Minneapolis: University of Minnesota Press, 1990.

Menchú, Rigoberta. *I, Rigoberta Menchú: An Indian Woman in Guatemala*. Ed. Elisabeth Burgos Debray. Trans. Ann Wright. London: Verso, 1983.

Mignolo, Walter. "Colonial and Postcolonial Discourse: Cultural Critique or Academic Colonialism?" *Latin American Research Review* 28.3 (1993): 120–34.

O'Gorman, Edmundo. *The Invention of America: An Inquiry into the Nature of the New World and the Meaning of Its History*. Bloomington: Indiana University Press, 1961.

Rama, Angel. *La ciudad letrada*. Hanover, NH: del Norte, 1982.

———. *Transculturacion narrativa en America Latin*. Mexico City: Siglo 21. 1982.

Rulfo, Juan. *Pedro Paramo*. 1955. Trans. Margaret Sayers Peden. New York: Grove, 1994.

———. *The Burning Plain*. Trans. George D. Schade. Austin: University of Texas Press, 1967.

Said, Edward. *Orientalism*. London: Routledge, 1978.

———. *The World, the Text, and the Critic*. London: Vintage, 1984.

Seed, Patricia. "Colonial and Postcolonial Discourse." *Latin American Research Review* 26.3 (1991): 181–200.

Spivak, Gayatri Chakravorty. "The Rani of Simur." *Europe and Its Others: Proceedings of the Essex Conference on the Sociology of Literature, July 1984*. Ed. Francis Barker, et al. Colchester: University of Essex Press, 1985.

Turner, Bryan S. *Theories of Modernity and Postmodernity*. Cambridge: Polity, 1990.

Vidal, Hernán Vidal, "The Concept of Colonial and Postcolonial Discourse: A Perspective from Literary Criticism." *Latin American Research Review* 28.3 (1993): 112–19.

Viswanathan, Gauri. "The Beginnings of English Literary Study in British India." *Oxford Literary Review* 9.1–2 (1987): 2–25.

Wallerstein, Immanuel. *The Modern World System: Capitalist Agriculture and the Origin of the European World-Economy in the Sixteenth Century*. New York: Academic, 1974.

Introduction: The Linked Histories of the Globalized World   The Fascist Longings in our Midst   Queer with Class: Absence of Third World Sweatshop in Lesbian/Gay Discourse and a Rearticulation of Materialist Queer Theory   Cross-Mirrorings of Alterity: The Colonial Scenario and Its Psychological Legacy   Mythologies of Migrancy: Post-colonialism, Postmodernism, and the Politics of (Dis)location   Postcolonial DefferendDifferend: Diasporic Narratives of Salman Rushdie   At the Margins of Postcolonial Studies   Keeping History at Wind River and Acoma   Modernity's First Born: Latin America and Postcolonial Transformation

Postcolonial Theory and the "Decolonization" of Chinese Culture

10

Toward Articulation:
Postcolonial Theory
and Demotic Resistance

VICTOR LI

In an important article criticizing postcolonial theory's hegemonic ambition to represent or speak for the dominated and the oppressed, Simon During writes:

> [I]t is important not to forget that the postcolonial paradigm appeals largely to whites and diasporic Indian intellectuals working in the West. It does not appeal to those closest to the continuing struggle against white domination – to Koori activists in Australia or the South African PAC, say; to offer another instance, I do not think there is a Maori word for "postcolonialism." (348)

I will return to During's remark later in this essay, but, for the moment, I want to note that his statement – "I do not think there is a Maori word for 'postcolonialism'" – not only assumes lexical incommensurability but also forwards the argument that a concept or term such as *postcolonialism* is utterly foreign and irrelevant to the Maoris in their struggle for autonomy and self-determination. The Maoris, During implies, do not have a word for "postcolonialism" because they have no need for it. To defend the Maori struggle for autonomy from the totalizing tendencies of metropolitan theory, During utilizes a strategy of cultural separatism. Thus, on one side we are presented with Maori culture with its specific, local concerns, and on the other we have the academic culture of postcolonial studies, with its own separate and distinct agenda.

One can understand why During would want to oppose cultural separatism to the perceived threat of cultural assimilation and domination. Like many contemporary critics, During is suspicious of any discourse that seeks to explain or represent anything other than itself; thus, resisting what he suspects to be a universalizing tendency in metropolitan postcolonial theory, he invokes local cultural particularities. Like most cultural relativists, During also fears that powerful metropolitan cultures will swallow up peripheral ones, thereby destroying their distinctive, resistant cultural identity. Prompted by such fears, well-meaning anthropologists, museum curators, and supporters of indigenous struggles seek to protect a threatened culture by invoking, sometimes to the point of reifying, the culture's "authentic" identity.

However, such forms of cultural protectionism ignore two dangers: the danger that cultural separation may turn into the oppressive rigidity of apartheid and the danger of identifying cultural authenticity with an ahistorical and exotic cultural essentialism. The first danger is succinctly described by the French anthropologist Jean-Loup Amselle:

> Given all the philosophies of history and other sagas of human progress, American culturalist anthropologists along with Lévi-Strauss were right to stress the particularist nature and the relative character of the values promoted by different societies. But the flip side of this generous attitude is the erection of impermeable cultural barriers that imprison each group in its own singularity. [...] Far from being an instrument of tolerance toward, and liberation of, minorities as its proponents like to claim [...] [the notion of separate, distinct cultures] reveals instead all the wrongs of ethnological reason, and that is why it has been claimed by the "new right" in France. To isolate a community by defining a set of characteristic "differences" can lead to the possibility of its territorial confinement. [...] Ethnic labeling, and the assignment of differences, are self-fulfilling prophecies. (qtd. in Lionnet 107)

On the second danger, that of regarding cultural authenticity as unchanging essence, the American anthropologist James Clifford has this to say:

> I am especially sceptical of an almost automatic reflex [...] to relegate exotic peoples and objects to the collective past. [...] Exotic traditions appear [to the modern West] as archaic, purer (and more rare) than the diluted inventions of a syncretic present. In this temporal setup a great many twentieth-century creations can only appear as imitations of more "developed" models. [...] Many traditions, languages, cosmologies, and values are lost, some literally murdered; but much has simultaneously been invented and revived in complex, oppositional contexts. If the victims of progress and empire are weak, they are seldom passive. It used to be assumed, for example, that conversion to Christianity in Africa, Melanesia, Latin America [...] would lead to the extinction of indigenous cultures rather than to their transformations. Something more ambiguous and historically complex has occurred, requiring that we perceive *both* the end of certain orders of diversity and the creation or translation of others. [...] [We must begin to survey] hybrid and subversive forms of cultural representation, forms that prefigure an inventive future. (16–17)

The relegation of cultural authenticity to the past in effect freezes or halts the process of historical and cultural change and denies that a culture may be open to new ideas and new ways of doing things or that it may develop and grow through intercultural addition, adoption, or even appropriation. The attempt to salvage cultural authenticity can turn into the censorship of cultural innovation, as the following example demonstrates. After the Second World War, with the help of the Canadian government, Inuit craft-producing co-operatives were set up and directed to produce carvings that would be recognizably "traditional." A non-Inuit arts-and-crafts specialist was hired to screen out carvings deemed unsuitable. Among those deemed unsuitable was a soapstone sculpture of Elvis Presley, which escaped the sledge-hammer only because of the intervention of a perceptive official "who felt the piece reflected the reality of the Sugluk settlement with which he was familiar" (Brett 122). What this example shows is that "cultural correctness" does not appreciate cultural "border-crossings" or cultural hybridization. To the arts-and-crafts specialist, Elvis belonged firmly to the white world of the south, and the Inuit should only carve seals, bears, hunters, and the like. It probably did not occur to him that Elvis, heard through the radio or glimpsed through magazines and newspapers, may have been as much a part of Inuit everyday life as seals and bears. Moreover, he probably would have been surprised to learn that Elvis was himself a cultural hybrid, a Southern white boy whose rock-and-roll style was derived from Black American music, itself a hybrid of African and European musical idioms.

This phenomenon of cultural intermixing and exchange has been termed "transculturation" by Latin American critics and writers and has been taken up by literary theorists such as Mary Louise Pratt and Françoise Lionnet. In her study of travel writing and colonial encounters, Pratt argues that adopting a transcultural approach allows for a contact perspective that foregrounds "the interactive, improvisational dimensions of colonial encounters so easily ignored or suppressed by diffusionist accounts of conquest and domination" (7). A contact perspective, Pratt continues, "treats the relations among colonizers and colonized [...] not in terms of separateness or apartheid, but in terms of co-presence, interaction, interlocking understandings and practices, often within radically asymmetrical relations of power" (7). Of course, we should never lose sight of asymmetrical relations of power in any encounter between cultures, but a transcultural approach enables us to acknowledge as well that the subaltern culture is neither passive nor lacking in the power to resist, influence, or even redirect and shape the dominant culture.

To Françoise Lionnet, the concept of transculturation provides us with "a new vocabulary for describing patterns of influence that are never unidirectional" (103). She defines transculturation as "a process of cultural intercourse and exchange, a circulation of practices that creates a constant interweaving of symbolic forms and empirical activities among the different cultures that interact with one another" (103–04). The transcultural approach as described by Pratt and Lionnet allows us, for example, not only to accept the conventional view that African slaves were assimilated to "white" American culture but also to comprehend the truth of Kwame Anthony Appiah's claim that "there is [...] no American culture without African roots" (qtd. in Lionnet 102).

Language provides us with the best example of transculturation at work. As the transculturalist *par excellence*, Mikhail Bakhtin, puts it: "The word in language is half someone else's" (293). Even a quick examination of the English language bears out Bakhtin's point, revealing the extent of the language's transculturation. Words that we use in everyday life, such as *shampoo*, *pajamas*, and *ketchup*, or an important newsworthy word such as *tariff*, turn out to be transculturated words, words that have travelled from elsewhere and metamorphosed into English.[1]

The point I wish to make, for the moment somewhat elliptically, is this: adopting the stance of cultural relativism or separatism leads to a problematic politics of identity, while choosing a transcultural approach leads to an empowering politics of articulation (a concept that will be explained in more detail later in this essay). The debates that currently swirl around postcolonial theory, in my view, are debates over which approach to adopt or emphasize. It is to one of these debates that I now turn.

2

A central characteristic of postcolonial theory is its exertion of a certain historical vigilance, a wariness of all monocultural discourses and their colonizing imperative. Postcolonial theory's suspicion of Western narratives of enlightenment and progress is matched equally by its resolve to not be taken in by imagined or invented national allegories of native authenticity. Postcolonial theory's critical vigilance, moreover, is directed against itself, such that its institutional and geopolitical locations, locutions, and interests are all brought into question.

One of the questions postcolonial theory addresses to itself is that of its relation to its constituency, a question that quickly turns into the accusation that theory alienates itself from the very constituency on whose behalf it intervenes. In a somewhat simplified and schematic manner, the problem can be described as the perceived gulf between a highly literate metropolitan theory, with its institutionally privileged enunciative positions and modalities, and the generally disadvantaged demotic speech of marginalized populations. Thus critics such as Benita Parry, Timothy Brennan, and Simon During have all questioned theory in the name of what can be called "demotic resistance." Parry, for example, has accused postcolonial theorists such as Homi Bhabha and Gayatri Spivak of "an exorbitation of discourse" that is deaf to the "alternative text" of the native subaltern (43). In a similar vein, Brennan comments on theory's self-imposed distance from popular national resistance: "the increasing obtuseness, increasingly mandarin quality of metropolitan theory was an indirect way of dealing with the threatening engagements of the decolonized intellectuals' quest for recognition" (103). The most damaging accusation, however, comes from During, whose critical remarks on the irrelevance of postcolonial theory to indigenous struggles have already been cited here.

It can be argued, however, against Parry, Brennan, and During that their critical vigilance is in fact part of the problem they have defined so usefully. Their suspicion of postcolonial theory and their call for demotic resistance, after all, are couched in the same theoretical idiom and delivered from the same privileged locations as those of the postcolonial theorists they critique. There is, it seems to me, no way of avoiding such a performative contradiction as long as postcolonial theorists and their critics remain locked within the theoretical languages and institutional structures against which their vigilance is trained but from which their critical authority, their certification to speak, is nonetheless derived. As Vivek Dhareshwar points out, "Even a discourse that claims to deconstruct the West's constructions of the Other has to still circulate in the discursive space of the West; it remains positioned in that discursive space and its problematics get defined by the structure of address available in that space" (150). Similarly, Gayatri Spivak admits to the aporia of her own critical position, of having to say "'no' to a structure, which one critiques, yet inhabits intimately" (225).

I wish to argue that both postcolonial theory and its critiques land themselves in such a predicament because they reproduce in their arguments a stubbornly persistent binary opposition between the theoretical and the demotic, between theory's suspicion of the simplifications of collective identity and action and popular demotic resistance to the institutional and interpretative privileges accorded to theory. An opposition of this kind locks theory and theory's critiques into an unproductive cycle of vigilance, counter-vigilance, renewed vigilance, and so on.

Postcolonial theory and its demotic critiques are compelled to adopt a strategy of vigilance because of a tendency, often overlooked, in both camps to privilege a politics based on the concept of negative freedom. Negative freedom, a classic liberal ideal, can be defined as the belief in absolute self-determination free from all external constraints, interferences, or influences.[2] In demanding absolute autonomy, negative freedom activates a hermeneutics of suspicion that rigorously tracks down and uncovers any form of external influence or pressure that may compromise the autonomy of an individual or group. Such a hermeneutics of suspicion finds common cause with a politics in which identity remains autonomous and authentic by affirming its difference from others and by vigilantly guarding against external determinants. In relying heavily on a notion of autonomy founded on difference, postcolonial theorists and their demotic opponents find themselves adopting a discourse in which identity is based on separation, demarcation, exclusion, and non-contamination, a discourse of autonomy in which the other is not yet a "possible basis for agreement" (Glissant 97). Thus, in questioning the political and institutional motives of metropolitan postcolonial theory, critics such as Parry, Brennan, and During clearly seek to maintain, through the practice of separatist vigilance, what they regard as the autonomy and integrity of demotic resistance. From the other side, the insistence on the authenticity of the resistant demotic or native voice appears curiously like an indulgence in what Henry Louis Gates Jr. has called "the sentimental romance of alterity" (466). Yet even as postcolonial theorists accuse their demotic detractors of advocating the pure and autonomous identity of the other, their own accusation must assume a certain enunciative autonomy, an identity, however minimal, distancing it from the native or demotic scene it questions. Thus, for instance, even as Edward Said criticizes "nativism" for seeking an illusory autonomy and priority of identity, the cosmopolitan and ironic view that enables his critique appears to insist on a detached and somewhat superior perspective far above the embattled and strident fray of competing standpoints (see Said 275–76). In other words, Said's championing of cultural heteronomy and hybridity requires him, paradoxically, to maintain the autonomy and purity of a freelance, exilic consciousness. As Said has remarked in an interview, "[E]ven in the case of the Palestinian movement itself I've made it a point never to accept an official role of any sort; I've always retained my independence" (qtd. in McGowan 175). It appears that for Said the preservation of otherness in the same, of difference in identity, requires that the otherness or difference of the critic be kept free and separate in itself. But as John McGowan points out in his critique of Said's valorization of oppositional otherness, "[T]o imagine the other as distant and separate is profoundly undialectical [...] [since it] rests on an assumption of self-sufficiency, of an identity forged in the absence of social ties" (175). Thus, taking an ironic turn, Said's suspicion of purist identity politics depends on his acceptance of the pure and autonomous oppositional identity of the critic.

What should be clear, then, is that certain tendencies in both postcolonial theory and demotic critiques of postcolonial theory readily assume a concept of negative freedom, of autonomy from all external influences and relations, and thus lock themselves into rigid oppositions that exercise vigilance against external threats to that autonomy. It may be more productive in the long run to relax the opposition and shift the emphasis from the defensive autonomy of negative freedom (freedom *from*) to a more open, more relational and positive version of freedom (freedom *to*), a freedom enabled rather than constrained by social relationships. To go beyond the ultimately paralyzing mode of theoretical self-vigilance will require the thought of relationality or transculturation and the practice of articulation, the productive though always provisional and uncertain colligation of different elements. Stuart Hall, who has done much to promote the theory of articulation, defines it thus:

> In England, [articulation] has a nice double meaning because "articulate" means to utter, to speak forth, to be articulate. [...] But we also speak of an "articulated" lorry: a lorry where the front and back can, but need not necessarily, be connected to one another. The two parts are connected to each other, but through a specific linkage that can be broken. An articulation is thus the form of the connection that *can* make a unity of two different elements, under certain conditions. It is a linkage which is not necessary, determined, absolute and essential for all time. You have

to ask, under what circumstance *can* a connection be forged or made? So
the so-called "unity" of a discourse is really the articulation of different,
distinct elements which can be rearticulated in different ways because
they have no necessary "belongingness." (53)

Hall's description of articulation allows us to rethink and reinvent the
possibility of linkage where opposition and difference may seem only too
firmly entrenched. Rather than falling into the frozen certainties of political
identities or the stalemated opposition of different ideologies, the practice of
articulation reopens the dimension of agency, change, risk, and uncertainty.
In short, it enables us to make our own history even under conditions not
of our choosing. Thus, instead of privileging theory at the expense of the
demotic or vice versa, or defending the purity of demotic resistance against
the cosmopolitanism of theory or vice versa, or allowing the perceived
antagonism between theory and the demotic to settle into an unavoidable
aporia, we should attempt to grasp them relationally, placing and articulating them in the same space of struggle, judgement, and enunciation. Homi
Bhabha argues that such an emphasis on the activity of articulation produces
a shift from "the negative dialectics of the 'symptomatic reading' [or what I
have called theoretical self-vigilance], to an attention to the place and time
of the enunciative agency" ("Postcolonial Authority" 57). The emphasis on
agency and articulation allows us to go beyond vigilance and the guilt and
suspicion that generate vigilance, and to redirect our energies instead to the
more difficult and uncertain task of cultural creation and collective social
action.

This is why I think social activists and politically engaged writers have
been ahead of academics in their awareness of the need to question the strict
separations necessary to the desire for absolute cultural or critical autonomy
and to engage instead in the political activity of articulation. I will thus turn
to the work of Rigoberta Menchú, Edouard Glissant, and Chinua Achebe and
briefly sketch how I think they can help us end the rift between institutionally
privileged discourses and the claims of the demotic.

3

The Nobel Peace Prize winner of 1992, the Guatemalan Indian activist
Rigoberta Menchú, ends her *testimonio* with these words:

[M]y commitment to our struggle knows no boundaries nor limits. This is
why I've travelled to many places where I've had the opportunity to talk
about my people. Of course, I'd need a lot of time to tell you all about my
people, because it's not easy to understand just like that. And I think I've

given some idea of that in my account. Nevertheless, I'm still keeping
my Indian identity a secret. I'm still keeping secret what I think no-one
should know. Not even anthropologists or intellectuals, no matter how
many books they have, can find out all our secrets. (247)

Though Menchú's insistence on safeguarding the autonomy and inviolability
of her Indian identity comes through very clearly, it is important to note as
well that she recognizes the need to publicize her people's plight and to gain
the solidarity of others. Though rooted in a constituency, she also realizes
that a wider audience is needed in the struggle waged for the survival of her
people. Moreover, as George Yúdice has pointed out, Menchú's affirmation
of her Indian identity leads neither to essentialism nor to a "romanticized
ancestral reconciliation" because it is part of a "cultural and political practice
necessary for survival" (226). This cultural and political practice requires
Menchú to engage simultaneously in the defence of autonomous identity and
the search for new articulations, for new forms of political struggle. We see
this when Menchú, in order to preserve her Indian identity and the ways of her
ancestors, decides to join a national peasant organization, thereby embracing,
as she puts it, "other things, other ways" (149). Menchú's double strategy of
defending autonomy through the practice of social or political articulation
is also evident in her attitude to education in general and the learning of
Spanish in particular. Thus Menchú agrees with her father's warning – "My
children, don't aspire to go to school, because schools take our customs away
from us" (169) – and adds, "[E]ven though a person may learn to read and
write, he should not accept the false education they give our people. Our
people must not think as the authorities think. They must not let others
think for them" (170). Yet Menchú's resistance to education is a resistance
to the hegemonic educational system imposed by the non-Indian central
government in Guatemala. She does not abandon the idea of learning; nor
does she deny the importance of learning Spanish. On the contrary, Menchú
says that although her life has taught her many things, "human beings are
also made to learn many more" (162). Further, with a pragmatism born out of
political activism, she adds: "Since Spanish was a language which united us
[that is, the different Indian groups] why learn all the twenty-two languages
in Guatemala? It wasn't possible, and anyway this wasn't the moment to do
it. [...] I learned Spanish out of necessity" (162).

Menchú's participation in a national peasant movement also taught her
to see beyond cultural and ethnic oppositions, which, as often as not, are
created by a shared history of political and material oppression. Thus, though
Menchú proudly proclaims her native identity, she is not a naïve nativist,
for she also understands that her own identity includes different elements,

different sub-constituencies, if you will, and that she has to participate fully in the struggle as "an Indian first, and then as a woman, a peasant, a Christian" (120). She also realizes that as a Guatemalan Indian she must try to articulate her struggle to that of the Spanish-speaking *ladinos*. Thus, in a moment of self-reflection and self-critique, she remarks:

> As I was saying, I'm an Indian*ist*, not just an Indian. I'm an Indianist to my fingertips and I defend everything to do with my ancestors. But I didn't understand this in the proper way, because we can only understand when we start talking to each other. And this is the only way we can correct our ideas. Little by little, I discovered many ways in which we had to be understanding towards our *ladino* friends and in which they had to show us understanding too. Because I also knew *compañeros ladinos* with whom we shared the worst conditions, but who still felt *ladino,* and as *ladinos* they didn't see that our poverty united us. But little by little, both they and I began discussing many very important things and saw that the root of our problems lay in the ownership of the land. All our country's riches are in the hands of the few. (166)

The most important lesson we can learn from Menchú's testimony is that the struggle to preserve the autonomy of cultural identity may require a further thinking beyond autonomy toward social and political articulation; or as Menchú puts it, "[W]e have to erase the barriers which exist between ethnic groups, between Indians and *ladinos*, between men and women, between intellectuals and non-intellectuals, and between all the linguistic areas" (233).

4

Like Menchú, the Martinican writer and critic Edouard Glissant advocates resistance to the "all-encompassing world of cultural sameness, effectively imposed by the West." He too asserts the importance of preserving the identity of one's culture from that "universal humanism that incorporates all (national) peculiarities" (97). Thus, like Menchú, Glissant initially calls for a protective vigilance, for "[a]n identity on its guard, in which the relationship with the Other shapes the self without fixing it under an oppressive force. That is what we see everywhere in the world: each people wants to declare its own identity" (169). Again, however, like Menchú, Glissant affirms the autonomy of cultural identity precisely in order to open it out to a world of cultural diversity and cultural interchange, to what Glissant terms the recognition of "la Relation" (xii). Thus, even as Glissant asserts the need for "an awareness of our place in the world," he also adds that we must reflect "on the necessary and disalienated relationship with the Other" (169). Autonomy once attained, in Glissant's view, should not lead to isolation or separation but to a poetics of productive relationships and creative articulations. As he puts it, "To declare one's identity is to write the world into existence" (169).

Glissant's views on creolization are instructive in this regard. Glissant approaches Martinican Creole without any romantic illusions about its status as both a language of resistance and a language of powerlessness. Creole as a language of resistance is also Creole as powerless language. What does Glissant mean by this? First of all, Creole, in its present form in Martinique, is an anti- or counter-language. It is a language that produces through "fits and starts [...] an attempt to deny the Other's total and corrosive hold" (159). The Other, of course, is the colonizer's language, French. Like his fellow countryman, Frantz Fanon, Glissant is aware that France's granting of citizenship, of *departement* status, to Martinique is a concession and an imposition that has trapped Martinicans in greater dependency and that the only response to such a "benevolent" imposition is to resist it. As Glissant puts it,

> The only source of light ultimately was that of the transcendental presence of the Other, of his Visibility – colonizer or administrator – of his transparency fatally proposed as a model, because of which we have acquired a taste for obscurity, and for me the need to seek out obscurity, that which is not obvious, to assert for each community the right to a shared obscurity. (161)

As an obscurity directed at the dominant Other, Creole is a language of resistance. As Glissant goes on to argue, however, to base the identity of Creole solely on resistance, on a form of negative freedom, is to declare in a sense its powerlessness; it is to base identity on *reaction* to the Other rather than *action* for oneself. Thus Creole as linguistic or poetic resistance "will be insignificant unless it is an integral part of a resolute collective act – a political act" (163). That resolute collective act implies not only Martinique's political self-determination but also Martinique's cultural emancipation from France. Such a cultural liberation would require, as a first step, the transformation of Creole from an anti- or counter-language based on resistance to French to a Creole that can affirm and celebrate its own identity without having to defer to, and thus without having to resist, the authority of French. In other words, Glissant wants to replace the negative reactional freedom, on which Creole's present linguistic identity is based, with a more positive concept of freedom that affirms Creole's identity as diversity and not as a language that has failed to attain purity. As Glissant explains,

> The idea of creolization demonstrates that henceforth it is no longer valid to glorify "unique" origins that the race safeguards and prolongs.

> [...] To assert peoples are creolized, that creolization has value, is to
> deconstruct in this way the category of "creolized" that is considered as
> halfway between two "pure" extremes. [...] Creolization as an idea means
> the negation of creolization as a category [that is, the category of Creole
> as impure French, a category imposed by the French and tacitly accepted
> by Martinicans in their use of it to resist official French], by giving priority
> to the notion of natural creolization, which the human imagination has
> always wished to deny or disguise (in Western tradition). (140–41)

Glissant's rethinking of creolization allows him, therefore, to see cultural or
linguistic identity as multiply determined, as always-already transculturated.
One's cultural or linguistic autonomy is thus, for Glissant, never fixed and
isolated but always an ongoing articulation of differences. One of these differences that has been articulated in Creole, not as an instance of a pure or
superior identity but as merely another equal element in a new collectively
formed language, is French. In Glissant's words: "If, therefore, when we deal
with our own history, we adopt (we Caribbean people) the various European
languages and adapt them, no one will teach us how to do this. We will
perhaps be the ones to teach others a new poetic and, leaving behind the
poetics of not-knowing [or the counter-poetics of a counter-language], will
initiate others into a new chapter in the history of mankind" (169).

Following Glissant's lead, a younger generation of writers, Jean Bernabé,
Patrick Chamoiseau, and Raphael Confiant, in their manifesto "In Praise
of Creoleness," argue that Creoleness is always-already transcultural or
translingual:

> Creoleness is not monolingual. Nor is its multilingualism divided
> into isolated compartments. Its field is language. Its appetite: all the
> languages of the world. The interaction of many languages (the points
> where they meet and relate) is a polysonic vertigo. [...] Living at once the
> poetics of all languages is not just enriching each of them, but also, and
> above all, breaking the customary order of these languages, reversing
> their established meanings. (901)

Glissant and Bernabé, Chamoiseau, and Confiant, therefore, repudiate the
binary opposition that would put Creole in its demotic place and install
French on the plane of high culture; they argue instead for a Creole that
articulates linguistic relationships in all kinds of unsuspected ways, as Glissant
explains:

> It is the unknown area of these relationships that weaves, while
> dismantling the conception of the standard language, the "natural

texture" of our new baroque, our own. Liberation will emerge from this cultural composite. The "function" of Creole languages, which must resist the temptation of exclusivity, manifests itself in this process, far removed from the [...] fire of the melting-pot. (250)

5

Glissant's meditations on the diversity that constitutes cultural, national, or linguistic identity are very similar to Chinua Achebe's concerns in his novel *Anthills of the Savannah*. Glissant's remark – "Diversity needs the presence of peoples, no longer as objects to be swallowed up, but with the intention of creating a new relationship" (98) – could well sum up Achebe's rethinking of postcolonial national identity in his novel. *Anthills of the Savannah* describes the dissolution of an authoritarian nationalist discourse no longer in touch with the realities of the common people and shows how that dissolution leads to the political awakening of the novel's three main characters – Chris Oriko, Ikem Osodi, and Beatrice Nwanyibuife – who begin to unlearn their own isolated elitist premises and privileges. All three characters, highly placed in the social hierarchy, undergo a transformation as they shed their "been-to" stance of superiority as graduates of London University. All three become "wide-eyed newcomer[s]" (201) to the ways of their own country, a fictional West African state named Kangan. Far from being the administrators and intellectuals who have the knowledge to guide their society, they learn, to their surprise and humility, that they are alienated from their own people and that they have to be taught the demotic wisdom they have so long ignored. Thus Chris, for example, in his flight from the country's dictator (his former classmate, Sam) has to be instructed in the art of street survival by the taxi driver, Braimoh. Recognizing the value of the instruction he has received, Chris says humbly to Braimoh: "Thank you [...] I must remember that [...] [t]o succeed as small man no be small thing" (194).

The novel argues that for too long the dominant nationalist discourse of Kangan has centred around an elite male clique that has claimed to represent the nation; but as Beatrice angrily reminds Chris: "Well, you fellows all three of you [Chris, Ikem, and the dictator, Sam], are incredibly conceited. The story of this country, as far as you are concerned, is the story of the three of you" (66). In turn, Beatrice learns that the national discourse should include not only educated women like her but also the likes of Ikem's half-literate mistress, Elewa, and Beatrice's own Christian maid, Agatha (184–85). The failure of Kangan nationalist discourse is therefore the failure of its exclusions, the failure, as Ikem observes, "of our rulers to re-establish vital inner links with the poor and dispossessed of this country" (141). We must note, however, that the novel's increasing inclusion of the voices of the poor and dispossessed and of the pidgin they use does not lead to a rejection of the intellectual's role in society. The intellectual, to be sure, is no longer *the* centre of authority. Yet, at the same time, the intellectual becomes part of a new articulation of national identity and authority. I want to look at two set pieces in the novel in which this new articulation takes place.

The first is Ikem Osodi's lecture to a university audience in which he recounts the Abazon Elder's fable "The Tortoise and the Leopard" as an example of political struggle. Though Ikem's use of the Elder's fable reveals his respect for the traditional lore of his people, his respect does not condemn the fable to a quaint folklorish status; there is no ideology of salvage, no attempt at preserving the exotic elements of the tale in Ikem's retelling. The traditional tale is adapted by Ikem for a modern university audience and in the process an articulation is achieved linking the Abazonian struggle to the problems besetting Kangan society as a whole. Moreover, the work of articulation is not solely that of the intellectual. The Abazonian Elder, in telling Ikem the story in the first place, shows his awareness that the tale would travel well and that, through Ikem, he can link his Abazonian constituency to a more diverse Kangan audience. The Elder's understanding that Abazonian identity depends on articulation rather than separation or isolation from the rest of Kangan is expressed clearly when he rebukes one of his fellow Abazonians for criticizing Ikem's absence from Abazonian social ceremonies:

> Go on with your meetings and marriages and naming ceremonies because it is good to do so. But leave this young man alone to do what he is doing for Abazon and for the whole of Kangan; the cock that crows in the morning belongs to one household but his voice is the property of the neighbourhood. You should be proud that this bright cockerel that wakes the whole village comes from your compound. (122)

Ikem's lecture at the university thus provides an example of a successful articulation of the traditional and the modern, the regional and the national, the demotic and the academic. It is possible, Achebe appears to be saying, for the intellectual to remain an intellectual and yet learn from the people and be of service to the people. The intellectual is most herself or himself when she or he becomes a model of social articulation; as Ikem Osodi puts it,

> There seems no way I can become like the poor except by faking. What I know, I know for good or ill. So for good or ill I shall remain myself, but with this deliberate readiness now to help and be helped. Like those complex, multivalent atoms in Biochemistry books, I have arms that reach out in all directions – a helping hand, a hand signalling for help. (142)

The other example of social articulation occurs at the end of the novel, in which Beatrice holds a naming ceremony for the baby daughter of Elewa and the murdered Ikem. The gathering can be read as Achebe's reimagining of the Nigerian nation, a reimagining in which differences are included and articulated in new and creative ways and not simply elided as they would have been in an elitist, masculinist nationalism. The gathering illustrates Glissant's statement that "the nation is not based on exclusion; it is a form of disalienated relationship with the other, who in this way becomes our fellow man" (250). At the naming ceremony we find different ethnic groups, Muslim and Christian, men and women, old and young. Moreover, the gathering, which is described as an "ecumenical fraternization" (224), though traditional in its observation of ritual, is also innovative in that Beatrice gives the baby girl a boy's name: Amaechina, "May-the-path-never-close" (222). The name is conferred at a traditional ceremony; but, in turn, through Beatrice's uncoupling of name and gender, tradition is transformed, given new life and reoriented toward the future – "May-the-path-never-close." This simultaneous observation and transformation of tradition is what Elewa's roguish old uncle admires when he says,

> Do you know why I am laughing like this? I am laughing because in you young people our world has met its match. Yes! You have put the world where it should sit [...]. My wife here was breaking her head looking for kolanuts, for alligator pepper, for honey and for bitter leaf. [...] And while she is cracking her head you people gather in this whiteman house and give the girl a boy's name. [...] That is how to handle this world. (227)

Again, what we have in the uncle's guarded approval of Beatrice's action is a recognition of the need for articulation between the generations, between the genders, between the past and the present, between the old medicine-man uncle and Beatrice, the London University graduate with a "walloping honours degree in English" (62). In a recent interview, Achebe describes his own practice of articulation in the following way: "We do have several traditions. We have the indigenous tradition, the oral tradition, the vernaculars, the ancient tradition of literature before, but we also have today. You can't disappear back into the past, so we need to create a synthesis of these two. That is the issue" ("Interview" 79–80).

6

With the examples of Menchú, Glissant, and Achebe in mind, in conclusion I would like to return to Simon During's remark that postcolonial theory "does not appeal to those closest to the continuing struggle against white domination" (348) and that there is no word in Maori for "postcolonialism."

During's remark is useful in cautioning us against postcolonial theory's ambition to be the avant-garde of political struggle. But from the point of view that I have adopted in this essay, During's comment is problematic not only because it assumes, rather patronizingly, to know the real interests of the Maoris but, more importantly, because it forecloses the possibility of articulating local Maori struggles to a wider national or transnational arena of struggle, thereby disallowing the possibility of forging larger solidarities, stronger political blocs. It seems to me that if postcolonial theory should learn, as During rightly suggests, to curb its ambition and recognize that the discursive ambiguities and complexities it so elegantly formulates must be tempered by the cruder and harsher but no less ambiguous and complex demands of local political struggles, then it is equally the case that local political activists may find the arguments and strategies of postcolonial theorists to be of some use in their struggle. Thus, *contra* During, it can be argued that although "postcolonialism" may not exist in the lexicon of Koori and Maori activists, its addition may be welcomed by those activists if only because it widens the scope of their struggle and adds to their arsenal of strategies.

Why, then, does During insist on keeping metropolitan postcolonial theory separate from Maori political activism? It is, I suspect, partly because he fears that any contact between the two will result in an unequal exchange leading to the co-optation of the latter by the former. Arif Dirlik expresses a similar concern in his critique of postcolonial theory when he argues that the postcolonial valorization of hybridity conceals an asymmetry of power relations that favours metropolitan-based postcolonial intellectuals. Yet although Dirlik is right in insisting that "not all positions are equal in power" (343), both he and During underestimate the ability of the "weaker" party to confront, appropriate, change, and adapt the dominant discourse to suit its own needs. Thus, while Dirlik and During can only observe the silencing of the subaltern demotic voice by metropolitan theory, the assimilation of the other into the same, a more sensitive analysis can detect subtle ways in which the subaltern other can take up the dominant discourse and, through a process of critical mimicry, work its changes on that discourse. As Homi Bhabha points out, when a statement from one institution is transcribed in the discourse of another, a process of destabilization and innovation occurs, since "any change in the statement's conditions of use and reinvestment, any alteration in its field of experience or verification, or indeed any difference in the problems to be solved, can lead to the emergence of a new statement: the difference of the same" (*Location of Culture* 22). According to Bhabha's analysis, concern over the metropolitan co-optation and assimilation of the subaltern is challenged by the subaltern's subversive mimicry – fear over the making same of the different mocked by the making different of the same. In his study of how the Kwaios of the Solomon Islands resisted British colonialism, Roger Keesing usefully reminds us that "[e]ven when they appear to be appropriating the structures and categories and logics of colonial discourse, subaltern peoples progressively but ultimately radically transform them, in the very process of transgression and in their deployment in a counter hegemonic political struggle" (238).[3]

However politically well-intentioned, the desire to protect the subaltern demotic voice from metropolitan theory, ironically, can end up preventing the establishment of coevalness between the two. In seeking to defend the subaltern Other's autonomy, metropolitan critics like During find themselves implicated in the very situation of dominance they wish to dismantle. By their logic, the subaltern's autonomy is predicated on the subaltern's unchanging structural position as the Other of the West. However, this "othering," which ensures the subaltern's autonomy, also betrays the vulnerability of subaltern identity, its problematic unchanging role as reactive opposition to active Western domination, for, as Bhabha has warned, "the site of cultural difference can become the mere phantom of a dire disciplinary struggle in which it has no space or power [...] [and in which] the Other text is forever the exegetical horizon of difference, never the active agent of articulation" (*Location of Culture* 31). Asked to function as the deconstructive limit of Western knowledge, the subaltern Other, more often than not, is constructed into being by dissenting factions of the West. As such, the Other is frozen in an antithetical, adversarial role, its identity forever dependent on its difference from the West. Essentialized and preserved in theoretical aspic, the Other is made to function as the conscience of the West, turned into an allochronic entity whose history is controlled by the deconstructive needs of the Western academy rather than its own. Coeval historical agency, innovation, and change are denied to the Other in order that it can remain forever as the limit-text of the West. Thus, whenever a non-Western subaltern Other is told not to take up Western knowledges or discourses because to do so would be to betray his or her indigenous culture, what some anthropologists have called "the salvage paradigm" is activated and the model indigenous culture is denied historical agency in order that it can be salvaged and displayed in all its purity and autonomy *by* and *for* the West.

Is there a Maori word for "postcolonialism"? The answer, I hope it is clear, should not be "no and there is no need for such a word," but "not yet." Depending on Maori needs, *postcolonialism* may well become a loanword inserted into the Maori lexicon, a metropolitan word that will become locally inflected, ceding its identity as it becomes articulated to Maori exigencies. A continent away from the Maori struggle, the Mayan peasants of Chiapas launched their rebellion on the same New Year's Day that the North American Free Trade Agreement (NAFTA) took effect. NAFTA entered the lexicon of the Zapatista rebels because they understood that the struggle for their indigenous rights and for their very livelihood had to be engaged not only on their own local ground but also on a nation-wide and transnational basis. Shedding the image of what Alcida Ramos has called "the hyperreal Indian," the Indian created in the image of predominantly white-staffed indigenist movements – the Indian who is "dependent, suffering, a victim of the system, innocent of bourgeois evils, honourable in his actions and intentions, and preferably exotic" (163) – the Mayan rebels of Chiapas launched what Roger Burbach has called a "postmodern rebellion" (113). They skilfully utilized the media for their own ends, and Burbach reports that when he visited the region with an international delegation in March, 1994, a few months after the uprising, he was struck by the sophisticated nature of their demands:

> In a meeting with many of the community members, it was striking that the women's organization took the lead in discussing the community's needs and plans as well as the obstacles it faced. They wanted decent schools, medical services, assistance so they could attend nearby technical colleges, and the right to elect their own representatives at the municipal and state level. They also wanted lands from the nearby cattle estate to augment production [...] but were fully cognizant of the fact that these lands could only be farmed with appropriate technologies to avoid impoverishing the delicate soil of the region. (123–24)

The Chiapas uprising proves that in order for subaltern or dominated peoples to be other than objects of study or recipients of action by well-meaning post-colonial theorists, rock stars, or metropolitan political activists, they must be seen as they see themselves – not as isolated, vulnerable peoples (though they can be that too) whose authentic way of life needs to be protected, preserved, or salvaged by external powers but as theoretical and cultural coevals and co-actors who are interested in metropolitan knowledges, techniques, and goods and who can freely articulate these with their own local, historical needs and practices. As Rigoberta Menchú puts it, arguing for resistance as articulated action rather than piecemeal reaction: "We need to be on the constant lookout for new techniques. [...] [E]verything must have a reason or we might do things we want to, but without knowing why we're doing them" (130).

Notes

1 "Shampoo" comes from the Hindi verb *champna* ("to press") and its familiar imperative, *champo.* "Pajamas" is derived from the Hindi word for a type of loose trousers, *pajama,* itself borrowed from the Persian compound word made up of *pai* ("foot") and *jamah* ("garment clothing"). "Ketchup" travelled into English from a Chinese regional dialect term for shellfish sauce – *Kӓe* ("shellfish" or "seafood") and *tsiap* ("brine" or "sauce"). Finally, "tariff" comes from a Turkish variant of the Arabic word *tarif* ("notification, explanation"). For extended discussions of the etymology of these and other transculturated words in English, see Louis G. Heller, Alexander Humez, and Malcah Dror, *The Private Lives of English Words.*

2 For an excellent critique of the uses of negative freedom in postmodern and postcolonial criticism, see John McGowan's *Postmodernism and Its Critics,* especially chapter 3.

3 In a similar vein, Anuradha Dingwaney Needham has argued that C.L.R. James critically appropriated the colonial sport of cricket and turned it into a symbol of West Indian self-determination: by seizing upon a symbol of English (*i.e.,* the colonizer's) national character – cricket – to represent West Indian (*i.e.,* the colonized's) self-definition, James, in effect, abducts "Englishness" (as defined by cricket) and makes it not the exclusive property of the colonizers but rather the means by which the colonized peoples of the Caribbean set themselves free (288).

Works Cited

Achebe, Chinua. *Anthills of the Savannah.* London: Picador, 1988.

———. "Interview with Feroza Jussawalla." *Interviews with Writers of the Post-Colonial World.* Ed. Feroza Jussawalla and Reed Way Dasenbrock. Jackson: University of Mississippi Press, 1992.

Bakhtin, Mikhail. *The Dialogic Imagination.* Ed. M. Holquist. Trans. C. Emerson and M. Holquist. Austin: University of Texas Press, 1981.

Bernabé, Jean, Patrick Chamoiseau, and Raphael Confiant. "In Praise of Creoleness." Trans. Mohamed B. Taleb Khyar. *Callaloo* 13.4 (1990): 886–909.

Bhabha, Homi K. *The Location of Culture.* New York: Routledge, 1994.

———. "Postcolonial Authority and Postmodern Guilt." *Cultural Studies.* Ed. Lawrence Grossberg, Cary Nelson, and Paula A. Treichler. New York: Routledge, 1992. 56–68.

Brennan, Timothy. "Black Theorists and Left Antagonists." *The Minnesota Review* 37 (1991): 89–113.

Brett, Guy. "Unofficial versions." *The Myth of Primitivism.* Ed. Susan Hiller. New York: Routledge, 1991. 113–36.

Burbach, Roger. "Roots of the Postmodern Rebellion in Chiapas." *New Left Review* 205 (1994): 113–24.

Clifford, James. *The Predicament of Culture:Twentieth-Century Ethnography, Literature, and Art.* Cambridge, MA: Harvard University Press, 1988.

Dhareshwar, Vivek. "Toward a Narrative Epistemology of the Postcolonial Predicament." *Inscriptions* 5 (1989): 135–57.

Dirlik, Arif. "The Postcolonial Aura: Third World Criticism in the Age of Global Capitalism." *Critical Inquiry* 20.2 (1994): 328–56.

During, Simon. "Postcolonialism and Globalization." *Meanjin* 51.2 (1992): 339–53.

Gates, Henry Louis Jr. "Critical Fanonism." *Critical Inquiry* 17.3 (1991): 457–70.

Glissant, Edouard. *Caribbean Discourse: Selected Essays.* Trans. J. Michael Dash. Charlottesville: University Press of Virginia, 1989.

Hall, Stuart. "On Postmodernism and Articulation: An Interview with Stuart Hall." *Journal of Communication Inquiry* 10.2 (1986): 45–60.

Heller, Louis G., Alexander Humez, and Malcah Dror. *The Private Lives of English Words*. Tarrytown, NY: Wynwood Press, 1991.

Keesing, Roger M. *Custom and Confrontation: The Kwaio Struggle for Cultural Autonomy*. Chicago: University of Chicago Press, 1992.

Lionnet, Françoise. "'Logigues métisses': Cultural Appropriation and Postcolonial Representations." *College Literature* 19.3/20.1 (1992/93): 100–20.

McGowan, John. *Postmodernism and Its Critics*. Ithaca: Cornell University Press, 1991.

Menchú, Rigoberta. *I, Rigoberta Menchú, An Indian Woman in Guatemala*. Ed. Elisabeth Burgos-Debray. Trans. Ann Wright. London: Verso, 1984.

Needham, Anuradha Dingwaney. "Inhabiting the Metropole: C.L.R. James and the Postcolonial Intellectual of the African Diaspora." *Diaspora* 2.3 (1993): 281–303.

Parry, Benita. "Problems in Current Theories of Colonial Discourse." *Oxford Literary Review* 9 (1987): 27–58.

Pratt, Mary Louise. *Imperial Eyes: Travel Writing and Transculturation*. New York: Routledge, 1992.

Ramos, Alcida Rita. "The Hyperreal Indian." *Critique of Anthropology* 14.2 (1994): 153–71.

Said, Edward. *Culture and Imperialism*. New York: Knopf, 1993.

Spivak, Gayatri Chakravorty. "Poststructuralism, Marginality, Postcoloniality and Value." *Literary Theory Today*. Ed. Peter Collier and Helga Geyer-Ryan. Ithaca: Cornell University Press, 1990. 219–44.

Yúdice, George. "Marginality and the Ethics of Survival." *Universal Abandon? The Politics of Postmodernism*. Ed. Andrew Ross. Minneapolis: University of Minnesota Press, 1988. 214–36.

Introduction: The Linked Histories of the Globalized World   The Fascist Longings in our Midst   Queer with Class: Absence of Third World Sweatshop in Lesbian/Gay Discourse and a Rearticulation of Materialist Queer Theory   Cross-Mirrorings of Alterity: The Colonial Scenario and Its Psychological Legacy   Mythologies of Migrancy: Post-colonialism, Postmodernism, and the Politics of (Dis)location   Postcolonial DefferendDifferend: Diasporic Narratives of Salman Rushdie   At the Margins of Postcolonial Studies   Keeping History at Wind River and Acoma   Modernity's First Born: Latin America and Postcolonial Transformation   Towards Articulation: Postcolonial Theory and Demotic Resistance

Postcolonial Theory and the "Decolonization" of Chinese Culture

WANG NING

In current Chinese critical and academic circles, "postist" (*hou zhuyi*) issues such as postmodernism, post-Confucianism, post-Intellectualism, post-Chinese studies, post-Enlightenment, and postcolonialism are much discussed and debated among scholars, literary critics, and other intellectuals of the humanities and social sciences.[1] These terms frequently appear in various academic journals or literary magazines, puzzling ordinary readers as well as some old-fashioned intellectuals of humanistic tendencies. Strangely enough, scholars very often discuss these terms without quoting or referring to the original works. In the case of postcolonialism, for instance, they ignore the primary texts of such eminent theorists of postcolonialism in the West as Edward Said, Gayatri Spivak, and Homi Bhabha, let alone analyze them in a critical and profound way in order to carry on a theoretical dialogue with international scholarship in the field of postcolonial studies.[2] Of course, the misuse of theoretical terminology is largely attacked by both domestic critics and overseas scholars, even though it has helped to produce new meanings, distinct from those in the West.[3] This is particularly true of the terms *postmodernism* and *postcolonialism*. To my understanding, postmodernism and postcolonialism are two distinct – albeit overlapping – discourses that share the common theoretical ground of poststructuralism and the common Western cultural context. So we should first of all make a careful study of these concepts and phenomena before applying them to current Chinese cultural and literary studies. This essay starts with a redescription of postcolonial theory from the perspective of an Oriental or Chinese scholar before dealing with the issue of the "decolonization" of Chinese culture.

Postcolonial Theory Reconsidered

Postcolonialism has prevailed even during the high tide of international postmodernism, particularly in regard to issues concerning Third World culture or Third World criticism. I would like first to outline briefly my approach as a Chinese scholar to the various postcolonial theories constructed by such Western scholars of Oriental background as Edward Said, Gayatri Spivak, and Homi Bhabha before questioning such problematic constructions as those of Orientalism and Third World criticism from my own perspective. Obviously, postcolonial theory is taken almost exclusively from English criticism and is "changing so rapidly and involves so many positions that it can only be spoken about in the singular as a collective noun" (Hart 71). It is certainly controversial in meaning as well as uncertain in connotation. As a theoretical or critical term, its meaning is undoubtedly indeterminate and thereby rouses frequent attacks from mainstream Western critical circles as well as from critics of Oriental or Third World countries. It is actually, according to some Western scholars, "a collection of theoretical and critical strategies with which to look at the culture, literature, politics, and history of the former colonies of the European empires and their relation to Europe and the rest of the world" (Hart 71). In this way, to scholars of Oriental or Third World countries, postcolonial theory is a "highly complex study of the cultural, political, and historical differences among the European imperial powers and from their former colonies" (71–72). It is obviously a long-standing process of deterritorialization of the Western empire from within as well as from without. As Deleuze and Guattari put it in describing the anti-Oedipus (decentralizing) process,

> [T]he process of deterritorialization here goes from the center to the periphery, that is, from the developed countries to the underdeveloped countries, which do not constitute a separate world, but rather an

essential component of the world-wide capitalist machine. It must be
added, however, that the center itself has its organized enclaves of
underdevelopment, its reservations and its ghettos as interior periphery.
(231)

So those advocating postcolonial strategies in the West are actually trying to
undermine the power from within the hegemonic empire. In so doing, they
have touched upon the issues of the Third World's anti-colonialist struggle;
however, they are not very concerned with this struggle. Admittedly, postcolonial theory is a product of Western critical discourse; thus, it is by no
means appropriate to be used in the Chinese cultural context. At the same
time, many Chinese scholars are worried about the "colonizing" of Chinese
culture and literature since the May Fourth period (1919), which actually
marked the beginning of new Chinese culture and literature and the break
from tradition.

Postcolonialism is in effect a metamorphosed version of postmodernism
in relation to the anti-colonialist and decolonizing practice in Oriental
and Third World countries. During the heyday of postmodernism, postcolonialism was almost overlooked or even deliberately marginalized by
mainstream Western critical circles. The theorists in postcolonial studies
are mostly scholars who have an Oriental or Third World background or
have relationships with people from Oriental or Third World countries who
have prestigious teaching positions in Western universities. These theorists'
Western and non-Western national and cultural identities undoubtedly
account for their mobile positions in the theoretical debates. They cannot
but confront such an insurmountable dilemma: since they live in the West,
they have to write of their own experiences either directly or indirectly in
the English language, and they achieve success by first of all identifying
themselves as Westerners; but they have to speak up on behalf of the Orient
or the Third World in a particular way in a multicultural society so as to
work in their own as well as their countrypeople's interest. Consequently,
their political tendency is often complicated and even uncertain, and their
criticism of the cultural hegemony of the First World often cannot fairly
represent the interest of Oriental and Third World intellectuals because of
their insufficient knowledge and understanding of the practical situations in
these countries and because of the problematic ideologies in their research.
Thus their construction of the Orient and the Third World is usually based
on incomplete understanding, or even misreading, rather than on first-hand
personal experiences in an Oriental or Third World country.

However, in spite of all these shortcomings, postcolonial theory is still a
forceful cultural strategy and a challenging theoretical discourse opposed

to mainstream Western culture and critical discourse, helping to correct Western people's long-standing prejudice against the Orient, to popularize Oriental studies in the West, and to promote academic dialogue between the East and West. Postcolonialism, if applied in an appropriate manner, could also be adopted by Third World intellectuals in their decentralization of the "totalitarian" ideology and academic discourse. Therefore, we have to observe this complex phenomenon in a dialectical way and deal with different postcolonial theorists in different ways.

Edward Said, the postcolonial theorist best known for his description and construction of the so-called Orient and Orientalism, is quoted and discussed frequently in Chinese cultural contexts. He has pointed out correctly that the Orient in the eye of Western people actually has nothing to do with the "geographical Orient" or Oriental people themselves. For quite a few Western scholars, "[t]he Orient was almost a European invention, and had been since antiquity a place of romance, exotic beings, haunting memories and landscapes, remarkable experiences. Now it was disappearing; in a sense it had happened, its time was over" (*Orientalism* 1). So it is a "constructed" Orient rather than the "real" or geographical one – obviously a Western means of representation. Since the Orient constructed in Western discourse has nothing to do with the geographical East, there have appeared a number of versions of Orientalism, including a Freudian one, a Spenglerian one, and a Darwinian one (22), but none constructed from the perspective of any Oriental culture. Thus Orientalism exists only in Western discourse, and this makes it problematic and uncertain (Wang, "Orientalism" 905–10). It is also true that Said has criticized severely the unequal relationship between the Orient and the Occident and the falsehood of Oriental studies in the West: "[T]hat Orientalism makes sense at all depends more on the West than on the Orient, and this sense is directly indebted to various Western techniques of representation that make the Orient visible, clear, 'there' in discourse about it" (*Orientalism* 21–22). Obviously Said's severe critique has warned us that the so-called Orient or Orientalism exists only in the eyes of Western people or in the means of representation in Western culture. So in my view it is of vital significance for us to observe Orientalism as an ideology as well as a discipline in the Western context.

Gayatri Spivak, another influential representative of postcolonial theory in the West, is known in China primarily for her translation of Jacques Derrida's book *Of Grammatology*. She actually plays a double role in American academic circles and in her own native country. Her challenge against and criticism of mainstream Western culture is still within the framework of Western culture itself although she sometimes refers to the practical condition in her native country, India, and tries to speak for Third World intellectuals. But as she herself puts it in describing her "mobile" stand, "I am not interested in defending the postcolonial intellectual's dependence on Western modes: my work lies in making clear my disciplinary predicament. My position is generally a reactive one. I am viewed by the Marxists as too codic, by feminists as too male-identified, by indigenous theorists as too committed to Western theory" (*Postcolonial Critic* 69–70). Furthermore, from her haughty attitude toward Third World scholars both from India as well as from other countries, we can hardly recognize her cultural identity as a Third World critic or intellectual. It would appear that she simply wants to attract the attention of the mainstream Western scholarship so as to fulfill her "anti-Oedipus" enterprise to move from periphery to centre and attempt to deconstruct the sense of centre. If ever she completes this task, she (or someone else) will no doubt manifest herself (or himself) as a cultural elitist of more or less Third World background. Perhaps herein is the unique value and significance of these postcolonial theorists represented by Spivak: they have some Oriental roots but have received more education in the Occident. Since they have received education in the West, they usually have a solid foundation of Western culture rather than their own culture. But, ironically, they appear in the West always as "others" (from the Third World) due to their Oriental national identity. When they come to the East, they also cannot deny the strong impact of Western culture in which they are deeply rooted, and so they are then viewed as "others" in the East. This is a predicament that many of these hybrid Western–non-Western postcolonial critics cannot help but be confronted with.

Bhabha is different from Said and Spivak. Younger than his two colleagues, his attitude appears to be more flexible. He tries to playfully undermine the hegemony and authority of Western discourse by parodying the Western way of thinking and writing. On the one hand, he does express his sympathy toward the anti-colonialist struggle waged by Third World people:

> The struggle against colonial oppression changes not only the direction of Western history, but challenges its historicist "idea" of time as a progressive, ordered whole. The analysis of colonial depersonalization alienates not only the Enlightenment idea of "Man" but challenges the transparency of social reality, as a pre-given image of human knowledge. ("Remembering Fanon" 114)

On the other hand, however, unlike Said or Spivak, he always looks upon postcolonial discourse as polemic rather than antagonistic and as a meta-discourse through which the hegemony of Western discourse is undermined or deconstructed. Since the Third World discourse is an "other" to the imperial discourse, it exists only in relation to the latter, without which this "other" is obviously meaningless. Hence his attitude on many occasions is more playful than serious, and his works are always written in an ambiguous way, open to different interpretations.[4] So understandably, because of his playful, ironic attitude toward Western cultural hegemony, he can hardly make people believe the real intention of his deconstructive effort. In contemporary China, Bhabha's critical practice has been more and more attractive, not just to postcolonial scholars but to some young critics and writers of postmodern and poststructural persuasion as well.[5]

Since postcolonial theorists have such complicated political and cultural backgrounds, they cannot avoid confronting an inherent dilemma: on the one hand, they always promote their academic research by constantly criticizing Western culture and theory from their unique (Oriental or Third World) perspectives; on the other hand, they cannot escape the shadow of Western discourse and influence now that they live in the West and use exclusively Western languages – or more specifically, the English language – which is different from the indigenous "English" used by the "real" Oriental and Third World intellectuals. Nor can they have equal dialogue with non-Western academics. So to Third World people, they are actually playing a double role: as critics of colonialism in the West and as advocates (and examples) of a sort of neo-colonialism in the East. Their criticism of Western culture is nothing but a strategy of deconstruction in the course of which a neo-colonial discourse is gradually constructed in a unique way. Their decolonizing practice "occurs on the periphery, but it occurs at the center and at the core as well" (Deleuze and Guattari 237) – or more specifically, in the First World rather than in the Third World. Notwithstanding this ambivalence, postcolonialism has come onto the scene of Chinese culture and literary criticism and has had a certain influence on our cultural strategy and writing discourse. Thus, in talking about postcolonialism in Third World countries such as China, one must associate it with the practical situation of the native countries; otherwise, it could only produce something "other" to the Western audience.

Decolonizing Chinese Culture?

The phrase "Third World culture" is often discussed in China largely because of Fredric Jameson's influence (and his reading of the Third World text as a national allegory) and because of the ongoing debates on postcolonialism in academic circles. Economically speaking, China is still a developing country belonging to the Third World although its economy has been advancing beyond expectation in recent years. So it is not surprising that Chinese scholars and critics usually identify their culture as that of the Third World. But with regard to the so-called Third World culture discussed in the Western context, the term, like that of *the Orient,* or *Orientalism*, usually refers to the colonized culture of Third World countries. It is also an invented phenomenon as an "other" to the West. Unlike the phenomenon of the Orient or Orientalism, it is created both by Westerners and Third World people themselves. In this respect, Chinese culture and literary discourse are said to have been colonized since the beginning of this century, or more specifically the May Fourth period, when various Western cultural trends and academic thoughts flooded into China, exerting strong influence on modern Chinese culture and literature (Wang, "Confronting" 905). Almost all the major writers and literary scholars at the time were more or less involved in the Chinese modernist literary movement or cultural modernity. As a result, comparatists usually research the literature of this period by adopting the method of influence-reception study rather than parallel study, as they do in observing classical Chinese literature, which is almost independent of any Western influence. If we recognize the May Fourth period as the first colonization of Chinese culture and literature, then the practice in the 1980s should be regarded as the second colonization, which occurred after a long period of Soviet doctrinal domination of Chinese culture and literature. For since then, Western cultural trends and literary thoughts have not only entered China but also permeated almost every aspect of Chinese people's lives, including consumer culture, mass media, and advertising enterprises.

A particularly significant change occurred in the Chinese literary language, which used to be characterized as classically elegant and fluently concise, full of allusions and images and rhythms; since the first and second colonizations, this literary language has been hybridized and even "Europeanized" (*ouhua*). Scholars, writers, and literary critics cannot avoid using the "borrowed" language and theoretical terms in the Chinese context, largely because of the easy accessibility of translations of Western works. Translated literature is more popular than created literature to many young people. A present-day avant-garde novelist puts it frankly: "When writers like our generation began to write, we were most indebted to translated novels rather than classical Chinese literature, let alone modern Chinese literature. I have always been thinking that the contributions made to the construction and development of a new Chinese language should be first of all attributed to those translators, who have found an intermediary way of expression between the Chinese language and foreign languages."[6] This "intermediary way" between the "pure" Chinese language and the totally (translated) "foreign" languages is surprisingly not regarded as a sort of colonized cultural phenomenon. The same is true of the critical discourse used by some young avant-garde or scholarly critics in their writing. Thus, the Chinese language is hybridized – even colonized, confronted as it is with Western influence – while translated literature is the direct consequence of Western cultural colonialism. To such writers as the novelist quoted above, the colonization of the Chinese literary language is in effect an innovation of the literary discourse that will help contemporary Chinese literature approach the main trend of world literature. Therefore, it is an absolutely necessary step in the process of China's modernization. To those adhering to traditional Chinese literary doctrines, however, it is nothing but a phenomenon of cultural colonization, which can be traced back to the radical innovation of the May Fourth new cultural movement in which traditional Chinese culture and its sage, Confucius, were severely criticized. And this brings us to the following questions: Is it true that Chinese culture is a colonized one? Is it necessary to wage a struggle to decolonize our culture and literary discourse? This has become a stimulating topic, heatedly debated among the current Chinese culture and literary circles.[7]

History advances despite the resistance of individuals, and this is true of the evolution of language. China should, according to most Chinese intellectuals as well as ordinary people, catch up with and even surpass the advanced Western countries, economically and scientifically as well as culturally. The same is true of the Chinese language, which certainly should be modernized in order to facilitate communication with the international community – particularly in this age of cyberspace. In the contemporary era, no society, no culture, be it Oriental or Occidental, can avoid the influence of, or even colonization by, other societies or cultures; interpenetration and mutual influence among different cultures have become inevitable trends. The fact that hundreds of Chinese scholars have teaching positions in North American universities in the fields of comparative literature or East Asian studies has undoubtedly changed the traditional essence of Orientalism or Oriental studies in the West, inserting into it some fresh methodologies and ideas. (Could we regard such a phenomenon as a kind of colonization of North American culture?) In the process of international communication, any culture will undoubtedly lose something, which is absolutely necessary in order to influence others and renew itself. Whether our language and literary discourse have become colonized or modernized is a question for further study. But we should distinguish between colonization and modernization: the former is passive, meaning that we could not but receive the (Western) influence, thus making our language Westernized (colonized); but the latter is active, which indicates that the Chinese language should also be popularized and simplified along with China's modernization in order for us to communicate more easily with the international community. The state of the art of contemporary Chinese culture and literary language obviously belongs to the latter case. So we should observe such a phenomenon in a dialectical way: on the one hand, such a colonization, if it continues to exist, will help promote the revolution and modernization of Chinese culture and language so as to allow Chinese literature to gradually be accepted in the canon of world literature. On the other hand, the national character of Chinese culture and language cannot help but be obscured or even more-or-less lost. In this respect, the postcolonial strategy of opposition to mainstream Western culture is identical with the Chinese attempt to struggle against the imperial hegemony of the West, politically, economically, and culturally.

In contemporary China, along with brief references to Western postcolonialism, different manifestations of postcoloniality in cultural and literary circles have appeared: first, postmodern studies, which aims to prove that postmodernity is not an exclusively Western product, for it can produce metamorphosed versions in some Oriental or Third World countries where the general condition is modern or even premodern;[8] second, post-Chinese studies (*hou guoxue*), which is viewed as a strategy to decolonize Chinese culture and literary discourse (but the approach that these scholars adopt is still a colonized one, for they borrow Western ways of thinking to reinterpret Chinese culture, thus producing something "other" to the West); and third, Third World criticism, which attempts to help demarginalize Chinese literature and criticism so that it can enter the mainstream of world literature, or have dialogues with international critical circles, on an equal footing. Although these positions are angled differently, as are approaches within postcolonial studies, they are summarized misleadingly by certain overseas Chinese scholars as the joint attempts of Chinese cultural conservatives.[9] Of course, these apparent attempts have raised the controversial question of whether Chinese culture should be decolonized, and if the answer is "yes," how this is to be achieved.

Such manifestations of cultural conservatism are apparently different, though more or less oriented toward decolonization/deterritorialization. The first practice aims at carrying on an equal dialogue on the same plane of postmodern studies with international scholarship; the second attempt is made to carry on dialogues with overseas Sinological studies, making traditional Chinese culture known to the world; and the last is aimed at distinguishing indigenous Chinese critical discourse from that of the West. The ultimate goal is still aimed at opening up more space for scholars and intellectuals to activize their academic dialogues with international scholarship rather than isolate themselves again. Nevertheless, to criticize all three phenomena without careful distinction and profound analysis is to be blind to the complexities of cross-cultural communication. Careless and superficial criticism will only harm communication on an international scale. Ours is an age of information as well as cultural globalization, and the global village is by no means a myth. There is no such thing as the colonization of Chinese culture and literary discourse, for China has never been a colonial country;

moreover, Chinese culture has been deeply rooted in the soil of the Chinese nation, so it is unnecessary to wage any struggle against such a colonization. The misleading attempt to decolonize Chinese culture can only harm international academic dialogue and cross-cultural communication.

Toward an Age of Dialogue

What will characterize the new century? Will it be like the situation described by Samuel Huntington in his controversial essay "The Clash of Civilizations"? Or will the contrary situation arise, as described by some Chinese scholars who envisage the new century as belonging to the Orient or, more specifically, to China?[10] My answer is neither, for since the end of the Cold War, the world has entered a so-called post-Cold War period in which the main trend is characterized by different forces co-existing, complementing each other, and being in dialogue rather than maintaining opposition. This is probably one of the reasons why the long-ignored idea of cultural relativism has again attracted scholars' attention and has become a hot topic for comparatists to deal with. In Western society, especially in North America, which is characterized by multiculturalism, postcolonialism functions as one of the different voices, a contrapuntal one, which always remains within the limited sphere of academic studies and does not influence government policy, whereas in China scholars discuss how postcolonialism will lead China to a new isolated state from the outside world and to a new opposition between the East and the West. Since Chinese people have suffered a great deal from the state of isolation, we need more understanding from and communication with the outside world, including the West. Thus, it is definitely not the time to decolonize our culture, for Chinese cultural identity will receive increasing recognition from people of other countries even though that identity is often misunderstood by Westerners. According to the new significance of cultural relativism, all cultures exist in relation to other cultures. No culture will forever dominate the world. In the past, Oriental culture was marginalized and appeared mysterious to the West, but it nevertheless survived the period of Eurocentrism and has begun to flourish again in the past decade. If Western culture has failed to overcome Oriental culture, then neither has the latter dominated the former. Any attempt to reunify world culture with any kind of Oriental culture or ideology is bound to fail; so, what we need most at the moment is dialogue rather than opposition. My essay therefore intends to show that it is unnecessary to wage a struggle to decolonize Chinese culture and literary discourse. However, postcolonialism can still be viewed as a field of academic study in which we discuss significant theoretical issues and, in doing so, link ourselves to international scholarship.

Notes

1 One can read essays in such journals published in China's mainland and Hong Kong as *Dushu* [Reading], *Dongfang* [The Orient], and *Ershiyi shiji* [Twenty-First Century], which show the hot debate carried on by domestic and overseas Chinese scholars concerning the relationship between postcolonial theory and Chinese culture and literature.

2 Apart from the essays published in Chinese, I should mention the two conferences at which dialogues between the East and West were carried on concerning the issue of postcolonialism: The International Conference on Cultural Studies: China and the West (August 1995, Dalian), at which such scholars as Terry Eagleton, Ralph Cohen, and Jonathan Arac addressed topics relevant to postcolonial theory; and The International Conference on Cultural Dialogue and Cultural Misreading (October 1995, Beijing), at which such scholars as Douwe Fokkema, Mario Valdds, and Gerald Gillespie touched upon this topic. On these two occasions, Chinese scholars were able to discuss some academic issues directly in English with their Western colleagues.

3 To most Western scholars, postcolonialism is viewed as rather radical, while in China it is regarded (especially by Zhao Yiheng and Xu Ben) as conservative, having something in common with government policy.

4 Along with the debate and discussion about the issue of postcolonialism in the Chinese context, we find that Bhabha has exerted more and more influence on some young avant-garde Chinese critics, especially Zhang Yiwu and Chen Xiaoming, who are regarded as two of the major postmodern critics in current China and whose ways of writing are more closely related to that of Bhabha than that of Said or Spivak.

5 In this aspect, cf. particularly Zhang Yiwu's publications in the Hong Kong journal *Ershiyi shiji*, published between 1994 and 1996. Unfortunately, he is often misunderstood by overseas Chinese scholars as a spokesman of official Chinese discourse.

6 See Yu Hua's conversation with Pan Kaixiong on the first day of the new year, in *Zuojia* [Writers] Number 3, 1996. I do not doubt that many other young writers share his opinion.

7 One can read articles dealing with or criticizing postcolonialism and the colonization of Chinese culture in such leading Chinese newspapers as *Guangming ribao* [Guangming Daily], run by the government, and in such authoritative academic journals as *Beijing daxue xuebao* [Journal of Peking University].

8 Along with the deepening of the debate on postmodernism in the Third World, particularly in China, more and more Western scholars have realized that postmodernity is not a typical Western model. It could generate some different versions in some underdeveloped Oriental or Third World countries – for instance, in China. One example is the special issue on postmodernity and China co-edited by Arif Dirlik and Zhang Xudong for the journal *boundary 2* 24.3 (fall 1997).

9 See especially Zhao Yiheng's challenging article "Post-Isms and Chinese New Conservatism" ['houxue' yu Zhongguo xin baoshouzhuyi]; the Chinese version appeared in *Ershiyi shiji* 2(1995): 4–17.

10 In this respect the most influential idea is put forward by Ji Xianlin, an eminent Oriental scholar and comparatist, who predicts that the twenty-first century will be that of the Orient and that Oriental culture will dominate world culture.

Works Cited

Ashcroft, Bill, Gareth Griffiths, and Helen Tiffin. *The Empire Writes Back: Theory and Practice in Post-Colonial Literatures.* London: Routledge, 1989.

Bhabha, Homi. "Of Mimicry and Man: The Ambivalence of Colonial Discourse." *October* 28 (Spring 1984): 125-133.

———. "Remembering Fanon: Self, Psyche and the Colonial Condition." *Colonial Discourse and Postcolonial Theory: A Reader.* Ed. Patrick Williams and Lauren Chrisman. New York: Columbia University Press, 1994.

Barker, Francis, *et al.*, eds. *Literature, Politics, Theory: Papers from the Essex Conference 1976–84.* London: Routledge, 1987.

Deleuze, Gilles, and Félix Guattari. *Anti-Oedipus: Capitalism and Schizophrenia.* Trans. Robert Hurley, *et al.* New York: Viking, 1977.

Hart, Jonathan. "Traces, Resistances, and Contradictions: Canadian and International Perspectives on Postcolonial Theories." *Arachne* 1.1 (1994): 69–85.

Huntington, Samuel. "The Clash of Civilizations?" *Foreign Affairs Reader* 72.3 (1993): 22–49.

Knight, Dianna. "Barthes and Orientalism." *New Literary History* 24.3 (1993): 617–33.

Said., Edward. *Orientalism.* New York: Vintage, 1979.

———. *Culture and Imperialism.* London: Vintage, 1993.

Spivak, Gayatri C. *In Other Worlds: Essays in Cultural Politics.* New York: Routledge, 1988.

———. *The Post-Colonial Critic: Interviews, Strategies, Dialogues.* Ed. Sarah Harasym. New York: Routledge, 1990.

Wang, Ning. "Confronting Western Influence: Rethinking Chinese Literature of the New Period." *New Literary History* 24.4 (1993): 905–26.

———. "Dongfangzhuyi, houzhiminzhuyi he wenhuabaqaunzhuyi pipan: aidehua saiyide de houzhirninzhuyi lilun pouxi [Orientalism, Postcolonialism and the Critique of Cultural hegemonies: A Theoretic Anatomy of Edward Said's Postcolonial Theory]." *Beijing daxue xuebao* [*Journal of Peking University*] 2 (1995): 54–62.

———. "Orientalism versus Occidentalism?" *New Literary History* 28.1 (1997): 57–67.

Zhao, Henry. "'Houxue' yu Zhongguo xin baoshouzhuyi [Post-isms and Chinese New Conservatism]." *Ershiyi shiji* [*Twenty-first Century*] 2 (1995): 4–17.

———. "Post-isms and Chinese New Conservatism." *New Literary History* 28.1 (1997): 31–44.

Introduction: The Linked Histories of the Globalized World   The Fascist Longings in our Midst   Queer with Class: Absence of Third World Sweatshop in Lesbian/Gay Discourse and a Rearticulation of Materialist Queer Theory   Cross-Mirrorings of Alterity: The Colonial Scenario and Its Psychological Legacy   Mythologies of Migrancy: Post-colonialism, Postmodernism, and the Politics of (Dis)location   Postcolonial DefferendDifferend: Diasporic Narratives of Salman Rushdie   At the Margins of Postcolonial Studies   Keeping History at Wind River and Acoma   Modernity's First Born: Latin America and Postcolonial Transformation   Towards Articulation: Postcolonial Theory and Demotic Resistance   Postcolonial Theory and the "Decolonization" of Chinese Culture

BILL ASHCROFT is the Head of the School of English at the University of New South Wales in Sydney, Australia. His book *The Empire Writes Back*, co-authored with Gareth Griffiths and Helen Tiffin, was one of the first to examine a field that is now recognized as postcolonial studies. Other research interests include Australian literature, Australian cultural studies, critical theory and postcolonial theories, African literature, and Indian literature.

REY CHOW is the Andrew Mellon Professor of Humanities in the Department of Modern Culture and Media at Brown University. She is the author of many works, including *Women and Chinese Modernity* (Minnesota, 1991), *Writing Diaspora* (Indiana, 1993), *Primitive Passions* (Columbia, 1995), and *Ethics After Idealism* (Indiana University Press, 1995).

ROB COVER is a lecturer in the School of English, Film, Theater and Media Studies at Victoria University of Wellington in New Zealand. His research interests currently focus on media theory, reception, and performative identity, as well as queer theory, media theory, sexuality, and youth suicide.

WENDY FAITH teaches for Luther College and the Department of English, University of Regina. Her interests include theories of metaphor, contemporary rhetorical analysis, and strategies of social empowerment. She recently published a feminist cognitive-linguistic response to poststructuralist language philosophy. At present, she is researching the casualization of university teaching and lobbying to improve the working conditions of sessionals.

MONIKA FLUDERNIK is a Professor of English at the University of Freiburg. She is the author of *The Fictions of Language and the Languages of Fiction* (Routledge, 1993), *Towards a 'Natural' Narratology* (Routledge, 1996), which won the 1996 George and Barbara Perkins Prize, and *Echoes and Mirrorings: Gabriel Josipovici's Creative Oeuvre* (Lang, 2000). Her text *Narrative Structure, 1250-1750: A Genre-by-Genre Analysis* is forthcoming.

REVATHI KRISHNASWAMY is an Assistant Professor in the Department of English at San Jose State University in California. Her research and teaching interests include nineteenth- and twentieth-century British fiction, colonial and postcolonial literatures and critical theory.

MARY LAWLOR is an Associate Professor of English and the Director of American Studies at the Muhlenberg College. She is the author of *Recalling the Wild: Naturalism and the Closing of the American West* (Rutgers University Press, 2000). Her text *Public Native America: Tribal Representations in Museums, Powwows and Casinos* is forthcoming and will also be published by Rutgers.

VICTOR LI is an Associate Professor in the Department of English at the University of Toronto. His teaching and research interests include contemporary theory and criticism, postcolonial theory and literature, Modern British literature, and globalization and culture. Li's current research is focused on neo-primitivism in contemporary critical thought.

PAMELA MCCALLUM is a Professor in the Department of English at the University of Calgary. She is the author of *Literature and Method,* and her research interests include literary theory and narrative, the representation of history, and twentieth-century British literature. Her annotated edition of Raymond Williams's *Modern Tragedy* is forthcoming from Broadview Press. She is currently editor of *ARIEL*.

VIJAY MISHRA is a Professor of English and Comparative Literatures at Murdoch University in Australia. Among his publications are *Dark Side of the Dream: Australian Literature and the Post-Colonial Mind* with Bob Hodges (Allen & Unwin Pty. Limited, 1992), *The Gothic Sublime, Devotional Poetics and the Indian Sublime* (SUNY, 1998), and *Bollywood Cinema: Temples of Desire* (Routledge). He has recently completed a book-length study of the literature of the Indian Diaspora.

KALPANA SHESHADRI-CROOKS is an Associate Professor of English at Boston College, as well as Director of the Women's Studies Program. She specializes in postcolonial theories, Anglophone literatures, and critical theory with an emphasis on Marxism and psychoanalysis. Presently she is working on a book on the concept of the "other" which will be entitled "The Other Difference."

WANG NING is a Professor in the Department of Foreign Languages at Tsinghua University. His major areas of research are concerned with modern and postmodern Western critical theories, Anglo-American literature, comparative literature and cultural studies, translation and media studies, and sinological studies.

A

Aboriginal peoples. *See* indigenous people; Native Americans
academy, 34, 92, 216
  academic discourse, 6
  academic freedom, 93
  academic politics, 5, 7
  canon of the West, 36
  Chinese critical academic circles, 231
  indiscriminate valorization of persons of colour, 7, 35–36
  metropolitan academic institutions, 93–94, 96, 190, 192
Achebe, Chinua, 15, 198, 216, 223
  Anthills of the Savannah, 221
Acoma Pueblo (museum), 11, 168, 174–76, 178, 182
  teaching history at, 183
Adam, Ian, and Helen Tiffin, *Past the Last Post*, 18
aesthetic/sacred opposition, 130, 137
aesthetics
  commodity, 49
  diasporic, 129, 131, 137
  postmodern, 12
aesthetics of monstrosity, 22–24, 32, 39.
  See also fascism
affirmative action, 9, 150
AIDS. *See* HIV/AIDS
Aijaz Ahmad, 101, 134, 157, 159
  "Politics of Literary Postcoloniality, The," 156
  In Theory, 156
Akhtar, Shabbir, 136
Al-e A'hmad, Jalal, 127, 133
  Plagued by the West, 131–32
Allen, Paula Gunn, *Sacred Hoop, The*, 170
Althusser, Louis, 22
  "interpellation," 26–27

Altman, Dennis
  Homosexual Oppression and Liberation, 52
  Homosexualization, 51
  "On Global Queering," 53
American multiculturalism, 10
  postcolonialism and, 147
Americanization of the homosexual, 53
"Americanness" as global style, 14
Amin, Samir, 3, 146
Amselle, Jean-Loup, 210
Anand, Mulk Raj, *Untouchables*, 65, 68
Anderson, Benedict, *Imagined Communities*, 114
Anthills of the Savannah (Achebe), 221
Anti-Oedipus (Deleuze and Guattari), 24–25
anti-Oedipus (periphery to centre), 232, 235
Appadurai, Arjun
  "diasporas of hope, diasporas of terror, and diasporas of despair," 17
Appiah, Kwame Anthony, 92, 106, 212
appropriation, 199–200
  of language, 206
  "technocratic criticism," 191
  in *testimonio*, 202
Apter, Emily, 146
ARIEL (A Review of International English Literature), 18
Armstrong, Nancy, 37–38
articulation, 222–23
  theory of, 215–16
Ashcroft, Bill, 4, 11–13, 103, 245
Australia, 51, 56
authenticity, 10–11, 147–48, 214
  cultural protectionism, 210–13
  fascist potential, 151
  in performative terms, 154
  as a spatial category, 153

authoritarianism, 24
authors
    author-as-genius, 9
    exiled writers, 8, 93
    immigrant postcolonial writers, 93, 106–7
    politically engaged writers, 216
autostereotypes, 63–64, 67
Ayodhya Affair, 133–34

B

Bakhtin, Mikhail, 136, 158, 212
banci kathoey, 53
Bandele, Biyi, *Brixton Stories*, 18
Barrios de Chungara, Domatila
    Let me Speak!, 197–98
Barthes, Roland, 22
Bass, Lee, 149
Basu, Shrabani, 132
Baumgartner's Bombay (Desai), 84
Bazin, André, "Stalin Myth in Soviet
    Cinema, The," 31–32
Beckford, William, *Vathek*, 75
belonging everywhere by belonging
    nowhere, 101
Bernabé, Jean, 220
Bersani, Leo, 47
Bevis, William, 174, 182
Bhabha, Homi, 8, 66–67, 70, 84, 130, 213, 216,
    231–32
    Ahmad on, 156–60
    "Difference," 66, 73
    gender blindness, 74
    Hardt and Negri on, 15
    hybrid Western-non-Western critic, 14
    hybridity, 68
    Location of Culture, The, 64, 224–25
    metaphor of the "trans-", 129
    on working class, 65
Bharatiya Janata Party (BJP), 133
Bhattacharya, Rimli, 127
binarism (in postcolonialism), 13
Black Atlantic, The (Gilroy), 117
Black Skin, White Masks (Fanon), 64, 69
black women. *See* persons of colour; women
blaming the victim, 65, 67
Bolivia, 197–98
Bombay film, 119
Border Dialogues (Chambers), 125
Brennan, Timothy, 104, 213–14
Britain, 113
    post-diaspora, 124
British Empire, 194

British imperialism, 11, 194
Britishness, 122–24, 126, 151
Brixton Stories (Bandele), 18
Brooks, Peter, 149
Brydon, Diana, 18
Buell, Frederick, 4
Burbach, Roger, 226
Burning Plain, The (Rulfo), 205
Butler, Judith
    Gender Trouble, 46
    Bodies That Matter, 46
Bye-Bye Blackbird (Desai), 64, 75, 84

C

Campaign, 56
capitalism, 3, 49–50, 152, 195–96, 198
    anti-capitalist movement, 2
    exploitation of labour, 6
    global structures of, 4
    hegemony of, 199
    laissez-faire, 51
    neo-colonial global capitalism, 97
    sweatshops, 49–50, 54–56
    Western bourgeois lesbian/gay
        communities and, 54
"Capitalism and Gay Identity" (D'Emilio),
    49
Cardinal-Schubert, Joanne, "Kitchen Works:
    sstorsiinao'si" (art installation), 17
Catholicism, 179–81
centre and periphery, 149–50, 152, 198–99,
    235–36. *See also* margins
    anti-Oedipus, 232, 235
    Chambers on, 152
Cernetig, Miro, 1
Chambers, Iain, 123–24, 147, 153–54
    Border Dialogues, 125
    on margin/centre dichotomy, 152
    Migrancy, Culture, Identity, 113, 151
Chamoiseau, Patrick, 220
Charbonneau, Toussaint, 168–69, 171–73
Chaudhuri, Nirad, 75
Chiapas uprising, 225
    as postmodern rebellion, 226
child labour, 54
China, 14–15, 236
    Japanese aggression, 22
    modernization, 14, 238
    new century, 240
    postmodern studies, 239
Chinese critical academic circles, 231
Chinese cultural identity, 240

Chinese culture and literature
    colonization, 14–15, 233, 237–38
    decolonizing, 232, 236–40
    Third World criticism, 232, 239
Chinese intellectuals, 14, 238
Chinese literary language, 238
    hybridized and "Europeanized" *(ouhua)*,
        237
Chinese/Western transculturation, 15
Chow, Rey, 5, 7, 245
cinema. *See* film
La ciudad letrada (Rama), 192
"Clash of Civilizations, The" (Huntington),
    240
class, 17, 49, 77, 95, 97
    and transnational corporatism, 55
    West/Third World differences, 50
class awareness, 52–53
class conflict, 158
"Class Politics" (Morton), 46
class theory, 47
Clifford, James, 93, 211
Clive, Robert, 11
Colas, Santiago, 189, 192–93, 195
colonial discourse theory, 190–91, 193
colonialism, 24, 37, 64, 66–68, 91, 189
    (black) women, 72–73
    colonial inferiority complex, 77
    internalized, 66
    Third World anti-colonialist struggle, 233,
        235
    white supremacy, 65
    women, 69–70, 72–74
"Colonialism and Postcolonialism as (Latin)
    American Mirages" (De Alva), 193
colonization, 192, 196
    of Chinese language and literature, 14–15,
        233, 237–38
    Latin America, 193–94
    Third World, 53
communications technology, 3, 53, 117
communist art, 29, 31
Communist Manifesto (Marx), 16
comprador intelligentsia, 92
Confiant, Raphael, 220
Conquest, The (Dye), 170
constructionist trends (of queer theory), 46
contingency, 156, 158–60
cosmopolitan celebrities, 93, 106.
        See also writers
cosmopolitanism, 216
Cover, Rob, 6, 245

"Creole" (Žižek), 192–93
creolization, 219–20
cross-cultural communicaton, 15, 239–40
"Crusoe" (Rushdie), 115
cultural alienation, 8
cultural authenticity. *See* authenticity
cultural conservatism, 239
cultural doubling, 181
cultural hybridity. *See* hybridity
cultural identity. *See* identity
cultural integration, 17
cultural materialism, 18
cultural pluralism, 35–36.
        See also multiculturalism
cultural relativism or separatism, 13, 210,
        212, 240
cultural rootlessness, 81
cultural studies
    postcolonial, 151, 171
"culturally oriented criticism," 191
Czechoslovakia, 105–6

D
"Dangerous Art Form" (Rushdie), 95, 100
Darwin, Charles, *Voyage of the Beagle*, 195
De Alva, Jorge Klor
    "Colonialism and Postcolonialism as
        (Latin) American Mirages," 193
De Certeau, Michel, 184
    Practice of Everday Life, The, 183
de-historicizing, 158, 160
decolonization, 96, 107, 148, 238–39
    Third World, 148, 192
decolonized intellectuals, 213
deconstructio, 161
Delany, Samuel R., *Motion of Light in Water,
        The*, 34
Deleuze, Gilles, 26, 232
    Anti-Oedipus, 24–25
D'Emilio, John, 50
    "Capitalism and Gay Identity," 49
    class awareness, 53
demotic resistance, 13, 213–16, 223
demotic voice, 225
demotic wisdom, 221
deregulation, 2
Derrida, Jacques, 46
    Of Grammatology, 234
Desai, Anita
    Baumgartner's Bombay, 84
    Bye-Bye Blackbird, 64, 75, 84
desire theory, 46, 49–50, 52, 58

deterritorialization, 2, 232, 239
Dhareshwar, Vivek, 214
diaspora, 8–9, 94–95, 99, 106, 113, 122
  of colour, 112
  "diasporas of hope, diasporas of terror,
    and diasporas of despair," 17
  diasporic aesthetic, 131, 137
  diasporic archive, 115
  diasporic avant-garde, 118–21
  diasporic consciousness, 93
  diasporic ideology, 136
  diasporic imaginary, 138–39
  dual narrative of, 127
  gender relations, 120–21
  Hinduism in, 127
  and the idea of the sacred, 126–27, 129
  Indian-Pakistani, 114–15, 124
  justice for, 139
  millenarianism, 125–26
  and the nation state, 130, 137
  postcolonial, 93
  Salman Rushdie's writing, 115–18, 126–29
  Spivak and, 155
Diaspora (journal), 114
"Difference" (Bhabba), 66
differend, 8, 114–15, 130–33, 137–38, 140
  India, 134
Differend, The (Lyotard), 137
Dirlik, Arif, 3–4, 95, 146, 224
Disney, 2, 55
During, Simon, 2, 13, 209–10, 213–14, 223–24
Dye, Eva Emery, *Conquest, The*, 170

E

economic refugees, 7
education, 199, 217
Elsaesser, Thomas, 27, 36
  "to be is to be perceived," 28
Emperor's new clothes, 34–36
Empire (Hardt), 15–16
Empire Writes Back, The (Ashcroft *et al.*), 4,
  103, 193
Englishness. *See* Britishness
Enlightenment, 133, 135–36, 194–96, 199
essentialism, 13, 54
ethnic identities, 124, 127. *See also* race
  exclusion in lesbian/gay media, 57
ethnic/minority studies, 9
Euro-American publishers and readers, 92
Eurocentrism, 4, 98, 194–95
European avant-garde, 118
European cities, 113. *See also* metropolitan

European modernity, 194
"Evidence of Experience, The" (Scott), 33
exhibitionism, 27
exile, 63, 76–81, 93–94, 99, 111
  and artistic consciousness, 101
  exiled writer, 8
  fatwa, 9, 115, 118, 127, 130, 136
  Rushdie's interpretation of, 102
  Said on, 215
  working class, 7
exoticism, 68–69, 75–76, 176, 182
experience
  in deconstructing universalist claims, 34,
  37

F

Faith, Wendy, 245
Faiyazuddin Ahmad, 135
Fanon, Frantz, 64–66, 70, 72, 84, 190
  Black Skin, White Masks, 64, 69
Faruqi, M. H., 135
"Fascinating Fascism" (Sontag), 29
fascism, 5, 34, 37, 123, 133, 151
  aesthetics of monstrosity, 22–24, 32, 39
  association with film, 26–28, 31, 33
  Foucault on, 21, 24
  as Freudian projection, 24–26, 28, 30
  Hitler and Mussolini, 24–25, 33
  idealizing tendencies, 22–23, 29–31, 33, 36
  "in us all," 24
  internalized violence, 25–26, 29
  Japanese, 22–23
  Nazis, 23–25, 33
  new liberal fascism, 5, 37–39
  technology and, 22–23, 27, 33
  visual associations, 22
fascist aesthetics.
    See aesthetics of monstrosity
fascist art, 29–30
Fassbinder, Rainer Werner, 27–28, 36
fatwa, 9, 115, 118, 127, 130, 136
Faurisson, Robert, 137
Fear of a Queer Planet (Warner), 46
female body
  about desiring, 57
  cheap labour, 97
  for reproduction, 57
  West *versus* non-West, 57
film, 26–28, 33, 39
  black British cinema, 152
  Bombay film, 119
  idealizing power of, 31

Fludernik, Monika, 6–7, 245
Foot, Michael, 136
forge, 17–18
Foucault, Michel, 21, 24, 46, 66, 156
    Order of Things, The, 155
    Power/Knowledge, 54
Fourth World narratives, 11
France, 113
free-labour system of the West, 49–50, 52
freedom of expression, 9
Freud, Sigmund, 27
Freudian projection, 24–26, 28, 30
Freudian psychoanalysis, 71–72
Fuentes, Carlos, "Words Apart," 136

G
G8, 2
Gandhi, Rajiv, 135
Gap clothing, 2, 55
Gates, Henry Louis, Jr., 214
gay/lesbian. *See* lesbian/gay
Gay Liberation Front, 53
gaze of history, 204
gender, 73–74. *See also* women
    in colonial scenario, 64, 69–70, 72–74
    in diaspora, 120–21
    immigration and, 95, 97
Gender Trouble, Bodies That Matter (Butler),
    46
Giddens, Anthony, 196
Gilroy, Paul, *Black Atlantic, The*, 117
Glassblower's Breath, The (Gupta), 82–84
Glissant, Edouard, 216, 218, 221, 223
    views on creolization, 219–20
global capitalism
    recirculation of old colonial categories, 7
global migration. *See* migrancy; migration
global professional elite, 81–82
global queer identity, 55
globalism, 196
globalization, 15, 18, 197
    cultural, 239
    euphemism for imperialism, 3
    implications for postcolonial studies, 2
    linguistic and discursive, 14
    new economics of, 2
Godwin, William, *Political Justice*, 129
Goteburg, 2
Gramsci, Antonio
    "Study of Philosophy, The," 158
"Great East Asia Co-Prosperity Sphere," 24
Griffiths, Gareth, 4

Guardian, The, 136
Guatemala, 217–18
Guattari, Félix, 24–26, 232
Guess clothing, 55
Guide, The (Narayan), 68
Gupta, Sunetra
    Glassblower's Breath, The, 82–84
    Memories of Rain, 65

H
Habermas, Jürgen, 160
    Philosophical Discourse, 195
Hall, Stuart, 152, 161, 215–16
Hardt, Michael, *Empire*, 15–16
Harvey, David, 3
Hebard, Grace, 169
Heidegger, Martin, 33
Hennessy, Rosemary, 49, 57
    Materialist Feminism, 50
    "Queer Visibility," 52, 55
hetero-normativity, 46
heterogeneity, 124, 138, 180.
    See also hybridity
    Kantian sublime as, 139
heterosexuality, 46
heterostereotypes, 64, 67
Hinduism in the diaspora, 127
Hirohito, Emperor, 32
Hiroshima, 32
historical gaze, 204
historicism, 203
historicization, 160
historiography, 184
history, 159, 167–68, 175–76, 178, 199–201, 203
    de-historicizing, 158, 160
    gaze of, 204
    Native American, 11, 167–83
    postcolonial theory, 192–93
Hitler, Adolf, 24–26, 33
HIV/AIDS, 47–48, 53, 55
Holland, 113
Holocaust, 137
"home," 112
homelessness, 151
"homing in," 174, 182
Homosexual Oppression and Liberation
    (Altman), 52
homosexualism. *See also* lesbian/gay
    Americanization, 53
Homosexualization (Altman), 51
Howard, Harold, 171
Hulme, Peter, 194

human rights, 54, 203
Huntington, Samuel, "Clash of Civilizations, The," 240
hybrid Western-non-Western postcolonial critics, 235
hybridity, 7, 11, 63, 67–69, 81, 115, 117–18, 130, 151, 153–54, 156–58, 211, 215, 237.
   See also creolization; heterogeneity among indigenous people, 182
Hyundai, 55

I

I, Rigoberta Menchú, 200
idealism, 22–23, 29–32
   in film, 33
identity, 34, 46, 147, 158, 160, 192, 218
   based on difference, 214–15
   Britishness, 122–24, 126, 151
   cultural doubling, 181
   cultural linguistic, 220–21
   ethnic, 57, 124, 127
   indigenous, 182
   lesbian/gay, 54–55
   Native, 10–11, 215
   postcolonial, 181
   social identities, 27, 130
"Identity, Authority and Freedom" (Said), 93
identity politics, 12, 112, 212, 215
Imaginary Homelands (Rushdie), 124, 137
"the imaginary puritan," 37
Imagined Communities (Anderson), 114
imagological analysis, 63–84
immigrant writers, 106
   uncritical privileging of, 107
immigrants. *See also* migrancy
   class/gender differentiated histories, 95, 97
   economic refugees, 7
   intellectuals, 96, 99
   New Commonwealth, 130
   postcolonial immigrant intellectual, 92, 98–99
   Third World, 93
   working class, 97
imperialism, 3–4, 122, 124, 194–96, 198
   contemporary Empire, 15
   cultural, 106
   Spanish, 11
"In Praise of Creoleness" (Bernabé), 220
In Theory (Ahmad), 156
India, 234
   differend, 134

exoticist discourse, 75
   orientalist stereotyping, 75
India Today, 132
Indian-Pakistani diaspora in Britain, 114–15
Indian Penal Code, 126, 134
Indian secular law, 135
indigenous people, 17, 182, 213.
   See also Native Americans
   culture, 2, 67
   displacement within settler societies, 16
   hybridity, 182
   kiva, 179–80
   Maoris, 210, 223–25
   Quiché Indians, 202
information revolution, 3
'intellectual other,' 192
intellectuals, 222, 224, 231. *See also* academy
   Chinese, 14, 238
   comprador intelligentsia, 92
   contemporary white liberal, 38
   decolonized, 213
   diasporic Indian intellectuals, 209
   embattled figures of exile, 101
   global professional elite, 81–82
   immigrant, 92, 96, 99
   intinerant postcolonial intellectual, 92
   metropolitan postcolonial intellectuals, 224
   migrant postcolonial intellectuals, 98–99
   Third World intellectuals, 36–37, 91, 94–95, 233–36
"Intellectuals in the Post-Colonial World" (Said), 161
intercultural homelessness, 64
internalized colonialism, 66
internalized violence. *See under* fascism
International Monetary Fund, 2
interpellation, 26–27, 33, 154
interpolation, 198, 200–204
Inuit craft-producing co-operatives, 211
Invention of America, The (O'Gorman), 191
Iran, 132
Irving, David, 137
Islam, 120, 136
Islamic fundamentalists/Western literati divide, 8

J

Jain, Madhu, 132
Jameson, Fredric, 3, 38, 94, 236
Japanese, 22, 26
Jefferson, Thomas, 173
Johnson, Barbara, 161

K

Kant, Immanuel, 133, 139
Kaplan, Alice Yaeger, 31
   Reproductions of Banality, 26
Keats, John, 139
Keesing, Roger, 225
Khomeini, Ruhollah, 99, 115, 118, 130, 135
"Kitchen Works: sstorsiinao'si"
   (art installation), 17
kiva, 179–80
Krishnaswamy, Revathi, 7–8, 245
Kundera, Milan, 105

L

labour, 6, 113. *See also* working-class
   child, 54
   female body as cheap labour, 97
   free-labour system of the West, 49–50, 52,
     58
   global division of, 3
   global trade in, 7
   sweatshop labour, 45, 49–50, 54–56
   Third World, 12, 50
Laclau, Ernesto, 26, 159–60
   Politics and Ideology in Marxist Theory, 25
Lady Chatterley's Lover, 131
laissez-faire capitalism, 51
language, 15, 191, 200, 205–6
   appropriation of, 198
   Chinese literary, 237–38
   creolization, 219–20
   cultural linguistic identity, 220–21
   English, 14
   linguistic and discursive globalization, 14
   metropolitan vernacular, 151
   power to construct and dominate, 192
   transculturation, 212, 220
   transparency of, 12
late capitalism, 152
Latin America
   Chiapas uprising, 225–26
   colonization, 12, 193–94
   economies, 197
   globalism, 196
   ideology, 192
   literary criticism, 190
   modernity, 194–95
   postcolonialism, 189–90, 192–93
   Spanish imperialism, 11
   testimonio, 12–13, 200–203, 206, 216, 218
   transculturation, 198, 200
Latin American historians and critics, 191

Latin American intellectual integrity, 191
Latin American Research Review, 190
Lawlor, Mary, 10–11, 246
lesbian/gay, 51. *See also* queer theory
   cash and, 52
   exclusion of women, 52, 57
   global queer identity, 55
   identity, 54–55
   marketing, 6, 55
   middle class, 51, 53
   "powergays," 52
   survival outside the family, 49–51
   sweatshop labour and, 45, 53–54
   Third World gay/lesbians, 53
   white middle-class male dominance, 52,
     58
lesbian/gay discourse, 56.
   See also queer theory
   lack of class analysis, 50, 52
   "Queer" in, 46
lesbian/gay media, 6, 46, 51–52, 56, 58
   exclusion of non-white ethnicities, 57
   exclusion of women, 52, 57
lesbian/gay studies, 48
Let me Speak! (Barrios de Chungara), 197–98
Levi Strauss (corporation), 55–56
Lewis and Clark expedition, 168–69, 171–73
Li, Victor, 13–14, 18, 246
liberal democratic societies, 53
liberal humanism, 9
liberal politics, 51
linguistic and discursive globalization, 14
Lionnet, Françoise, 212
Location of Culture, The (Bhabha), 64,
   224–25
Lolita, 131
"Lost Woman." *See* Sacajawea
Lyotard, Jean-François, 8, 115, 130–31, 138–40
   Differend, The, 137

M

Magee, John, 22
Magee's Testament (video), 22–23
magic realism, 13, 18
Mahabharata, 119
mainstream Western culture, 234
La Malinche, 170
Mao Zedong, 33
Maoris, 210, 223–25
Marcusean class/psychoanalytic theory, 53
marginality, 5, 9, 96, 155, 160
marginalized (divergent group), 16

margins, 100, 114–16, 150–51, 154, 156, 161, 200. *See also* centre and periphery
Martinique, 219
Marx, Karl, 18, 157
  Communist Manifesto, 16
Marxism, 156, 160
mass demonstrations, 2
Mass Psychology of Fascism, The (Reich), 25
Materialist Feminism (Hennessy), 50
materialist queer theory, 48–50, 56–57
materialist theory, 6
McCallum, Pamela, 246
McDonalds, 55
McGowan, John, 215
media, 37
  international media market, 92
  lesbian/gay media, 6, 46, 51–52, 56–58
Memmi, Albert, 64
Memories of Rain (Gupta), 65
Menchú, Rigoberta, 202–4, 206, 217, 223, 226
  testimonio, 216, 218
mestizos, 204
metaphor, 99, 113, 127, 205
  of nationhood, 156
  of the "trans-", 129
  of visibility, 34
metonymy, 204
metropolitan academic institutions, 93–94, 96, 190, 192
metropolitan postcolonial intellectuals, 224
metropolitan postcolonial theory, 210, 224
metropolitan theory, 213
metropolitan vernacular, 151
Middleman and Other Stories (Mukherjee), 93
Midnight's Children (Rushdie), 104–5
Mignolo, Walter, 191–92
migrancy, 7–8, 16, 91–106, 115.
  See also immigrants
  class and gender, 95, 97
  global politics of, 127
  postcolonial work on, 81
Migrancy, Culture, Identity (Chambers), 113, 151
migration, 10, 16, 63, 112–13, 119
millenarian narratives, 117, 120, 141n6
millenarianism, 125–26
mimicry, 15, 68, 102, 113, 224
Mishra, Vijay, 8–9, 246
misogyny, 71–72
mobility, 127
modernism, 101–2

modernist literary movements, 237
modernity, 12, 154, 194–99, 237
  European, 194
monocentrism, 4
monstrous aesthetics. *See* aesthetics of monstrosity
Montaigne, Michel de, "On Cannibals," 195
Morton, Donald, 47–50
  "Class Politics," 46
Motion of Light in Water, The (Delany), 34
Mowitt, John, 15
Moyer, Carrie, 51
Mukherjee, Bharati, 98, 102
  Middleman and Other Stories, 93
Mukherjee, Meenakshi, 103
Mulruan/Nash (advertising co.), 51
multiculturalism, 34, 122, 130, 146, 150, 240
  American, 10, 147
  idealizing tendencies of, 22
  Taylor's notion of, 148–49
multitude, 16
museum-archive, 168, 175
museum curators, 210. *See also* native-hosted museums
music, 78, 117, 119, 152, 154, 212
Muslim Sharia laws, 135
Mussolini, Benito, 24, 33
mysticism, 24

N
Nagasaki, 32
Naipaul, V. S., 102–3, 115, 126
Nair, Rukmini, 127
Nandy, Ashis, 127
Nanjing Massacre, 22
Narayan, R. K., *Guide, The*, 68
nation-states, 3–4, 130, 196–97
  crisis of, 149
  subjection to world capital, 14
  transnational nature of, 114
nation theory, 47
national subsistence, 3
nationalism, 67, 91, 148
Native Americans, 168.
    See also indigenous people
  feminine authority, 170
  history and identity, 10–11, 215
  maintaining history and culture, 168, 183
  self-representation in public culture
    (*See* Native-hosted museums)
  Shoshone people, 168–69, 171
native authenticity, 213

Native-hosted museums, 10–11
 Acoma Pueblo, 11, 168, 174–76, 178, 182–83
 tourism, 10, 176–77, 181
 Wind River, 11, 167–68, 171–74, 183
nativism, 13, 95, 151, 215
Nazis, 23–24, 26. *See also* fascism
needs theory, 46–50
negative freedom, 214–15, 219
Negri, Antonio, 15–16
Negritude, 151
neo-colonial global capitalism, 97
neo-colonialism, 3, 97, 106, 236
New Commonwealth immigrants, 130
new liberal facism, 5, 37–39
New York Times, 149
Ngugi wa Thiong'o
 Ngaahika Ndeenda (I Will Marry When I Want), 65
Nietzsche, Friedrich, 195
 ressentiment, 25
Nike running shoes, 2, 55
Ning, Wang, 246
Nobel Peace Prize, 216
noble savage, 11, 170, 182
North American academy. *See* academy
North American Free Trade Agreement (NAFTA), 226

O

Oedipus, 25
Of Grammatology (Derrida), 234
O'Gorman, Edmundo, 192
 Invention of America, The, 191
"On Cannibals" (Montaigne), 195
"On Global Queering" (Altman), 53
oral narratives, 15, 168, 201
Order of Things, The (Foucault), 155
Oriental and Third World intellectuals, 233, 236
Oriental archives in the West, 133
Orientalism or Oriental studies, 95, 232, 234, 236, 238
Orientalism (Said), 156, 190, 234
orientalist stereotyping, 75
 exoticist/orientalist scenario, 68–69
Ortega y Gasset, José, 24
Ortiz, Fernando, 200
Other, 7, 37–38, 130, 192, 219, 225
OutRage, 56
 "powergays," 52

P

Parry, Benita, 213–14
Past the Last Post (Adam), 18
patriarchy, 6, 49, 173
Pedro Paramo (Rulfo), 205
periphery, 198–99, 235–36
persons of colour, 37
 black women, 72
 indiscriminate embrace of, 39
 as self-evidently correct, 35
 white liberal enthusiasm for, 36
Philosophical Discourse (Habermas), 195
Plagued by the West (Ahmad), 131–32
Pocahontas, 170
political correctness, 36–37
Political Justice (Godwin), 129
politically engaged writers, 216
Politics and Ideology in Marxist Theory (Laclau), 25
"politics of criticism," 161
"Politics of Literary Postcoloniality, The" (Ahmad), 156
"Politics of Recognition, The" (Taylor), 147
"politics of representation," 153
politics of resistance, 18
populism, 24
post-Chinese studies *(hou guoxue)*, 239
postcolonial analysis, 205
postcolonial differend, 114, 130, 137
postcolonial literature, 92, 94, 104
postcolonial politics, 94–95, 107
postcolonial studies, 66, 146, 149, 161–62
 as academic radicalism, 160
 Oriental or Third World scholars, 233–34
 status as disciplinary field, 18
postcolonial theory, 115, 213, 233–36
 demotic resistance, 213–16, 223
 as hegemonic, 13
 metropolitan, 210, 224
 relevance to indigenous struggles, 213
 speaking for the oppressed, 209
postcolonialism, 12, 91, 103, 112, 151, 154, 196, 201, 232, 240
 association with postmodernism, 96, 158, 160
 China, 231–36
 connection with multiculturalism, 146–47, 149–50
 Latin American, 192–93
 Marxist criticism, 150, 156
 and poststructuralism, 190, 232

"Postcoloniality and the Boundaries of
   Identity" (Radhakrishnan), 160
postmodern and postcolonial "celebrities," 8
postmodernism, 91, 94, 96, 101–2, 104, 150,
   156–57, 160
   postmodern aestheticism, 12
postmodernity, 195–96
poststructuralist philosophy (Queer theory
   and), 46
poststructuralism, 74, 190, 192, 232
poststructuralism/postmodernism, 96, 101
Poulantzas, Nicos, 26
Powell, Enoch, 122, 124
Power and the Glory, The, 131
Power/Knowledge (Foucault), 54
"powergays," 52
Practice of Everday Life, The (De Certeau),
   183
Prague, 2
Pratt, Mary Louise, 212
Presley, Elvis, 211
progress, 54, 213
   bourgeois myth of, 12
Protestantism, 181

Q

Quayson, Ato, 15
Quebec City, 2
"Queer" in lesbian/gay discourse, 46
queer middle-class people. *See* lesbian/gay
queer theory, 46
   absence of "class," 45–46
   desire-based, 50
   lack of race in, 47
   materialist queer theory, 48–50, 56–57
   as over universalizing, 47
   Third World and, 45
"Queer Visibility" (Hennessy), 55
"Queer with Class" (Cover), 6
Quiché Indians, 202

R

race, 16. *See also* ethnic identities
   Britishness, 122, 124, 126, 151
   linguistic difference, 122
racialized politics, 127
racism, 69–70, 98, 182
   Euro-American, 7
   new racism in Britain, 122
Radhakrishnan, R., 161
   "Postcoloniality and the Boundaries of
      Identity," 160

Rama, Angel
   La ciudad letrada, 192
   *Transculturacion narrativa en America
      Latin*, 200
   transculturation, 205
Rama, myth of, 125
recognition, 147
Reich, Wilhelm, 26
   Mass Psychology of Fascism, The, 25
representation, 201
Reproductions of Banality (Kaplan), 26
residential schools, 17
resistance in a globalized world, 16
ressentiment, 25, 27
Riefenstahl, Leni, 29, 39
Roberts, John, 169
Rouse, Roger, 149
Rulfo, Juan, 206
   Burning Plain, The, 205
   Pedro Paramo, 205
Rushdie, Salman, 7, 93, 96–97, 113–14, 131
   anti-racist rhetoric, 125
   appropriation into British citizenry, 125
   classist and sexist biases, 104
   "Crusoe," 115
   "Dangerous Art Form," 95, 100
   fatwa, 9, 99, 127, 130
   formulation of migrancy, 98–103
   Imaginary Homelands, 124, 137
   Iranian furore against, 120
   Midnight's Children, 104–5
   politico-aesthetics, 99
   postcolonial immigrant intellectual, 92
   Satanic Verses, The, 8–9, 102, 104, 115–19,
      121, 124–32, 134–35
   Shame, 104–5
Rushdie Affair, 126, 130–38, 140

S

Sacajawea, 180, 182–83
   cultural value among Indian people, 170
   as figure of feminine independence, 174
   "homing in," 174
   icon of U.S. romantic nationalism, 170
   later life, 174, 182
   Lewis and Clark expedition, 168–69,
      171–73
   in mainstream history, 169
sacred, the, 126–27
Sacred Hoop, The (Allen), 170
Said, Edward, 13–14, 37, 146, 215, 231–32
   "Identity, Authority and Freedom," 93

"Intellectuals in the Post-Colonial World,"
161
Orientalism, 156, 190, 234
"Third World Intellectuals and
Metropolitan Culture," 93, 95
Satanic Verses, The (Rushdie), 8–9, 102, 104,
115–18, 121, 124, 127–31, 134–35
migration in, 119
responses to, 132
and the sacred, 126
scholastic postcolonialism, 6
Schor, Naomi, 146
Scott, Joan, "Evidence of Experience, The,"
33–34
Seattle, 2
Seed, Patricia, 190
segregation, 13
Seshadri-Crooks, Kalpana, 9–10, 13, 246
settler societies, 10, 12, 16–17
sexuality, 37. *See also* lesbian/gay
Euro-American discourse on, 53
heterosexuality, 46
homosexualism, 53
sexualization of women (commodity
aesthetics), 49
Shah Bano case, 135
Shahabuddin, Syed, 132–35
Shakespeare, William, *Tempest, The*, 195
Shame (Rushdie), 104–5
shared histories (or linked histories), 17
Shaw, Anna Howard, 170
Shoshone people, 168–69, 171
Shoshone Tribal Cultural Center, 167, 169,
172
Shree (film), 116, 119
Slemon, Stephen, 13
Smith, Anna Marie, 122
social activists, 216
social identities, 27, 130
socialism, 24
Solomon Islands, 225
Sontag, Susan, 30–31
"Fascinating Fascism," 29
Spanish imperialism (Latin America), 11
Spivak, Gayatri, 96, 118, 155–57, 194, 213–14,
231–32
"anti-Oedipus" (periphery to centre), 235
as "hybrid Western-non-Western" critic,
14
reputation in China, 234
"Stalin Myth in Soviet Cinema, The" (Bazin),
31–32

Stalinist trials
retroaction, 31–32
"Stonewall69," 53
subalternity, 5, 7
surveillance (and political correctness),
36–37
suttee, 69, 75
sweatshop labour, 49–50, 54–58
corporal punishment, 54–55
human rights, 54
in lesbian/gay discourse, 45

T
Taylor, Charles, 148–49, 154, 158
"Politics of Recognition, The," 147
"technocratic criticism," 191
technologies of cultural transmission, 3,
53, 117
technology, 22–23, 27, 33
Tempest, The (Shakespeare), 195
Tennenhouse, Leonard, 37–38
testimonio, 12–13, 18, 200–203, 205–6
appropriations, 202
"zone of indeterminacy," 200
Thatcher, Margaret, 124
"Third World culture," 236
Third World intellectuals, 36, 91, 94–95,
234–35. *See also* persons of colour
as other, 37
postcolonialism, 234
"Third World Intellectuals and Metropolitan
Culture" (Said), 93
"Third World Intellectuals" (Said), 95
Third World literature
as "national allegory," 38
Third World sweatshop. *See* sweatshop
labour
Tiffin, Helen, 4, 18
Tölölyan, Khachig, 114
tourism, 176–77
traditionalism, 179
"traffic in female flesh," 7
Transculturacion narrativa en America Latin
(Rama), 200
transculturation, 7, 15, 198, 200, 205–6, 212, 220
Chinese/Western, 15
language, 212, 220
transnational corporations
lesbian and gay marketing, 55
marketing strategies, 49
pro-lesbian/gay strategies, 47
sweatshop labour, 50

transnationalism, 149
transparency, 33
transparency of language, 12
truthfulness of the text, 12

U

Untouchables (Anand), 65, 68
U.S., 149, 173
    presidential campaigns, 33

V

Vathek (Beckford), 74
Vidal, Hernán, 190–91
Vietnam War, 2
violence, 29
    repressive violence (of Western society), 25
    against women in Third World, 49
Virilio, Paul, *War and Cinema*, 33
visual technology, 28. *See also* film
Voyage of the Beagle (Darwin), 195

W

Wadze-Wipe. *See* Sacajawea
Wallerstein, Immanuel, 197–98
Wang, Fengzhen, 14
Wang, Ning, 14–15
War and Cinema (Virilio), 33
Warner, Michael, 47
    Fear of a Queer Planet, 46
Western cultural hegemony, 50, 149, 234, 236
Western forms of knowledge
    dominance of, 15
Western hegemony, 153
"Western imperialism," 36
Western liberalism, 9, 133, 149
    multiculturalism in, 147
Western universities. *See* academy
Westernization, 131–32.
        See also Americanization
Wilton, Tasmin, 48
Wind River Indian Reservation, 11, 167–68,
    171–74, 183
women, 49, 55, 121. *See also* gender;
    lesbian/gay
    black, 72
    female body, 7, 57, 97
    migrancy, 97
    misogyny, 71–72
    position as immigrants, 97
    poverty of non-heterosexual women, 52
    in Salman Rushdie's writing, 104
    sexuality, 71

    sexualization, 49
    victim and monster stereotypes, 69
"Words Apart" (Fuentes), 136
working-class, 52, 65. *See also* labour
working-class exiles, 7
working-class immigrants, 97
World Bank, 2
world music, 152
World Trade Organization, 2
"worlding" of modern Europe, 194–95
writers
    author-as-genius, 9
    exiled writer as a "champion of the
        oppressed," 8
    immigrant postcolonial writers, 106–7
    politically engaged, 107

Y

Yudice, George, 150, 217

Z

Žižek, Slavoj, "Creole," 192